DEBENHAM & FREEBODY

Are now holding an Exhibition and Sale of Early Stuart, Queen Anne, and later periods of fine needlework, some being very rare specimens; also Laces and Drawn Work from the Convents of Italy and Spain; and many other interesting curios.   CATALOGUES FREE.

THE FINEST COLLECTION

OF

ANTIQUE · EMBROIDERIES

—— IN LONDON ——

Catalogue, Post Free.

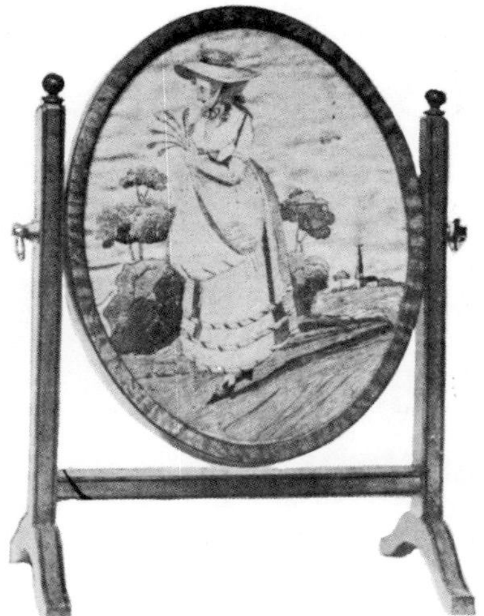

A Satinwood Oval Table Mirror with Old Embroidered Pictures on the reverse side. Size—8 ins. wide, 12 ins. high.   **£5 5 0**

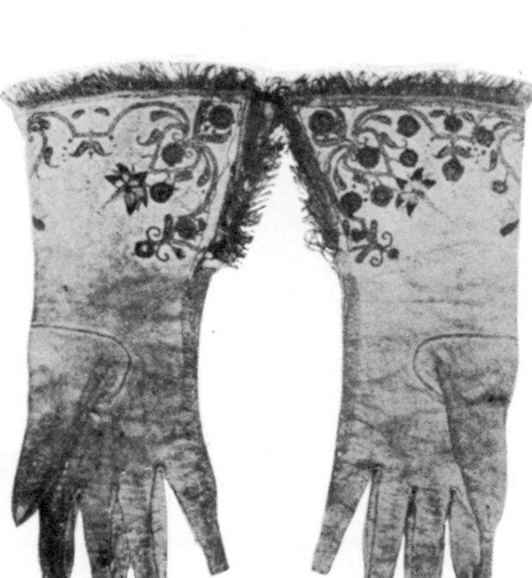
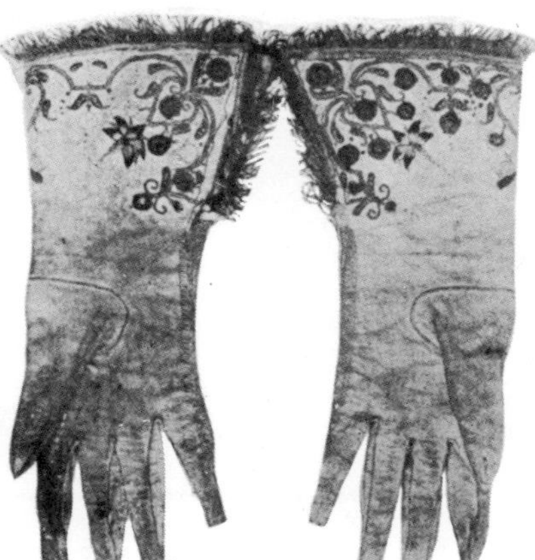

A Pair of Fine Old Embroidered Gloves, probably those left at Lacock Abbey by Queen Elizabeth when visiting there in 1574.   **£5 5 0**

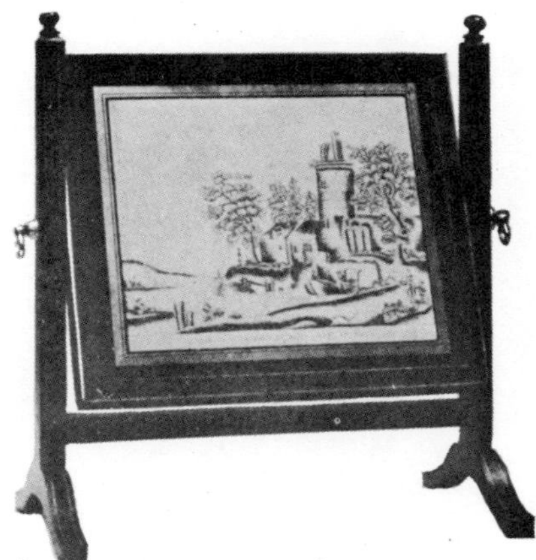

A Mahogany Table Mirror with Old Embroidered Picture in shades of brown and black silk and hair. Size—10 ins. wide by 11 ins. high.   **£5 5 0**

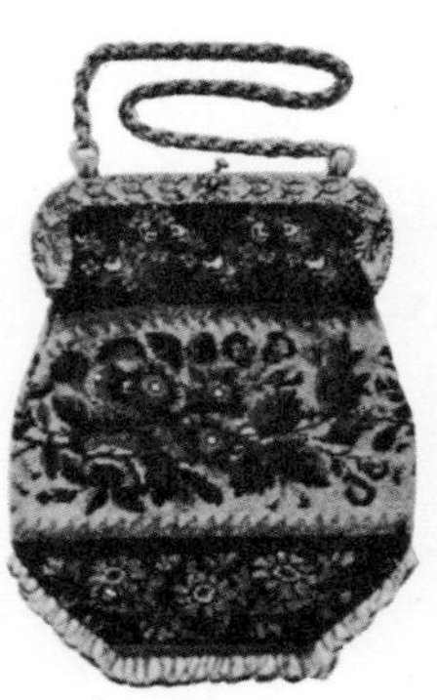

An Old English Bead Bag. Size—6 ins. by 8 ins.   **£8 18 6**

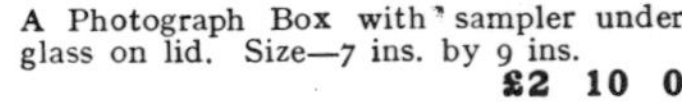

An Old English Bead Bag, with Pinch-beck Mount and Chain. Size—6 ins. by 7 ins.   **£10 10 0**

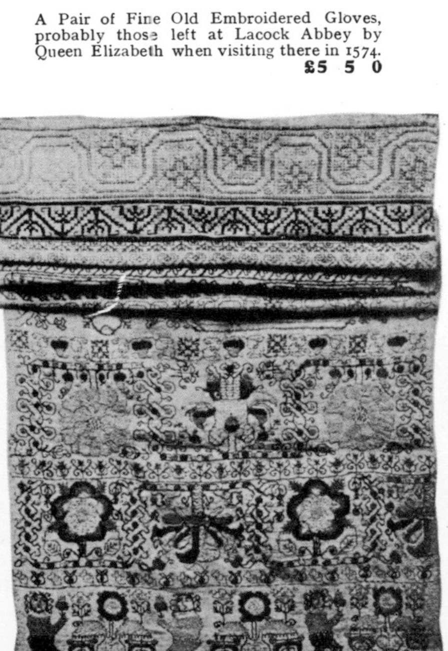

A Photograph Box with sampler under glass on lid. Size—7 ins. by 9 ins.   **£2 10 0**

A Curious 17th Century Sampler. Fine design and colouring. Size—10 ins. by 25 ins.   **£6 16 6**

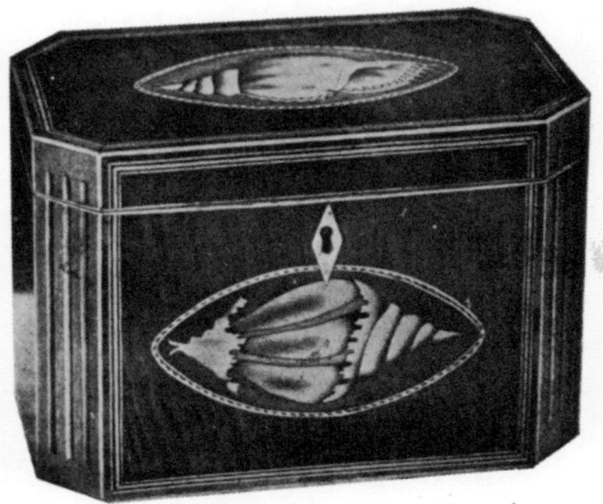

An Old Inlaid Tea Caddy. Shell design. Size—4 ins. by 7 ins.   **£2 2 0**

WIGMORE STREET, LONDON, W.

PETER ROBINSON'S, OXFORD STREET

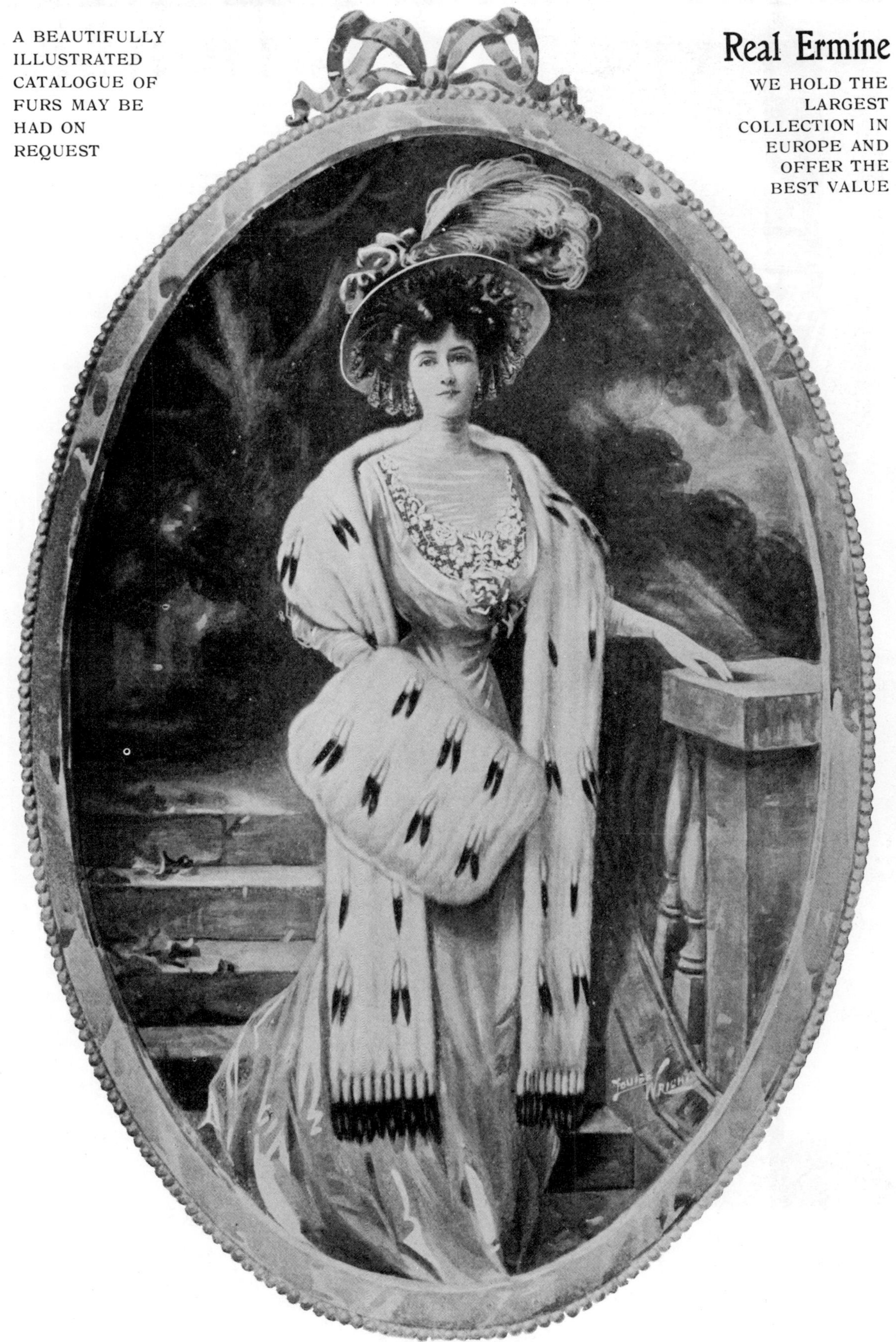

"THE QUEEN."

A Beautiful Scarf in finest Real Ermine.   Fur both sides with real Tails.   **33** Guineas.

Extra large Muff to match.   **16** Guineas.

Other Ermine Scarves, similar styles, in cheaper Skins.   **18, 21, 25** and **29** Guineas.

TABLE DAMASK

"Queen Anne"

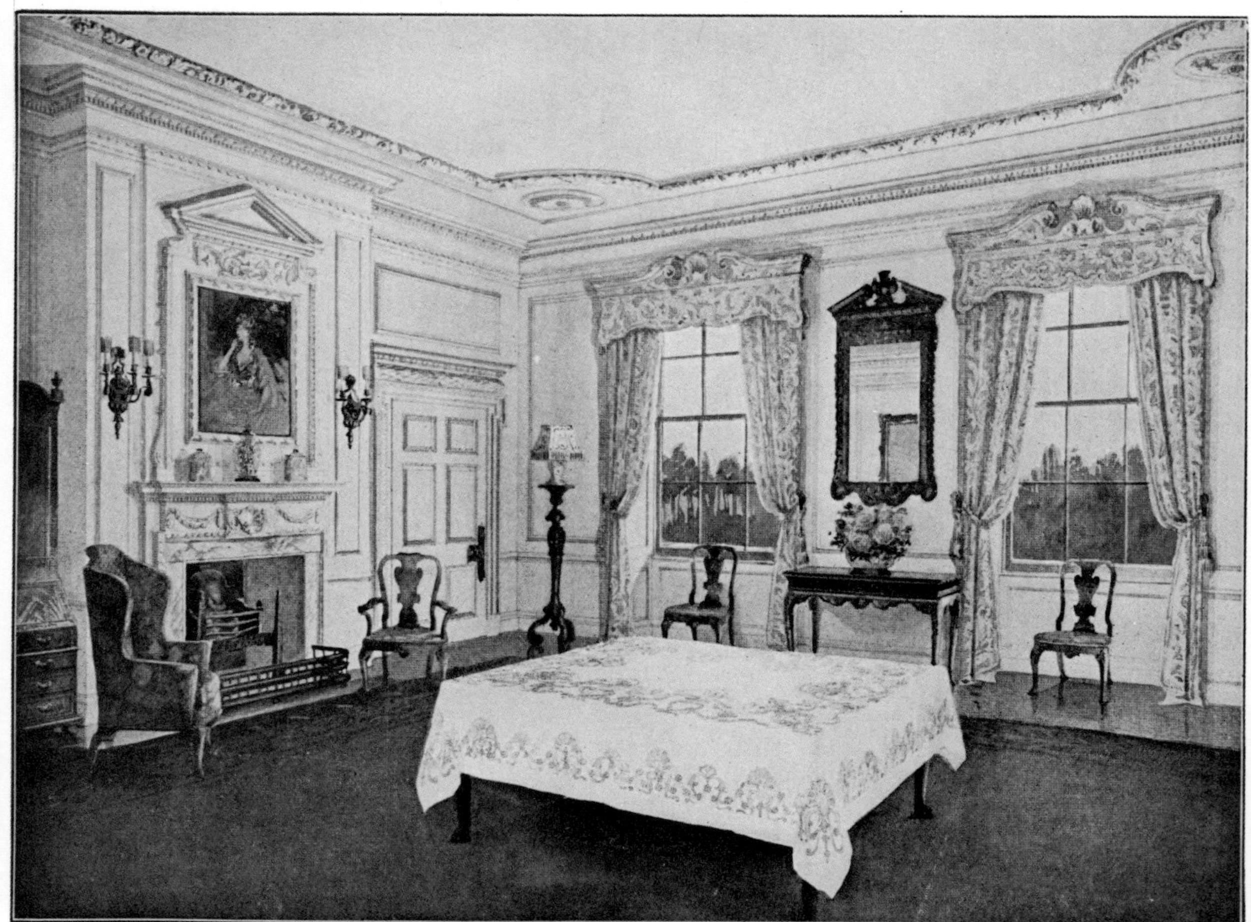

Owing to the great revival of taste and better appreciation of Decorative Arts in recent years, it has been possible to satisfy the most exacting cravings after the Antique, and enable those who aspire to truthfulness in detail of style to carry out same to the fullest extent. The English furniture periods have distinctive characteristics in line and decoration, by conforming strictly to which, produces that restfulness and balance so eagerly sought after in any decorative effect. Table linen, unlike all other decorative objects, has been slow to respond to the advanced taste, but Messrs. Robinson & Cleaver have just produced a series of period Damasks that for truthfulness of detail and artistic simplicity are unique. The above illustration represents Table Damask in a Queen Anne dining-room, and their other productions in Georgian, Chippendale, Sheraton, or Adam are equally true and characteristic. Their new list is now ready, a copy of which will be sent to applicants, specifying "Period Damasks."

ROBINSON & CLEAVER, BELFAST

LTD.

Linen Manufacturers to His Majesty The King.

LONDON AND LIVERPOOL

PERIOD FURNISHING

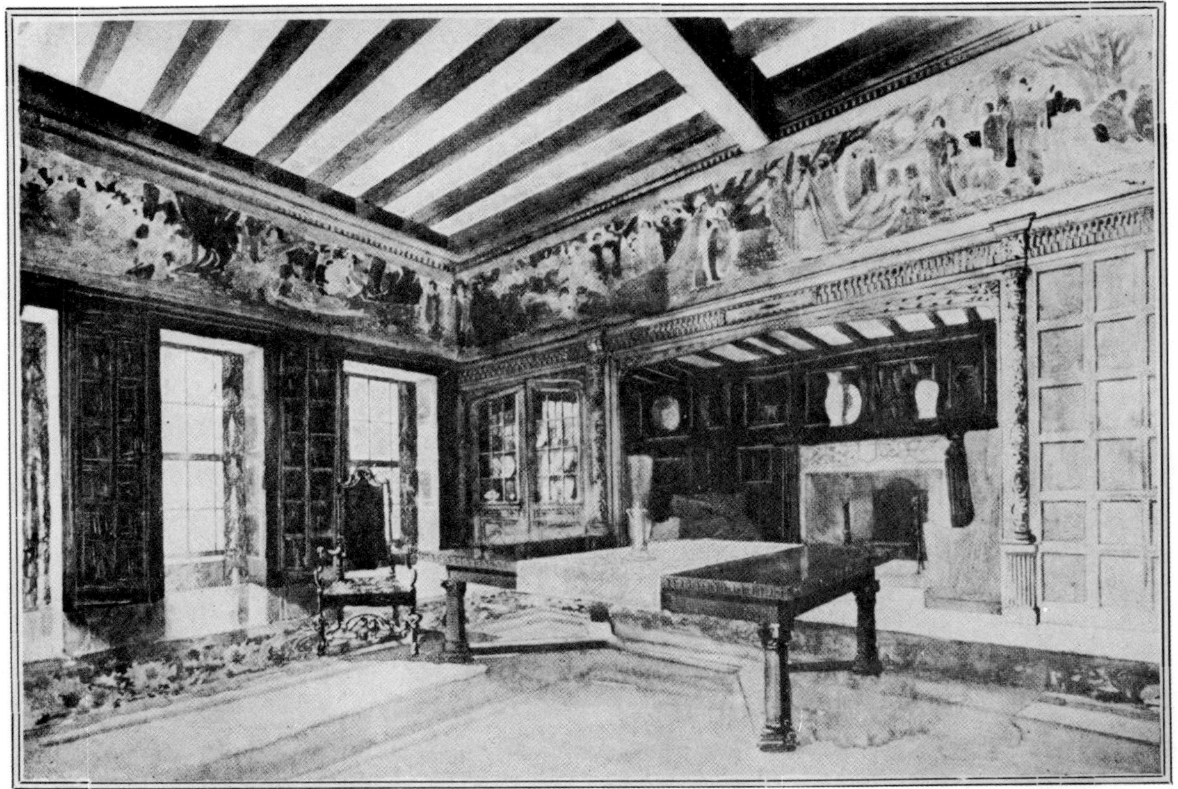

ELIZABETHAN DINING ROOM BY WARINGS

An Unique Exhibition of reproductions
of the best models of Old English Furniture, exquisitely fashioned, may be seen
at Warings' Salons of Decorative Art,
where everything for the decoration and
equipment of the home may be obtained

Persons of taste who desire to furnish their town or
country houses in the Period styles may entrust themselves with complete confidence to the guidance of

WARINGS

—— *DECORATORS TO H.M. THE KING* ——

WARING & GILLOW LTD   NEAR OXFORD CIRCUS

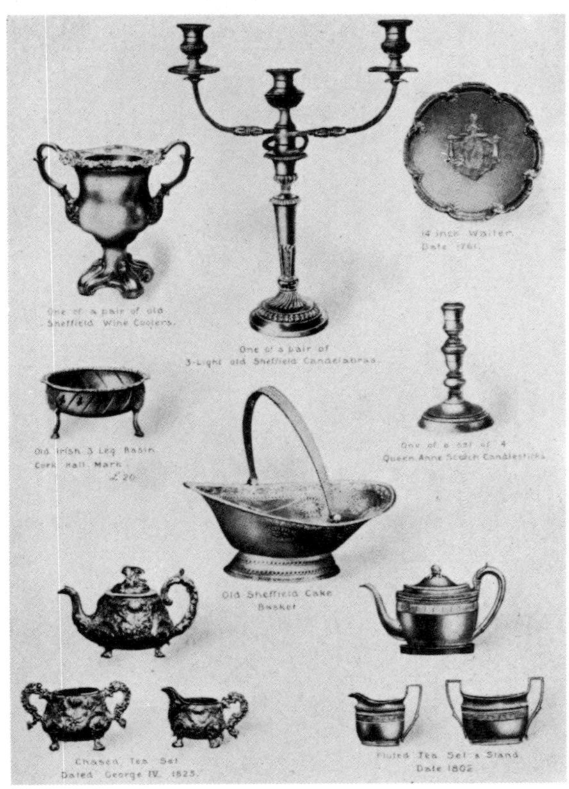

ELKINGTON

& CO., LTD.

Antique Silver and Old Sheffield Plate

Inspection invited of a fine collection at the Regent Street Show Rooms

GENUINE EXAMPLES
— bought for cash —
Utmost :: value :: given

London Show Rooms:
22, Regent Street, S.W.
(below Piccadilly Circus),
73, Cheapside, E.C.

| Birmingham | Liverpool | Montreal | Calcutta |
| Glasgow | Manchester | Buenos Aires | Rangoon |

Manufactory and Show Room: Newcastle.

OLD ENGRAVINGS

SPORTING — CLASSICAL — PORTRAITS —
MORLAND—BARTOLOZZI—BUCK—&c., &c.

FINE GENUINE OLD FURNITURE, CHINA,
SILVER, PAINTINGS, &c.   One of the largest
stocks in the West of England.   TRADE SUPPLIED.

J. P. WAY,

ANTIQUE ART GALLERY, 69, PARK ST.,
BRISTOL.

" A Short History of Bristol China and Pottery."
Illustrated. Send P.O. 7d.

WALTER PRATT

*House Decorator &
General Contractor,*

8, BARTLETT STREET,
and **35, GAY STREET,**

BATH.

*Estimates Free in
Town and Country.*   ＊   *Telephone Nos.
310 and 421 National.*

A GOOD SELECTION OF

Genuine Old English Furniture

OF VARIOUS PERIODS   PRICE LIST POST FREE FROM

J. W. PARTRIDGE,   ALVECHURCH,
Worcestershire.

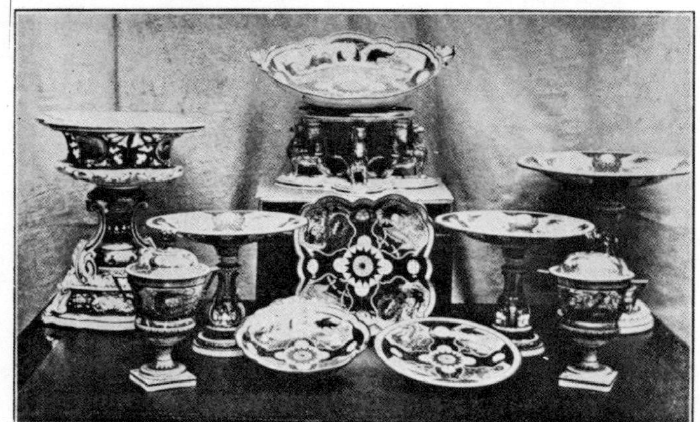

Fine Old Worcester Dessert Service, by Flight & Barr, decorated with dragons in rich colours, comprising 49 pieces.

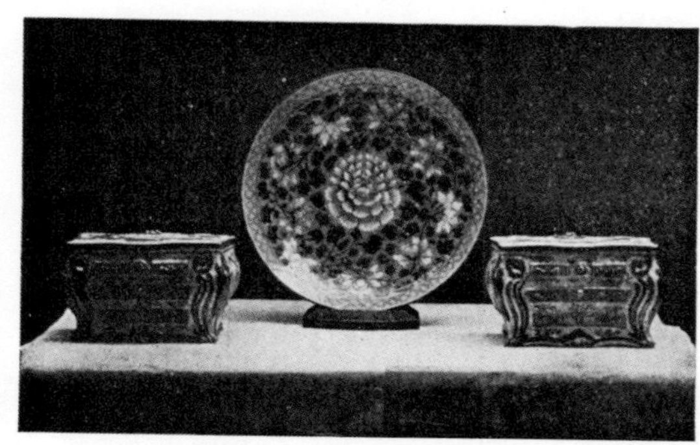

Pair of Continental commode-shape Jardinières, for bulbs or flowers, 5 ins. high, 8 ins. wide; unique specimens. Also a fine Oriental Dish, pink and green floral decorations, 13½ ins. diam.

GREAT
Clearance Sale!

Owing to EXPIRATION OF LEASE and Extensive Alteration of Premises, the ENTIRE STOCK is now being offered for sale AT A REDUCTION OF **20%** (**4/-** in the £) off marked prices for cash.

Genuine Antiques,

Fine Old Silver, Sheffield Plate, Enamels, China, Furniture, Pictures, and Works of Art generally.

— DESCRIPTIVE CATALOGUE POST FREE UPON APPLICATION. —

PLEASE NOTE ONLY ADDRESSES:

HENRY WELLS
15 & 19, High Street, SHREWSBURY.

Telegrams:—" Wells, Shrewsbury."   Under Royal Patronage.
National Telephone 55.   Enquiries and Inspection invited.

EXPERTS   *Estd.*   *1881*   **EXPERTS**

in Restoring, Relining, and Varnishing Oil Paintings.

in Restoring and Repairing valuable China and Glass.

Engravings, Prints, &c., Restored, Cleaned, Mounted and Framed.   Old Frames Restored and Re-gilt.

Also for Adapting and Mounting NEEDLEWORK for Screens, Pictures, Trays, &c.

Sporting Prints.

LAMBERT

Sporting Prints.

Antique China. Fine Old English Cut and Engraved Glass.

PICTURES of every description ON SALE.

Bronzes.   Old Brass.
Ivories.   Curios.

Also MOUNTED and FRAMED in any style.

Fine Old Prints.   Modern Engravings.

Best Workmanship.
Reasonable Charges.

THE WELLINGTON GALLERY,
100, KNIGHTSBRIDGE, S.W.

DANIEL EGAN,
26, Lower Ormond Quay,
∾ DUBLIN. ↶

Frame Maker and Gilder to the National Gallery of Ireland.

Modern and Antique Frames for Pictures and Looking Glasses.   Oil Paintings cleaned, lined, and restored. Prints cleaned and bleached. A large collection of Old Furniture, Paintings, Coloured Prints, and Drawings.

OLIVER BAKER,
STRATFORD=ON=AVON.

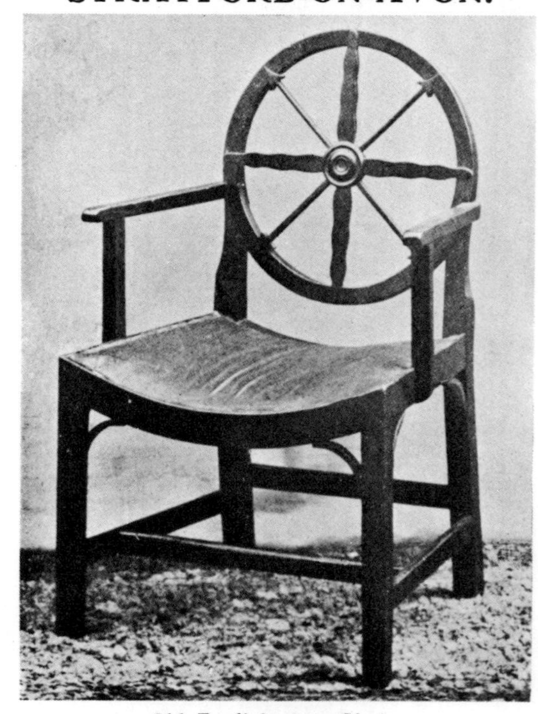

Old English Arm=Chair.

Old English Furniture
Pewter, Pottery, Brass, Ironwork, &c., &c.

Why not have your own Orchestra?

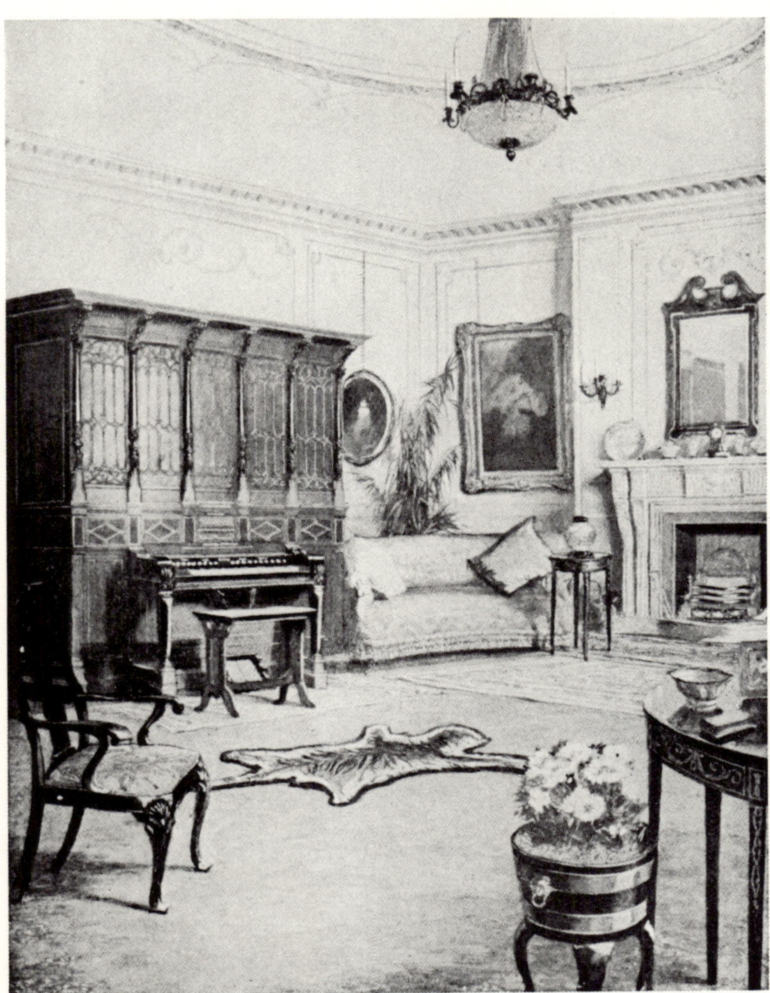

FOR your own recreation, for the entertainment of your guests, nothing will render you greater service than the

Orchestrelle.

On this wonderful instrument you can play the great symphonies, overtures, operas, etc., with full orchestral effect. You need not know a note of music ; all you need is the desire to play. You have only to call at Æolian Hall to understand how the Orchestrelle, an unique instrument, means to you practically the same thing as having a private orchestra always ready to play at your direction.

Fuller particulars are given in Catalogue 9, but you will find that five minutes of personal investigation will give you a better idea of the Orchestrelle than many pages of description.

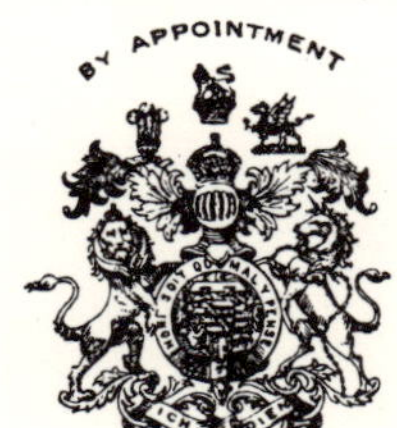

— THE —

Orchestrelle Company

Æolian Hall :: 135-6-7, New Bond St., London, W.

Old
Sporting
Prints

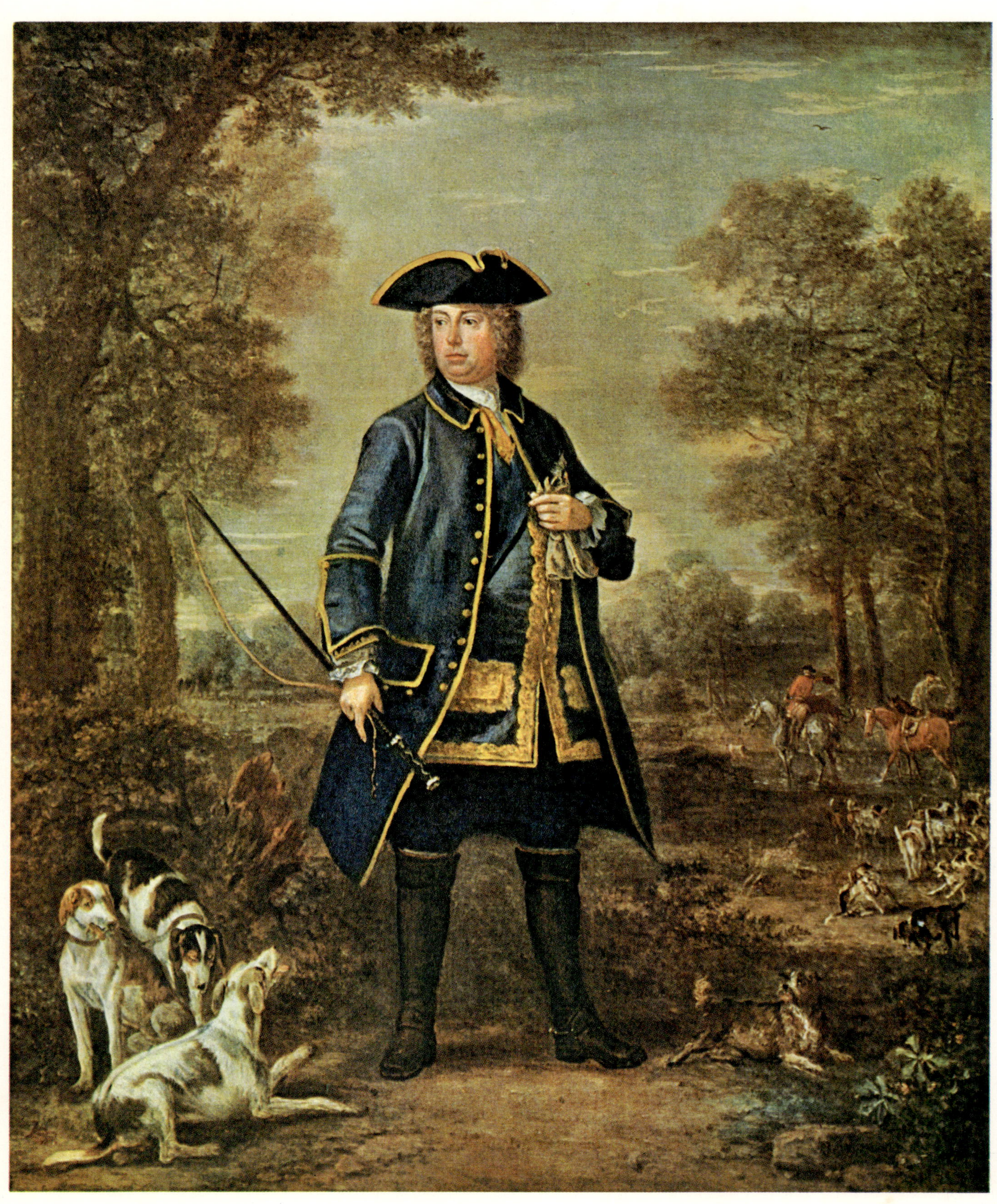

SIR ROBERT WALPOLE WITH HOUNDS
By John Wootton
From an Oil Painting in the possession of the Earl of Orford

Old Sporting Prints

Ralph Nevill

Spring Books

London · New York · Sydney · Toronto

Original edition published 1908
© National Magazine Company Limited, 1970

This edition published 1970 by
The Hamlyn Publishing Group Limited
London · New York · Sydney · Toronto
Hamlyn House, Feltham, Middlesex, England

Printed in Hong Kong by
Lee Fung Printing Company Limited

SBN 600 02893 3

This book was dedicated to
Sir Walter Gilbey, Bart.,
one of the greatest authorities on
English Sporting Pictures and Prints

CONTENTS.

LIST OF ILLUSTRATIONS.

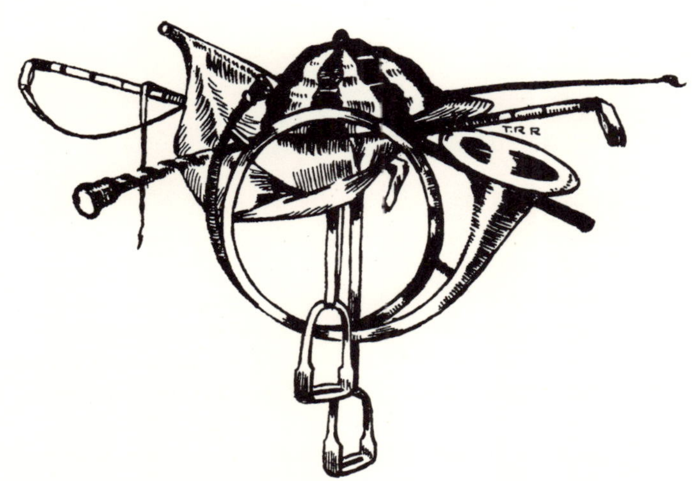

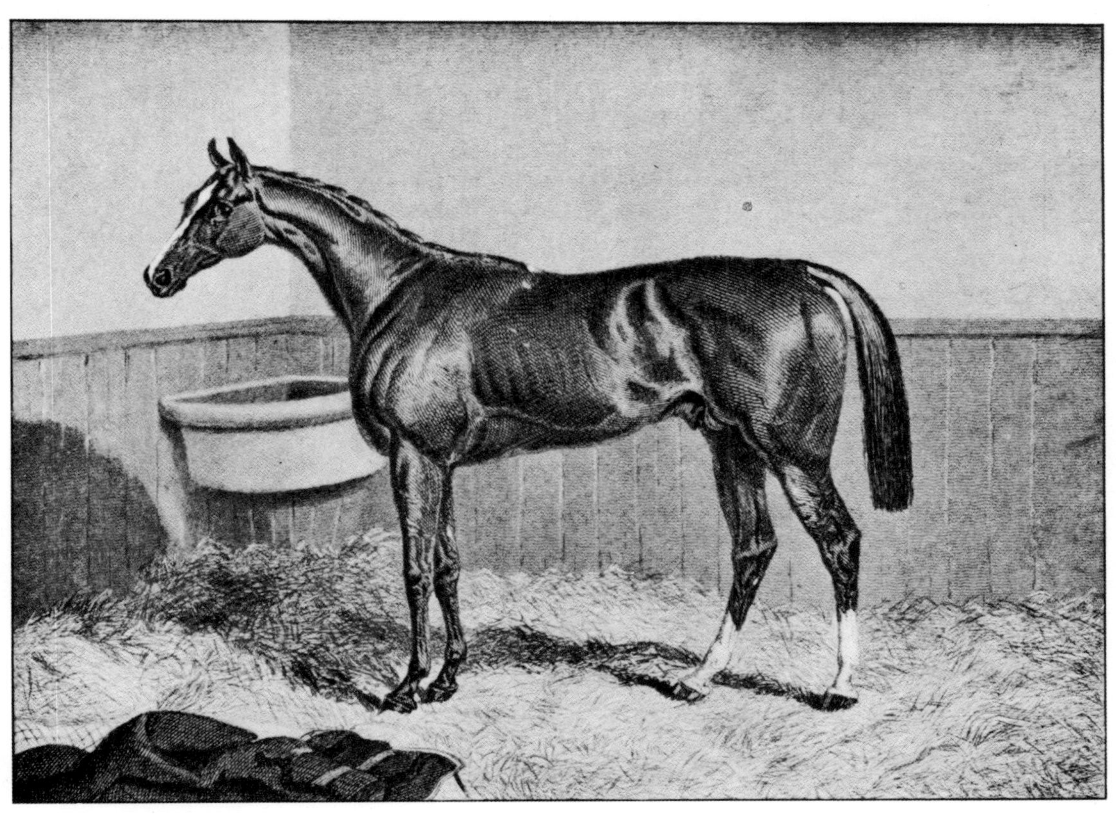

PYRRHUS THE FIRST.   WINNER OF THE DERBY, 1846
By Hacker, after J. F. Herring, Sen.

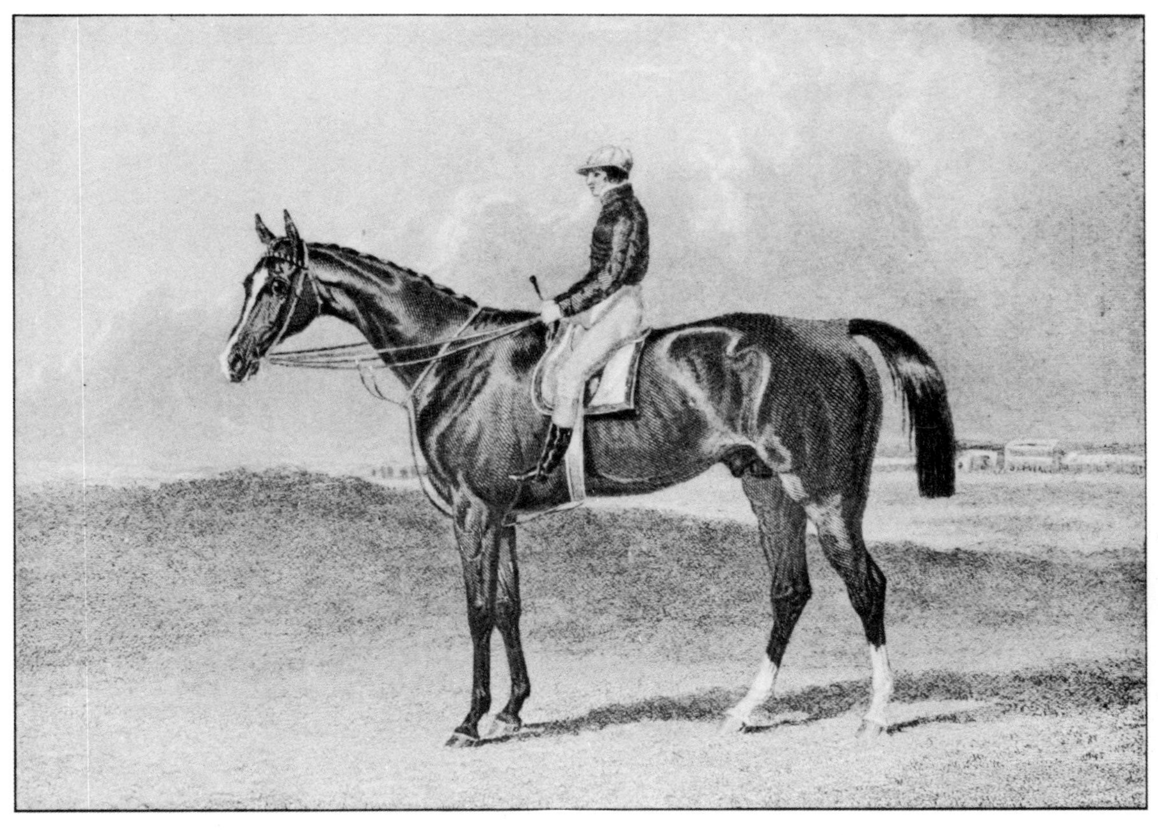

ORLANDO.   WINNER OF THE DERBY, 1844
By Hacker, after J. F. Herring

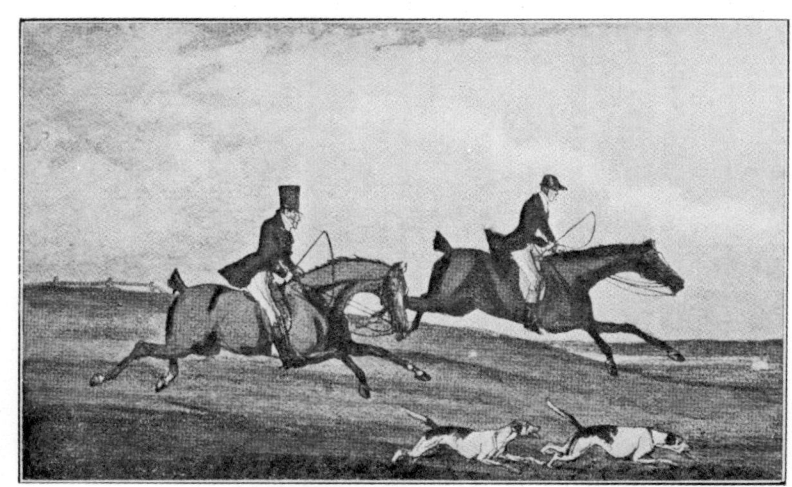

FOX HUNTERS
By Henry Alken

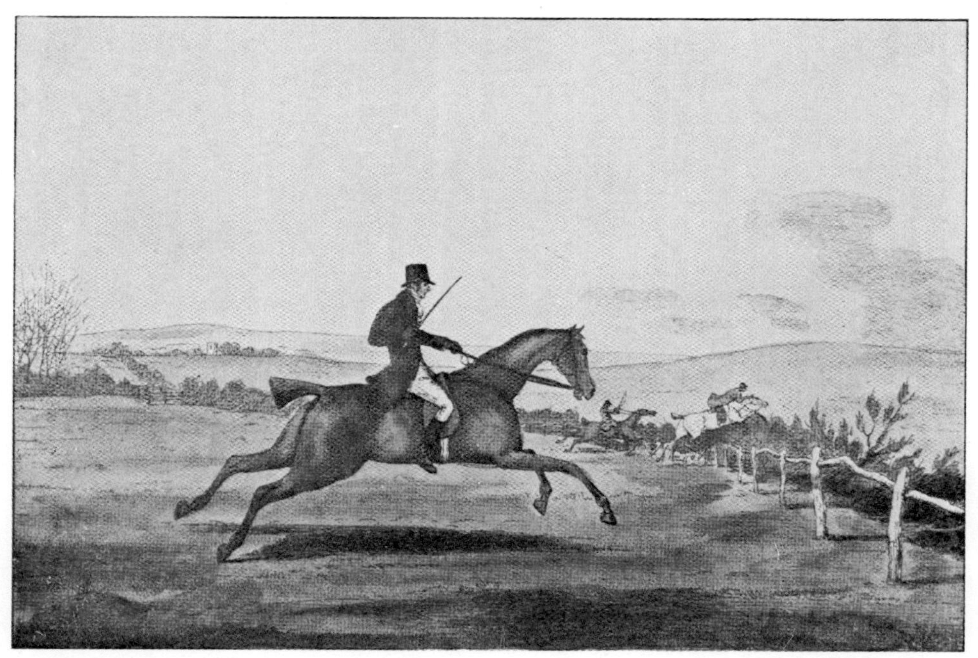

CHARGING AN OX-FENCE
Published by Humphreys, 1811

OLD SPORTING PRINTS.

Year by year old sporting prints are being accorded a larger measure of public appreciation. Considered in the past as little more than appanage of the passage and smoking-room they have for some time past been rising in general estimation and price, collectors paying comparatively large sums for good examples of this pleasant and animated form of pictorial art. To-day, many not sportsmen themselves or addicted to hunting, shooting, or racing, are included amongst the admirers of these old-world scenes, a number of which so vividly recall the full-blooded and robust life of a former generation, which in its amusements and habits differed so greatly from our own.

As a rule, attracting a glance even from those most indifferent to prints, these representations of the sportsman of the past in the hunting-field and by the covert side, possess a great deal of old-world charm. Here also may be seen the bucks of astounding costume, eager with excitement, amidst the rough and tumble of some country race-course or equipped in more workmanlike fashion piloting some good chaser over the fences of an impromptu steeplechase.

England at the end of the eighteenth and beginning of the nineteenth centuries was a sporting country in a different sense from to-day. The majority of hunting men, for instance, were squires who lived on their estates, a number of whom were well known as characters throughout the countryside. Hunting, with them, amounted occasionally to a sort of religion, and was not merely a pastime indulged in for purposes of relaxation and health. At the Gargantuan feasts, in which they delighted, songs in praise of the chase were much in vogue, whilst sporting toasts were drunk in bumpers amidst somewhat Bacchanalian shouts of enjoyment. A full-blooded jolly lot, not a few of them hardly visited London at all, being well content to live and die amidst the rural surroundings which they loved so well. The artistic tastes of this class were naturally limited, but they admired and liked striking representations of famous horses and hounds, whilst pictures of the incidents of a fox-chase, ending with an extremely spirited representation of the death of the fox, seldom failed to command their approbation.

A curious feature in eighteenth century hunting pictures is that instead of the short horn used in England at the present time a curly French horn, such as is still used in France, is often depicted as being carried. A print by Howitt, reproduced in these pages, is a case in point, whilst a proof of the French hunting horn having been used by the Royal Buckhounds is afforded by the frontispiece of the first number of the Old Sporting Magazine which was published in October, 1792. This shows the turning out of the deer for the Royal Hunt, a picture in which His Majesty, George III., is a conspicuous figure. With the dawn of the nineteenth century, the French hunting horn appears to have fallen into disuse, and at the present day a great many sportsmen are unaware that the instrument in question was ever a part of the equipment of the chase in this island.

Whilst sport in various forms is still an almost dominant factor in English life, it has assumed a somewhat different shape to that most popular in this country at the end of the eighteenth and beginning of the nineteenth centuries; the rough brutal pastimes in which our forefathers indulged having ceased to exist. Bear and Bull baiting, Cock- and Dog- fighting are things of the past, whilst the so-called glories of the prize ring do not ever seem likely to be revived.

Racing and hunting still flourish, though both are now sports appealing far more to the very rich than was the case in days gone by, when a spirit of unrestrained and somewhat rough merry-making held sway.

The happy-go-lucky spirit of careless jollity so conspicuous in the scenes pictured by Rowlandson has now long departed, and humorous incidents are rare amongst the crowds who flock to witness great cricket matches or contests between professional football teams. The picturesque is out of place in modern life, where everything, more or less, is affected by rule or regulation.

It is therefore but natural that old sporting prints, many of which are imbued with a spirit of vivacity and life, constitute a source of real attraction to those interested in a more individualistic past.

In a number of these engravings it is possible to discern many of the quaint and original characters who were well known to a by-gone generation, whilst in others the somewhat robust humours of the old English racecourse are prominent, together with many quaint sidelights on the life of a vanished age.

From these prints also can be reconstituted the travelling of past days, when the sound of the coach-horn enlivened many a country road, and the handling of the ribbons was an accomplishment at which many well-known sportsmen loved to shine.

In certain of these old prints we may witness great fights, the result of which was eagerly awaited throughout the country, whilst, if in a more serious mood, the burial of Tom Moody is there to claim our attention, the dying request of the old huntsman that six earth stoppers should give three rattling view-halloos in farewell, having been duly carried out, and the scene pictured by Dean Wolstenholme.

The school of artists which devoted its energies to the delineation of subjects of sport and the portrayal of animal life was essentially British in character, being in a very great measure dominated by the influence of George Stubbs, who was the first English animal painter to seek inspiration direct from nature. Previous to his day, nearly all pictures of the horse were painted

from the eye alone, the anatomy and muscular system of the horse
being more or less ignored.

As early as the eighteenth century there was in England a
great demand for pictures of horses and dogs. An old-time writer
in 1755 describes the sporting art of his day thus: "As soon as
a racehorse has acquired some fame, they have him immediately
drawn to the life. This, for the most part, is a dry profile, but
in other respects bearing a good resemblance. They generally
clap the figure of some jockey or other upon his back, which is
but poorly done."

It was at this time that John Wootton, the great English animal
painter, furnished the aristocracy of his day with pictures of their
favourite horses and hounds. Amongst his patrons was Sir
Robert Walpole for whom the portrait (now for the first time
reproduced, as the frontispiece to this volume) was executed. A
large number of hunting pieces, some of which were engraved,
were produced by Wootton, whose reputation being great, was
wont to obtain comparatively large prices for his works.

The portrait of Sir Robert was given by him to Dr. Ranby, one
of the Court Physicians, with the words, "Here, Ranby, is my
likeness." The costume is that of Master of the King's Staghounds, the scenery Windsor Forest. Sir Robert's favourite
terrier lies at his feet.

It may be mentioned that at Orford House, two miles from
Elsenham, a picture by Wootton, in a panel frame, is over one of the
mantelpieces. The work of this painter was very popular with
the sporting squires and nobility of his time, and whilst much of
it was admirable, he painted for those who were not too critical
in artistic matters.

The patrons of Wootton were not as a rule people who had
any knowledge of art or were possessed of much natural taste.
For the most part the hard riding, drinking and swearing top-
booted gentry of the day required a coloured chart of a horse,
with all his good points displayed as in a diagram, rather than a
picture, which at the same time should be a work of art.

An especially curious picture by Wootton met with destruction
at the burning of the Pantechnicon many years ago. This represented Sir Robert Walpole out hunting, a feature being the tame
magpie which used to go out with his hounds. This may be
verified from a sketch in the possession of the present Earl of
Orford, to whom the beautiful full-length portrait of Sir Robert also
belongs. As will be observed, this possesses considerable artistic
merit, being a specimen of the work of this artist at his best.

Sir Walter Gilbey, it may be added, possesses a picture of Sir
Robert standing by his hunter, painted by Wootton, together with
other works from his brush.

George Stubbs, A.R.A., the successor of Wootton as a painter
of animals, was born, the son of a surgeon, in 1724. His *Anatomy
of the Horse*, which was published in 1776, attracting some attention, Stubbs very soon became the fashionable horse painter of

his day, but his natural talent was too great to allow him to be satisfied with merely depicting horses in the mechanical lay figure style which so fully answered the requirements of the sportsmen of that time. Possessing a sound knowledge of anatomy, Stubbs never ceased to study, and went in a great deal for dissection; once, it is said, even carrying a dead horse on his back up a narrow staircase to his dissecting room. Though a man of great muscular strength this feat is difficult to credit. The animal was in all probability merely a small pony. Stubbs's works were engraved by Woollett, Earlom and Green.

A peculiarly attractive engraving, it may be added, executed by Woollett after Stubbs, is that of the *Spanish Pointer*, which shows a typical English landscape undulating in the background. The print in question, which is uncoloured, is by no means common, especially in the proof state, though ordinary impressions can be obtained for something between six and eight pounds.

With regard to the *Anatomy of the Horse*, by Stubbs, it should always be remembered that the plates in the original edition, published in 1766, alone are worthy of attention, those appearing in subsequent issues being very inferior. The failure of Stubbs to secure the services of an engraver caused him to undertake the task himself and during a period of from six to seven years all his spare time was given to this work.

A man of quite unusual bodily vigour, this artist retained his activity to the end of his life. He was a pedestrian of no mean powers, and walked eight or nine miles the day before his death, at the age of seventy nine, in 1806.

In 1790, George Stubbs was offered £9,000 for a series of portraits of famous English racehorses, but the outbreak of war with France brought the series to a premature conclusion when only sixteen portraits had been executed. These were, (1) *The Godolphin Arabian;* (2) *Marske, the sire of Eclipse;* (3) *Eclipse;* (4) *Dungannon;* (5) *Volunteer;* (6) *Gimcrack;* (7) *Mambrino;* (8) *Sweetbriar;* (9) *Sweet William;* (10) *Protector;* (11) *Shark* (12) *Baronet;* (13) *Pumpkin;* (14) *Bandy;* (15) *Gnawpost;* and (16) *Anvil.* The portrait of the Godolphin Arabian had been intended to form the frontispiece of the work. These sixteen pictures were exhibited at the Turf Gallery in Conduit Street in 1794. Afterwards they were engraved by George Townley Stubbs, the plates being of practically uniform size, and published in accord with the original design. Eleven plates of racehorses in colour after Stubbs by G. T. Stubbs were sold at auction some years ago for eleven guineas.

A painter of racehorses and sporting scenes who had a considerable reputation in his day was James Seymour, a contemporary of Wootton.

Seymour, who had originally been endowed with an ample fortune, dissipated it upon the Turf, and became a professional painter of equine portraits from necessity, receiving commissions from most of the prominent sportsmen of his day. His principal patron was Sir William Jolliffe, for whom, amongst other pictures, he painted two portraits of *Flying Childers*, another of the same famous horse being executed to the order of the Duke of Devonshire, an engraving of which by John Scott appeared in the Sporting Magazine of 1813. In Sir Walter Gilbey's collection is an interesting work of Seymour's, *Race at Newmarket (4th April, 1731)*, whilst a smaller picture by this artist, *The Old Weighing House at Newmarket*, is also at Elsenham. For the Duke of Queensberry, "Old Q," known late in life as "the Star of Piccadilly," James Seymour painted a representation of his famous carriage match. The picture in question, which bears the names of the horses and riders, only passed out of the Queensberry collection in 1897, when it was sold at Christie's. It is now said to be in the possession of Lord Rosebery.

"Old Q" late in life became a sort of tolerated West End scandal, his eccentricities originating a number of tales and witticisms, many of which were fantastic in the extreme. A curious work was published about him in 1808, which was called "The Piccadilly Ambulator, or Old Q [ueensberry], containing Memoirs of the Private Life of that Ever-green Votary of Venus, by T. P. Hurstone" (2 vols.). As a younger man the Duke (then Earl of March) had been a great frequenter of Newmarket and a rather successful patron of the Turf, displaying considerable shrewdness in the wagers on which he embarked.

In 1750 he made a wager of 1,000 guineas with Count O'Taafe (an Irish gentleman also notorious for his bets and oddities) that a carriage with four wheels could be devised capable of being drawn at the rate of not less than 19 miles within an hour. The machine for this match was built by Wright, of Long Acre, who exhausted all the resources of his craft to diminish the weight and friction as much as possible. In order to ensure lightness combined with strength, the harness was of quite a novel kind, silk being employed, artfully combined with leather. Four blood-horses of approved speed were next selected, with two grooms of small weight and tried skill to manage them. A course one mile in length was marked out at Newmarket, and after some trials, in which several horses are said to have been killed, the match was fixed to be run on August 29th, 1750. Bets amounting to several thousands of pounds depended on the result, but those who had wagered that the feat could not be performed lost their money, for the carriage was drawn over the appointed distance well within the hour. Three of the four horses which drew the machine had won plates. The two leading ones carried, including jockey, saddle and harness, about eight stone each, the wheel horses about seven, and the chaise with the boy that rode in it weighed about twenty-four stone.

The picture of this match, to which reference has been made, is said to have given a very fair idea of a sporting incident which attracted a great deal of attention. It was engraved many years later by J. Bodger, who inserted the following notice in the Racing Calendar of 1788 :—

"On or before the 1st March will be published *A Print* (in colours, from nature), executed in Bartolozzi's style of engraving. Honoured with the patronage of His Royal Highness the Prince of Wales, Noblemen and Gentlemen, members of the Jockey Club, etc., *J. Bodger* (land surveyor, Stilton, Hunts., and at 53 High Holborn) presents his dutiful respects to the nobility and gentry, and acquaints them that, at the request of many of his friends, he promises to publish by subscription a Print, as a companion to that of Twenty-four Courses, &c., on Newmarket Heath, representing His Grace the Duke of Queensberry's *Carriage Match*, with which will be given a particular account of the match, and the names of the horses and riders.

"The circumstances of the horses running away with their riders and carriages will be expressed in the Print, in passing by the King's Gap, from which place a new and picturesque landscape of the Heath, Beacon Hills, Upper and Lower Hare Parks, Four-mile Stables, and Choke Jade will be given; and a perspective view of horsemen and carriages coming over the B.C. Embellished with a section of the carriage; and, by particular desire, a representation of two horses going to run a trial. Also a Morning scene and an Auction Sale of Horses at the Coffee-house Gates, Newmarket.

" Conditions.

" (1) The size of the Plate will be 27 inches by 18 inches.

" (2) Price to subscribers for Prints of the horses, etc., in colours from Nature, one guinea; in black, 10s. 6d. Subscribers to have the first impressions.

(The print was also sold printed on silk, £1 5s.)

" The size of the horses, riders, and carriages is taken from the original painting by Mr. Seymour, now in the possession of the Duke of Queensberry, to whom the Print, by His Grace's permission, will be dedicated.

"An impression showing the present state of the Plate may be seen at Mr. Weatherby's, No. 7, Oxendon Street; also, by Mr. Bray, at Messrs. Tattersall's, London; at the Coffee-house, Newmarket; Mr. Monk, Chester; Mr. Harrop, Manchester; Mr. S. Hodgson, Newmarket; Mr. Tesseyman, York, and Mr. Smith, Oxford, of whom may be had prints, in colours, of twenty-four Courses, etc., and an emblem of a Sweepstakes coming in on Newmarket Heath, on which are given chronological memorandums of many extraordinary riding performances, as well as an Historical Account of the Races and the Devil's Ditch."

Bodger also executed an engraving of another picture by Seymour which was entitled, *Map of Newmarket Heath*. This was published in 1791, and shows a plan of all the different courses and exercising grounds upon the Heath, the situation of starting and winning post as well as the stands. At the bottom is an oval medallion containing a representation of the finish of a race, whilst historical accounts of the chief matches, dates and details of the

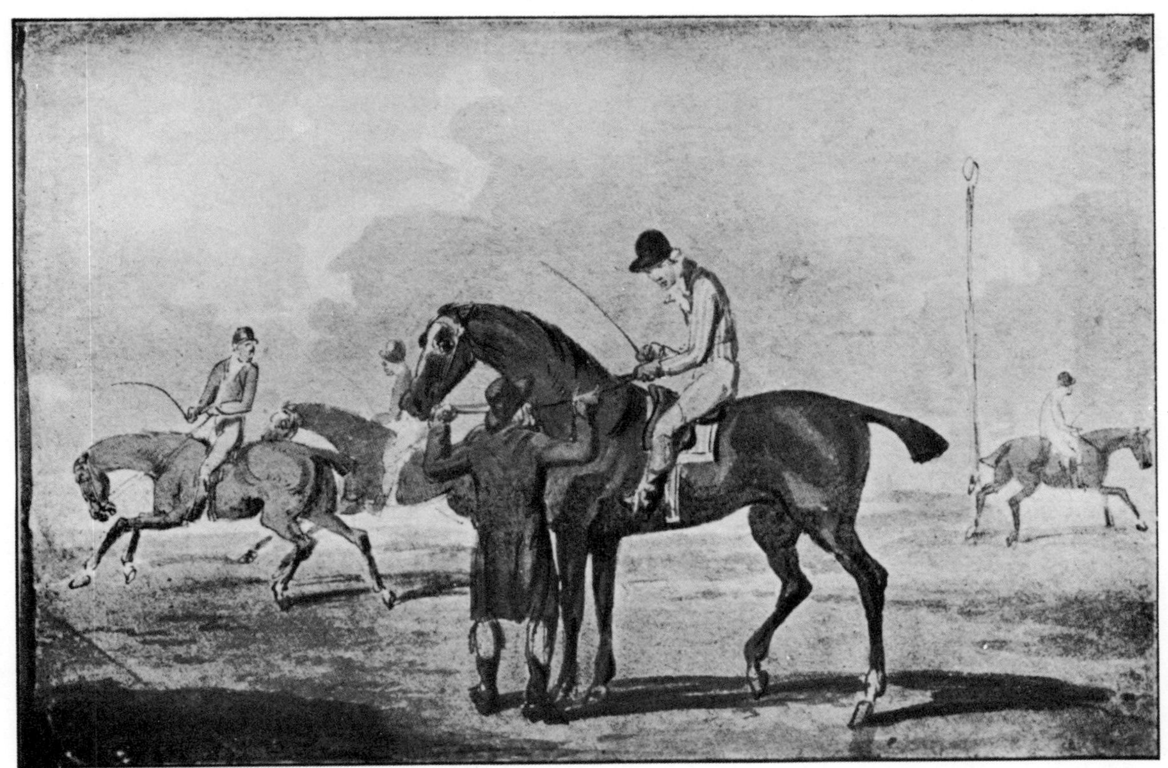

MOUNTING. *By Rowlandson.*

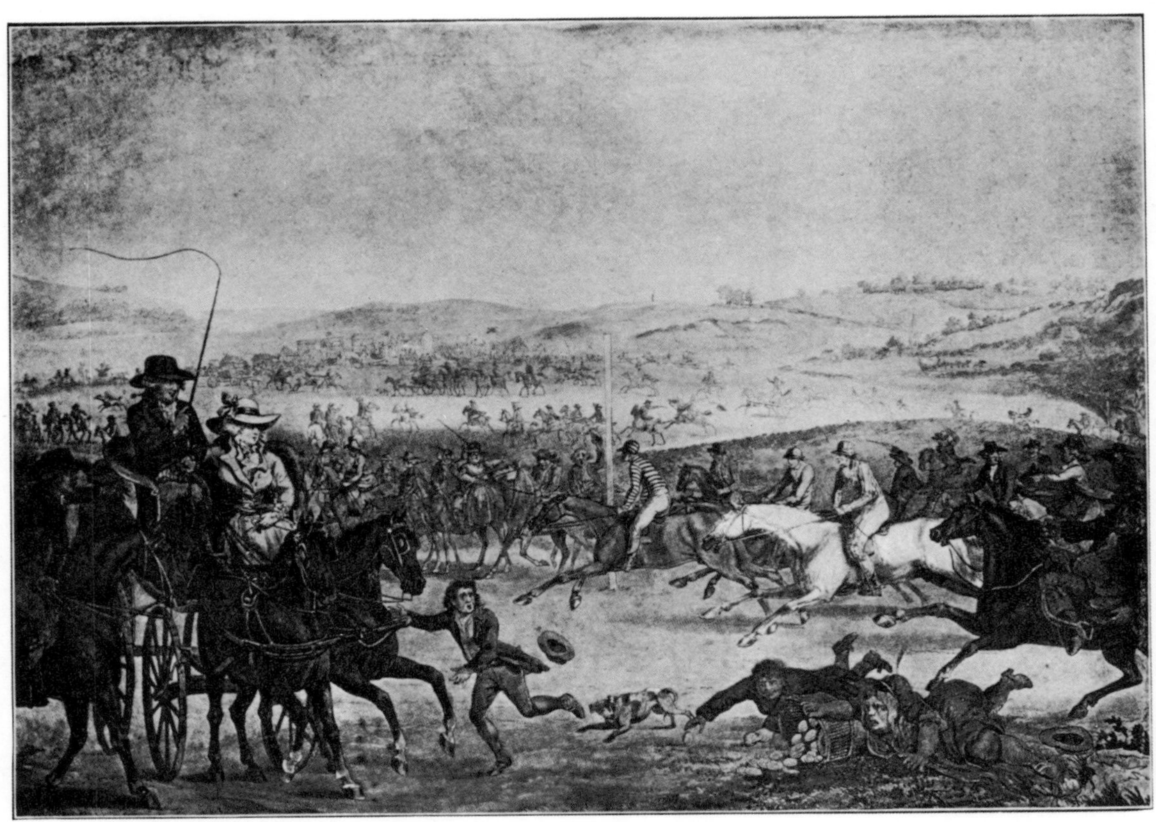

A COUNTRY RACECOURSE
By T. Jenkins, after W. Mason

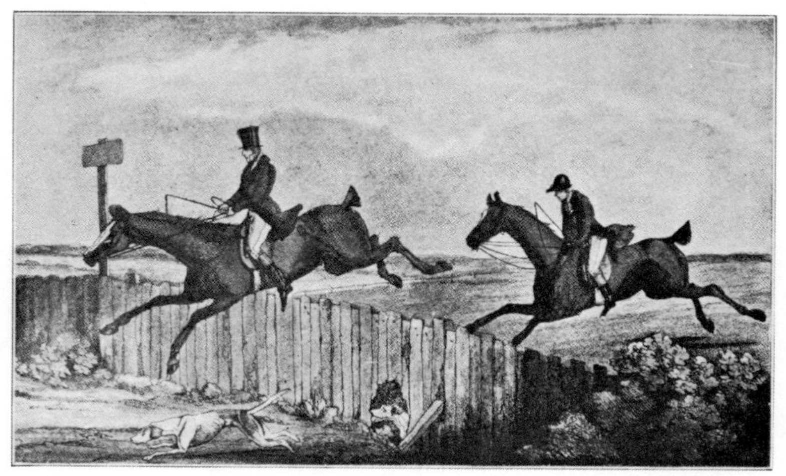

THE LEAP
By Henry Alken

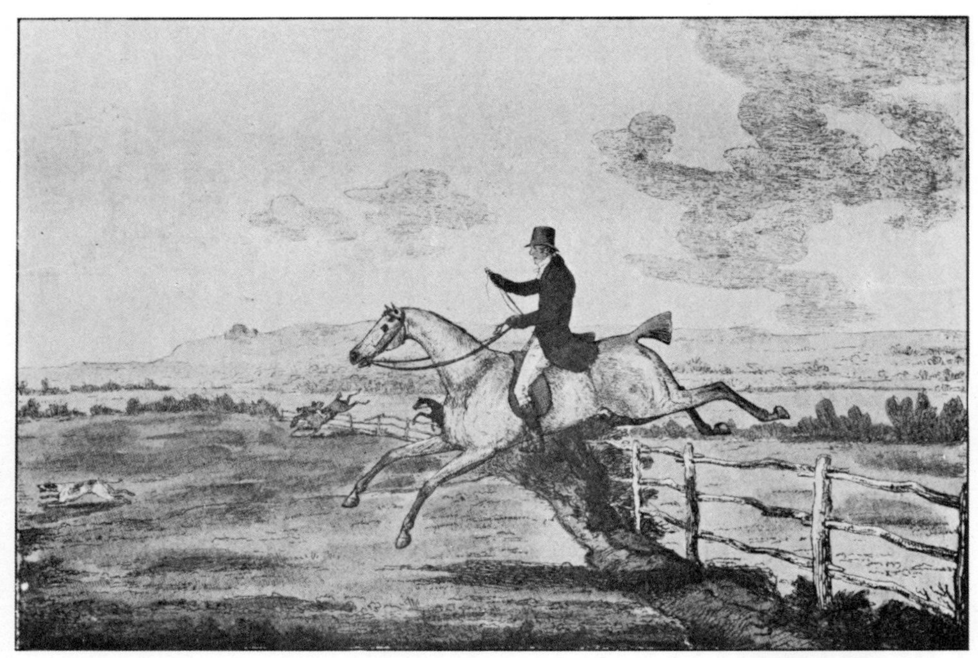

TOPPING A FLIGHT OF RAILS AND COMING WELL INTO THE NEXT FIELD
Published by Humphreys, 1811

annual meetings and the Royal Plates are also to be seen. This print, which, like the *Carriage Match* was printed upon silk as well as paper, was published at the same price.

Yet another print published in the same year by Bodger, after Seymour, is entitled *View of the Noblemen's and gentlemen's trains of running horses with the grooms and horses in their full liveries taking up their exercise up the Warren Hill, East of the Town of Newmarket*. This was dedicated to the Prince of Wales, whose arms are inscribed upon the engraving. It is a print of great interest, abounding in character. A conspicuous feature is the high four-wheeled gig drawn by six grey horses, the four first driven from the box seat, the leaders ridden by a post boy. The Prince is in a carriage on the left with the Princess by his side, her high hat being trimmed with feathers. In the background is seen a view of the town and Ely Cathedral, whilst in the distance a number of horses and jockeys complete the scene.

Like the two prints previously described a number of impressions were taken upon silk.

Amongst other hunting scenes Seymour painted a set of four pictures called *Fox Hunting*, which were engraved by J. Roberts. The huntsman on the grey horse going into cover, in the second of this series, is said to be a portrait of an old-world divine, the Reverend Mr. Fenning, a clergyman, who was devoted to hunting.

Of very independent spirit, this painter once administered a severe snub to the haughty Duke of Somerset with whom he had been staying for the purpose of painting portraits of his stud. The Duke, who had drunk Seymour's health, calling him Cousin Seymour, was very much offended at the latter claiming to be related to his family, and directed that the painter should be sent about his business, with the result that the equine portraits were left unfinished. Finding this exceedingly inconvenient, as no painter could be discovered equal to finishing the paintings in question, the Duke sent to Seymour asking him to return, receiving as answer the following disconcerting reply:

" My Lord, I will now, by declining to come, prove to you that I belong to your Grace's family."

Seymour drew exceedingly well, especially with the pen, and his delineations of horses are marked by much spirit and character. Unfortunately he was extremely lazy, and when he attempted to give more finish to his work his defects were very quickly apparent. From an artistic point of view the works of this painter are perhaps not worthy of any great esteem, but, as contributions to Turf history, they possess an undoubted value, owing to the light which they throw upon the manners and dress of a long-past age. By the art patrons of his own day Seymour was generally ranked as an artist far inferior to Wootton, who, however, it must be remembered, had been regularly trained for a painter's career.

It is curious to recall that in 1825 John Scott etched the portrait of a racehorse, *Old Partner*, which had been painted by Seymour some hundred years before. A number of plates of racehorses, after Seymour, were also engraved by R. Houston.

About the time of James Seymour's death in 1752 was born Thomas Gooch, who designed and engraved the agreeable set of coloured sporting prints which are known as *The Life and Death of a Racehorse.* The same artist appears to have painted more than one series of pictures dealing with the subject of an equine career. Gooch, whose particular specialities were portraits of horses and dogs, exhibited one set at the Royal Academy in 1783, whilst, in 1792, Jeffrey, of Pall Mall, published a folio volume containing, as the title page quaintly sets forth, " The Life and Death of a Racehorse, exemplified in his various stages of existence till his dissolution. The whole drawn and engraved in Aquatinta by Thomas Gooch, Esq." The titles of this set which Gooch himself engraved, differ considerably from those affixed to the pictures shown in the Academy. Another set of six engravings representing the same subject was, it must be mentioned, published in 1790, but some doubt appears to prevail as to the originals from which these were taken.

The Life and Death of a Racehorse should be in the possession of every collector, the size and general appearance of the six prints rendering them especially suitable for decorative purposes. A good set it may be mentioned should be procurable for from £10 to £15.

Not many of Gooch's pictures were engraved, whilst his career is enveloped in some obscurity, the exact date of his death being unknown.

Amongst sporting painters of the eighteenth century the four artists who bore the name of Sartorius occupy a conspicuous place. John Sartorius, who was born at Nuremberg in 1700, is the first. His chief works were a portrait of the celebrated mare, *Molly*, and of the racehorses *Looby*, *Old Traveller*, and *Careless*. Besides these he painted many other pictures of horses, sending no fewer than sixty-two works to the exhibitions of the Free Society of Artists, which were held from 1761 to 1783. He died in 1780. Francis Sartorius, the son of John, was born in 1734 and learnt the art of painting from his father, with the result that he eventually became the most celebrated member of his family. Acknowledged as the fashionable horse painter of his day, he executed more portraits of famous racehorses during the latter part of the eighteenth century than any contemporary artist. *Eclipse* was one of his most favourite subjects. John June engraved some of his works between 1760 and 1770.

In English country houses equestrian family portraits by Francis Sartorius are not infrequently to be found. At Aynho Park, Banbury, the beautiful seat of Mr. W. C. Cartwright, is a hunting piece representing three gentlemen, two of them the brothers Fermor, hunting in Aynho Park, whilst at Eridge Castle, Sussex, is a portrait of the grandfather of the present writer, painted when he was a boy of thirteen, mounted upon a big horse, with a little dog gambolling in the foreground. This was executed in 1773.

John N. Sartorius, son of Francis Sartorius, was born in 1755, and owing to the time in which he lived enjoyed advantages denied to his father and grandfather, whose opportunities for study had been somewhat limited. His pictures dealing with hunting, racing, shooting and other kindred sports, exhibit great animation and spirit, besides displaying signs of knowledge of the subjects dealt with. A frequent contributor to the Royal Academy from 1781 to 1821, he exhibited there about seventy-four pictures. One of his best works is a portrait of Sir William Rowley, with hunt servants and some of his favourite hounds. He was a frequent contributor to the *Sporting Magazine*, and there are many engravings from his works in the volumes published between 1795 and 1827. A fine hunting scene, painted by John N. Sartorius, is *The Death of the Fox*, a picture which formerly hung in Carshalton Park, Surrey. John Scott engraved a good many of his compositions, but perhaps his most successful efforts were the six engravings in *The Chase*, to which is added *Field Sports* by William Somerville, Esq., published in 1817 by Sherwood, Neely and Jones. The eldest son of John N. Sartorius, John F. Sartorius also devoted his talents to the delineation of sporting subjects. He was not a very prolific artist, and during his life-time had to compete with his father, whose work was very much superior. It is probable that in many cases the latter assisted his son, and consequently several sporting pictures exist which cannot for certain be assigned to any particular one of the two. John Scott also engraved the works of John F. Sartorios, and it is impossible to say whether the plates in the *Sporting Magazine*, signed simply " Sartorius," are by father or son.

An occasional exhibitor at the Royal Academy, where his pictures were sometimes refused by the Hanging Committee, one of his best works, shown in 1806, was *Coursing in Hatfield Park*, in which the famous Marchioness of Salisbury is a prominent figure. This lady, who was a very Diana of her day, established the Hatfield Hunt. A splendid and fearless rider, she continued to preside over its affairs up to the age of seventy, and even after this age rode in the park till she was eighty-six. In November, 1835, she met with a tragic end at Hatfield, being burnt to death through her cap catching alight from some candles on her writing-table.

Though not essentially a sporting artist, Thomas Rowlandson executed a number of designs connected with sport, many of the watercolour sketches, which he dashed off with such facility, representing incidents connected with either the turf or the chase.

It would however appear, from the numerous coloured prints after this artist, that the humorous and vivacious aspects of a sportsman's career appealed to him quite as much as sport itself. He executed quite a number of coloured prints of the same nature as those entitled *The Huntsman Rising* and *The Gamester Going to Bed*.

Born in 1756, when the world was not yet bitten with that love of uniformity, and the desire to reduce everyone and everything to a standard of dull and mediocre respectability, Thomas Rowlandson had little sympathy for the new conditions of life, which, during his old age, were beginning to make themselves felt. The change of dress and habits seem to have impaired his talents, for his later works can in no way compare with the brilliant sketches which, in his early period, he would dash off with such ease and facility. Towards the end of his life he became almost forgotten, and his death, in 1827, hardly aroused a languid comment.

When at his best, no artist, perhaps, ever conveyed a better idea of the hot-headed young Englishman and the buxom laughing English lass of the late eighteenth century. Severity has no place in his work except to be a butt for the sallies of red-coated ensigns and roguish damsels. The England he loved was a very different country to that existing to-day, when it has become rather like a huge factory, with set hours of play for the operatives. The sight of some of Rowlandson's drawings, replete with full-blooded life and unrestrained gaiety, cannot fail to make a few of us sigh for times which, if perhaps not so orderly, were more natural and entertaining than the entirely commercial trend of the present age.

Though many of the scenes pictured by Rowlandson are of a somewhat Bacchanalian character, the artist himself appears to have been a temperate man, the gaming table having appealed to him far more than the bottle. In this he differed from Gillray, who was a drunkard of a terrible description. In another respect also these artists were entirely different. Rowlandson, unlike Gillray, was never very severe towards the French. True is it that he executed several caricatures dealing with Napoleon, but none of them breathe that spirit of fierce hate which is so conspicuous in the work of his contemporary. For France, where he had received his education, he seems to have always kept a soft place in his heart, and no doubt the amusement and pleasure in which he had freely indulged whilst at Paris still lingered in his memory, and made him unwilling to make too fierce an attack upon a people with whom he had much in common. A hard, though not by any means a steady worker, the gaming-table absorbed most of the money which his reed pen brought to him, and the remainder was spent in entertaining that beauty of which he was such an ardent admirer.

Original sketches by Rowlandson are very often to be picked up in out-of-the-way country towns, and occasionally very good ones may be met with, for whenever this artist went upon a journey it was his practice to make drawings along the way, and as his was an extremely roving disposition, he produced a good deal of work of this sort.

Coloured drawings by this artist always command a good price, that is to say, if they have been done during his best period, which was, roughly speaking, between 1780 and 1810, though it must be

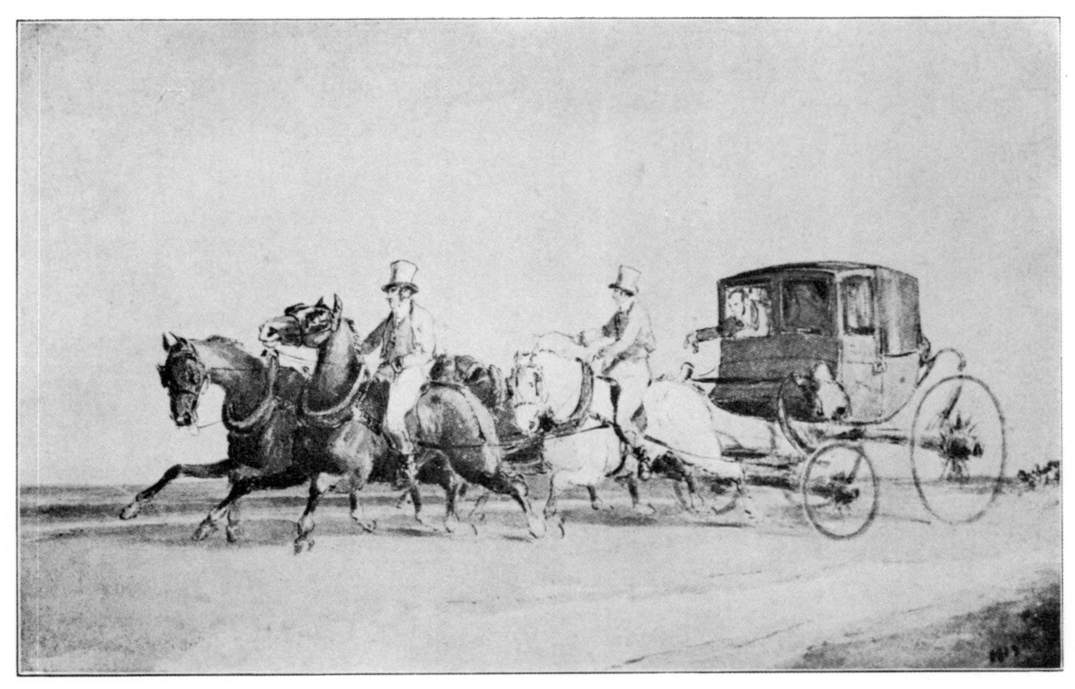

WATER COLOUR DRAWING
By Cooper Henderson

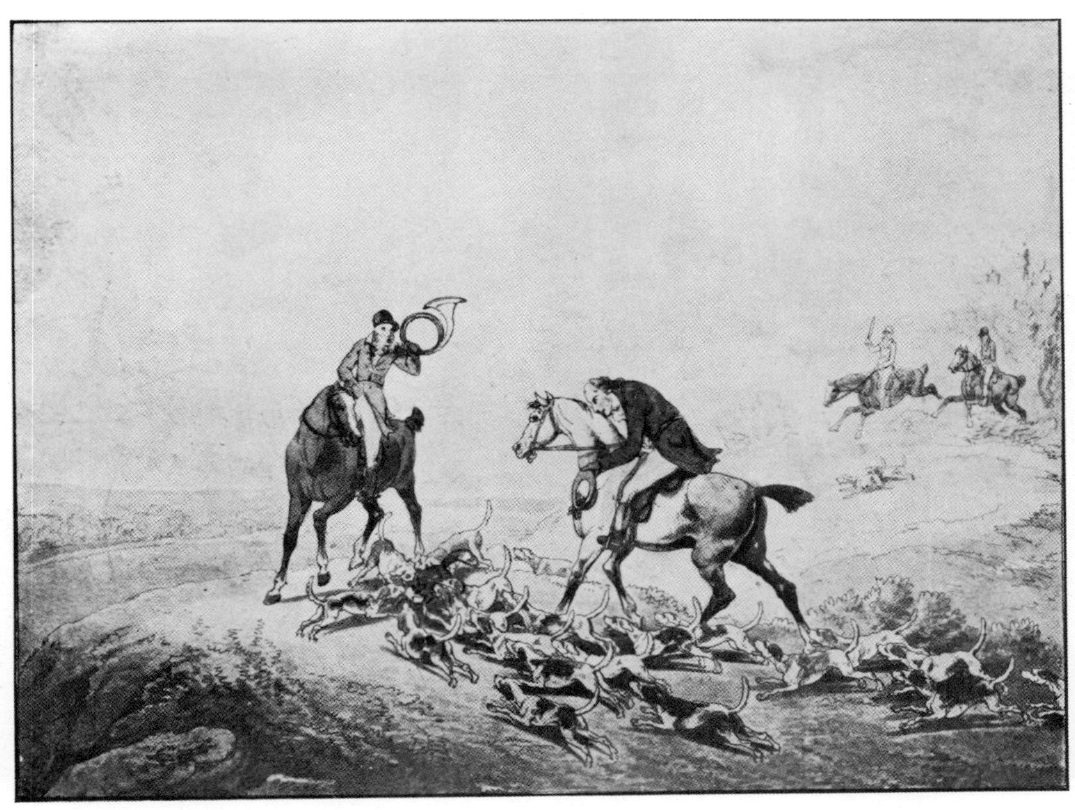

THE DEATH OF THE FOX
By Howitt

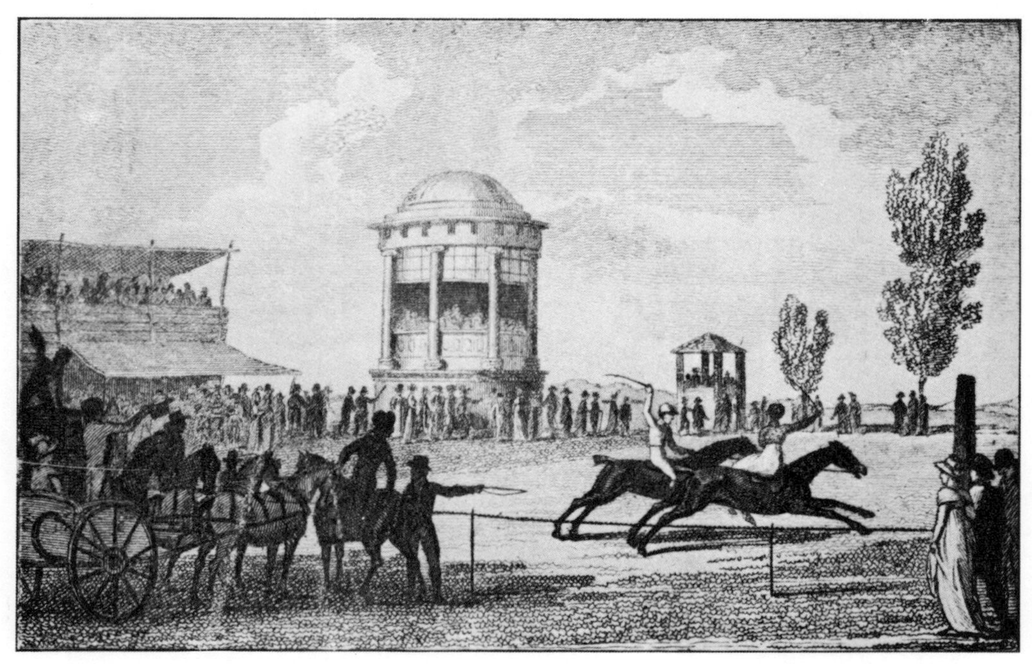

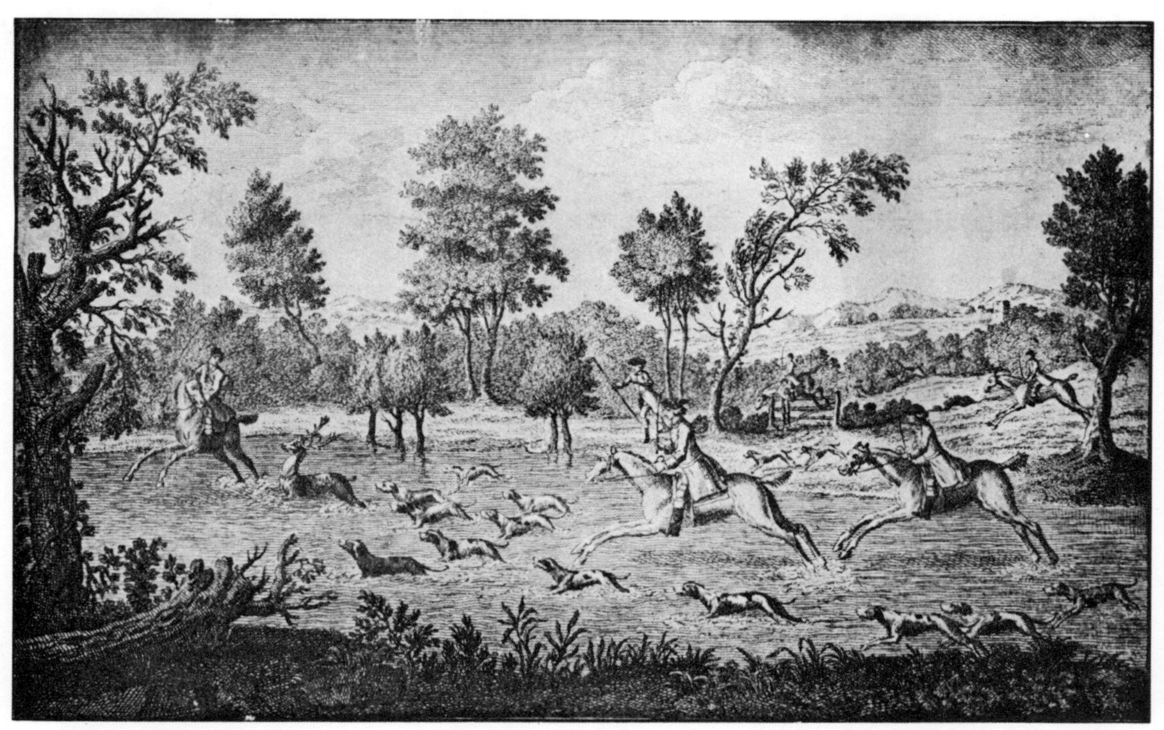

THE STAG TAKING SOIL
After Wootton

understood that his very best work was executed between a shorter time—1780 and 1790.

Many of his sketches of country towns, executed upon the spot, are quite delightful, and are still fairly easy to obtain. Nevertheless the very best are year by year becoming more rare. Characteristic scenes, showing well-known localities, should not be missed by any purchaser lucky enough to come across them. His book of coloured plates of London Volunteers, in a perfect condition, is worth a good deal of money, and there is little doubt but that, in a few years, it will increase in value, for examples of it are eagerly sought for by collectors.

Should any of our readers come across a copy of Rowlandson's *Imitations of Modern Drawings* at a moderate price, let them secure it, and they may then see what extraordinary versatility the artist possessed. It is a folio volume of imitations of various masters, in which the imitator's own individuality is completely sunk in that of the artist whose style and mannerisms are travestied.

Notwithstanding the undoubted talents of Rowlandson, it is not, however, everyone who appreciates his art. Of a free, careless, and somewhat extravagant disposition, he occasionally allowed himself to indulge in a license which is not to the taste of the present generation. Still there are many of his productions which must interest all who have any pretension to the possession of taste. His racing prints, for instance, are full of life and vigour, and will convey the idea of that robust vitality which was such a characteristic of English eighteenth-century life. A good example of his work in this style is the set of racing prints which made its appearance in 1789. Spirited and interesting, this set should not be overlooked when met with in a good condition.

The six prints are *Betting, Weighing, Mounting, Racing, Between Heats,* and *Running out of the Course.* This series, which is to be acquired with comparative ease, affords a capital representation of the incidents of racing as they existed some hundred years ago. Rowlandson, who was by nature more addicted to the pleasures of a town life than to rural sports, executed a good many sporting prints, but the greater number are practically caricatures, and are not very suitable for decorative purposes. Like Rowlandson, Morland dealt a good deal with sport, though somewhat indirectly. He was never, however, an accurate animal portrait painter. But ill-grounded in anatomy, he was most successful in portraying those animals whose forms were most dissimulated by their covering, such as pigs, sheep, rabbits, etc. It was his practice, whenever he painted a horse, to choose an aged one, not so much, probably, on account of thinking it picturesque, but by reason of the salient points of its form, which lent itself well to his peculiar genius. Morland's boon companions were his models—in *The Sportsman's Return,* "Dirty Brooks," the cobbler, one of the artist's drinking cronies and agents, is depicted leaning out of his stall.

Four fine sporting prints by Morland are a series of rare plates entitled *Fox Hunting,* which were engraved in colours by

E. Bell. *The Lucky Sportsman*, also in colours, engraved by F. D. Soiron, after the same artist, is another scarce print which in good condition realises somewhere about fifty pounds. *The First of September—Morning* and *Evening*—are an attractive pair of shooting prints by William Ward, after Morland, of which there are both coloured and uncoloured states. Other prints after Morland are: *Partridge Shooting* and *Duck Shooting*, by Charles Catton. *Morning, Partridge Shooting, Pheasant Shooting, Snipe Shooting, Duck Shooting,* and *Evening;* a set of large oblong folio plates, chiefly etched by Rowlandson, aquatinta by S. Alken, 1792. A set of these in colours commands something like thirty pounds, whilst uncoloured impressions should be obtained for two or three guineas.

A painter of sporting scenes whose style has some affinity to that of Rowlandson, was Samuel Howitt who married the sister of the latter, by whom he appears to have been very much influenced. Belonging to a family of Nottinghamshire Quakers, Howitt, who was originally possessed of independent means, took up his residence near Epping Forest, where the pursuit of field sports was his favourite occupation. His fortune however seems soon to have melted away, and finding himself in extremely straitened circumstances he became a drawing master at a school near Ealing, a post for which his artistic attainments, which had hitherto been only utilised for the purposes of amusement, fully qualified him.

About 1783 he appears to have obtained recognition as a talented artist, for in that year he exhibited a hunting picture in the Royal Academy. Much of Howitt's best work was executed in water colours, while he excelled also both as an engraver and etcher. In 1798 he contributed a certain number of engravings to Beckford's *Thoughts on Hunting*, whilst sixty illustrations in *Oriental Field Sports*, after Captain Williamson's designs, were his work. During his connection with the *Sporting Magazine*, Howitt engraved no fewer than 157 plates, whilst his productions in other quarters were also very large. As has before been said, this artist's style frequently shows a great resemblance to that of his brother-in-law Rowlandson, who, though a man of somewhat free life, appears to have been on terms of the closest intimacy with this artist of Quaker extraction.

Amongst sporting artists of the eighteenth century, Sawrey Gilpin, R.A. must not be forgotten. Gilpin painted both in oil and water colours, but though his pictures display great spirit his colouring is poor, whilst their execution is deficient in the higher technical qualities.

The famous Colonel Thornton, of Thornville Royal, was a friend and patron of this painter, who in 1793 painted for him *The Death of the Fox*, which was twice engraved eighteen years later by John Scott. One of the engravings it may be added was executed to serve as a companion print to *The Fox breaking Cover*, which Scott had engraved after Philip Reinagle. The pair of prints in question are amongst the best of the engraver's works. Ordinary impressions should be worth about £5, and proofs about double.

Amongst engraved portraits of racehorses after Sawrey Gilpin, *Highflyer* by F. Jukes, *Jupiter* and *Sir Peter Teazle* by W. Ward, are of some interest. An engraving of the last-named horse by John Scott, appeared in the *Sporting Magazine* for 1819. The portrait of Colonel Thornton's *Jupiter*, from which the print was taken, was exhibited at the Royal Academy in 1792. Three pictures illustrative of incidents in Colonel Thornton's Sporting Tour through the Highlands are in the Elsenham Collection and are of great interest, being the work of three different artists. Sawrey Gilpin painted the animals, George Barrett the landscapes, whilst the portraits were by Philip Reinagle one of the most celebrated sporting artists of that day.

A pupil of the Court Painter Allan Ramsay, Reinagle's work showed such a high degree of promise that Ramsay eventually appointed him as his assistant. On one occasion, it may be added, Reinagle was deputed by his principal (who had to go abroad for some time) to paint portraits of fifty pairs of Kings and Queens, the remuneration being ten guineas for each picture. On leaving the studio of Ramsay, the young painter seems to have entirely devoted his energies to portraiture, varied by the delineation of sporting subjects and landscape painting. Especially remarkable for his pictures of dogs, Reinagle made a particular study of what are now known as Clumber spaniels, which in his day were called "cock springers." Exhibiting two portraits of men in the Royal Academy of 1774, his first sporting contribution to this institution, of which he became an associate in 1787, was *Dead Game*. His Diploma picture on his election as an Academician in 1812, was *An Eagle and Vulture disputing with a Hyena*. Reinagle who continued to exhibit till 1832, showed altogether some hundred and thirty-eight pictures.

In 1796 he painted, in collaboration with Sawrey Gilpin, a portrait of Colonel Thornton, in which that redoubtable sportsman is shown roebuck shooting in the Forest of Glencoe, with the only twelve-barrelled rifle ever made ; in the background is a keeper crouching with a dog. This was engraved by M. W. Bate, and published by H. Mutlow, of Russell Court, in 1810. Colonel Thornton was a great patron of Reinagle, who, in 1803, exhibited, at the Royal Academy, a portrait of a great tench caught by the Colonel, a view of Thornville Royal being included as a setting for the same. In the first volume of Colonel Thornton's " Travels in France," is a frontispiece engraved by Mackenzie after a portrait which Reinagle specially designed. This is prettily embellished with attributes of the chase, whilst an oval beneath shows the famous match between Mrs. Thornton and her brother-in-law, Mr. Flint. The race in question was run on the last day of the York August Meeting, 1804, and resulted in the defeat of the lady, who took her beating with rather a bad grace. To Mrs. Thornton, it may be added, is attached the distinction of having been the only lady jockey ever mentioned in the " Racing Calendar."

Her feat is chronicled thus :—" Saturday, August 25th, 1804, Mr. Flint's Brown Thornville, by Volunteer out of Abigail, aged, rode by the owner, beat Col. Thornton's ch. h. Vinagrillio, aged, rode by Mrs. Thornton, four miles, 500 gns."

The weights for this race were what is known as catch-weights, that is to say that Mrs. Thornton was to ride her own weight against Mr. Flint's. An enormous crowd assembled at York to witness this very uncommon race, and at the appointed time Mrs. Thornton appeared dressed in a leopard-coloured body with blue sleeves, the rest buff, and a blue cap, in which dress she is represented in the print reproduced on p 38. Mr. Flint's colours were white. Before the race, odds of 5 and 6 to 4 were laid upon the lady, and in running the first three miles as much as 7 to 4 and 2 to 1 were wagered in her favour. During the last mile, however, it became evident that she would not win, and the odds veered round and were laid upon Mr. Flint. Notwithstanding that Mrs. Thornton displayed much excellent horsemanship, her opponent eventually won with much ease, to the great regret of the spectators, who were fascinated by her beauty and enterprise in taking part in such a sporting match. Over £200,000 is said to have changed hands over this race, which appears to have excited the liveliest interest in all parts of the country.

The Fox Breaking Cover was another picture by Reinagle painted for Colonel Thornton. This was engraved by John Scott, and, as has before been said, forms a pendant to *The Death of the Fox*, by Sawrey Gilpin.

Colonel Thomas Thornton, who has before been mentioned in connection with Sawrey Gilpin, was a celebrated figure in the sporting world of his day, and a liberal patron of art in its relation to sport. At times a daring gambler, Thornville Royal, his seat in Yorkshire (now the property of Lord Ripon), is said to have been purchased by him with money won at play. The estate in question was formerly known as Allerton Maulevrer, and was the property of the Duke of York, from whom Colonel Thornton bought it for £110,000 in 1789. Sixteen years later it was resold to Lord Stourton when the sporting owner took up his residence at Sype Park, Wiltshire, which he took on lease, the increase of cultivation having rendered hawking, which was the Colonel's favourite pastime, impracticable. Several portraits of Colonel Thornton, it may be mentioned, show him engaged in this sport. On leaving Thornville Royal the owner created a considerable sensation by the large retinue of huntsmen, grooms, keepers and falconers that followed in his train. In addition to a pack of hounds and numerous hunters, a regular menagerie of animals was included. Amongst a heterogeneous collection of roebuck, fallow deer, terriers, greyhounds and rare specimens of beasts connected with the chase were some French and Russian wild boar, received from the Emperor Napoleon in exchange for seventy couple of finely-bred English foxhounds.

Ten years later the Colonel determined to retire to France, where he bought the Chateau of Pon le Roi, which he resold in 1821. By this time his fame as a sportsman had become rather a

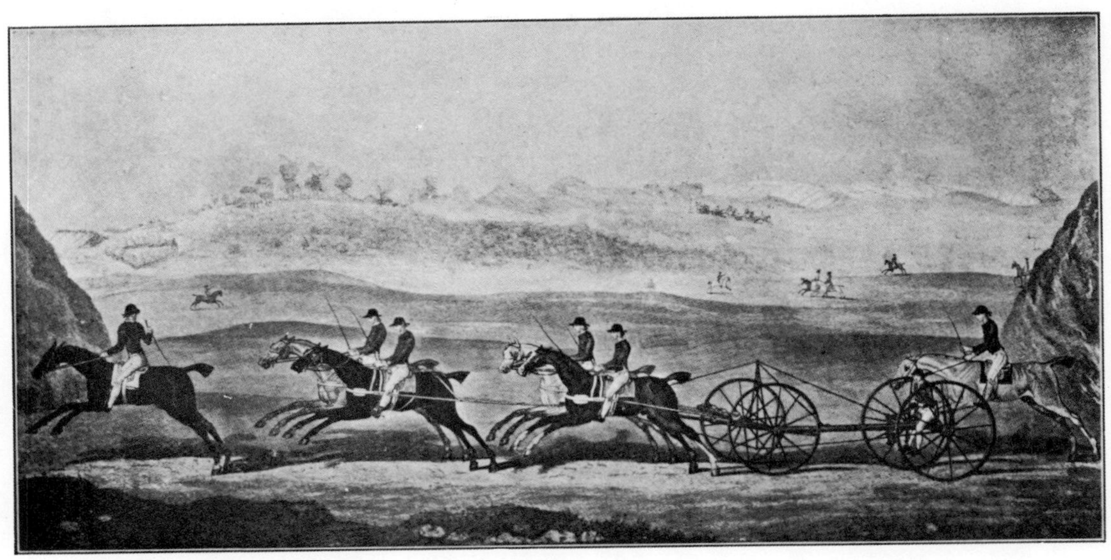

CARRIAGE MATCH AGAINST TIME, RUN AT NEWMARKET, AUGUST 29TH, 1750

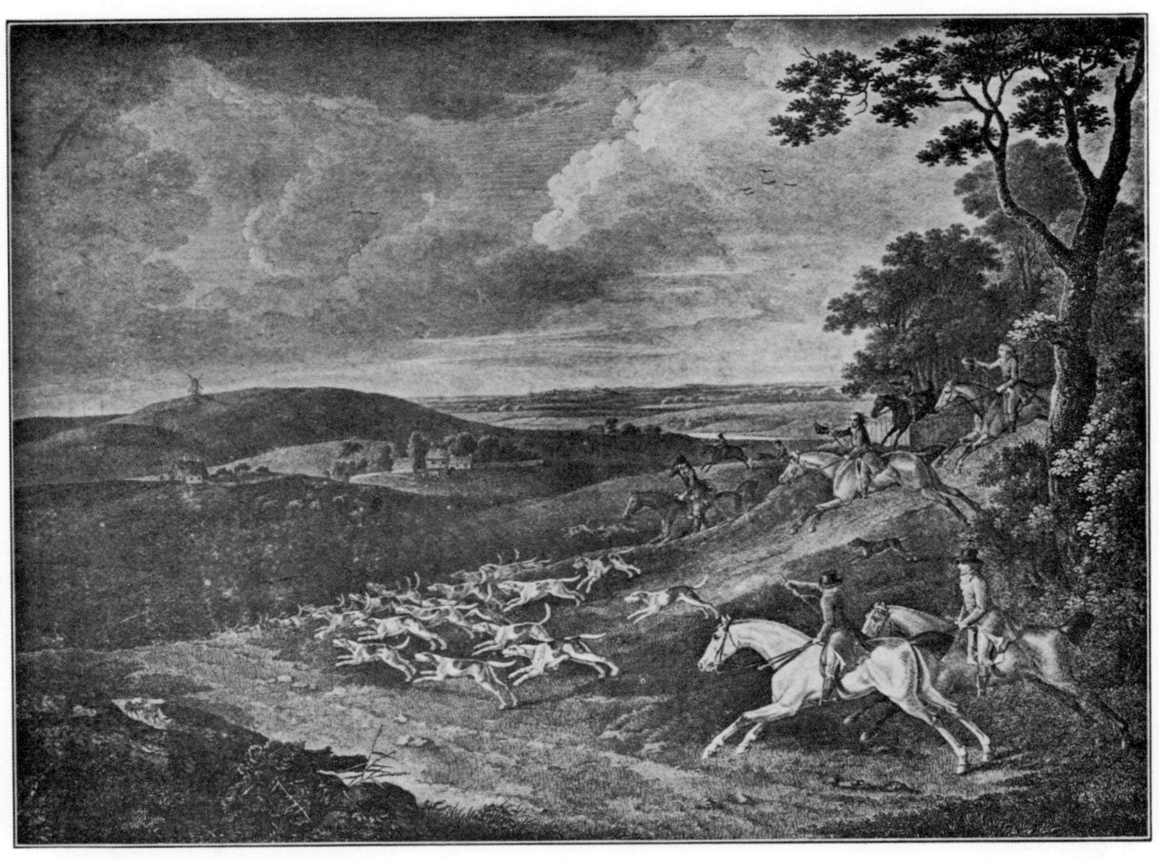

THE CHASE
By J. N. Sartorius.   Landscape by Peltro.   Figures Engraved by Neagle

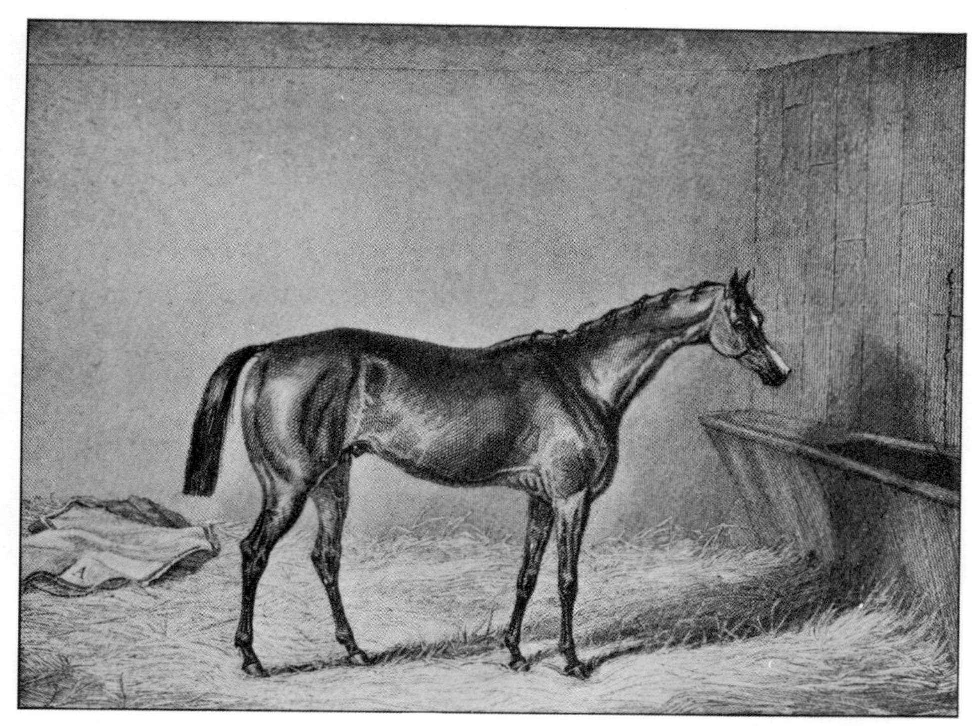

ATTILA.   WINNER OF THE DERBY, 1842
By Engleheart, after Laporte

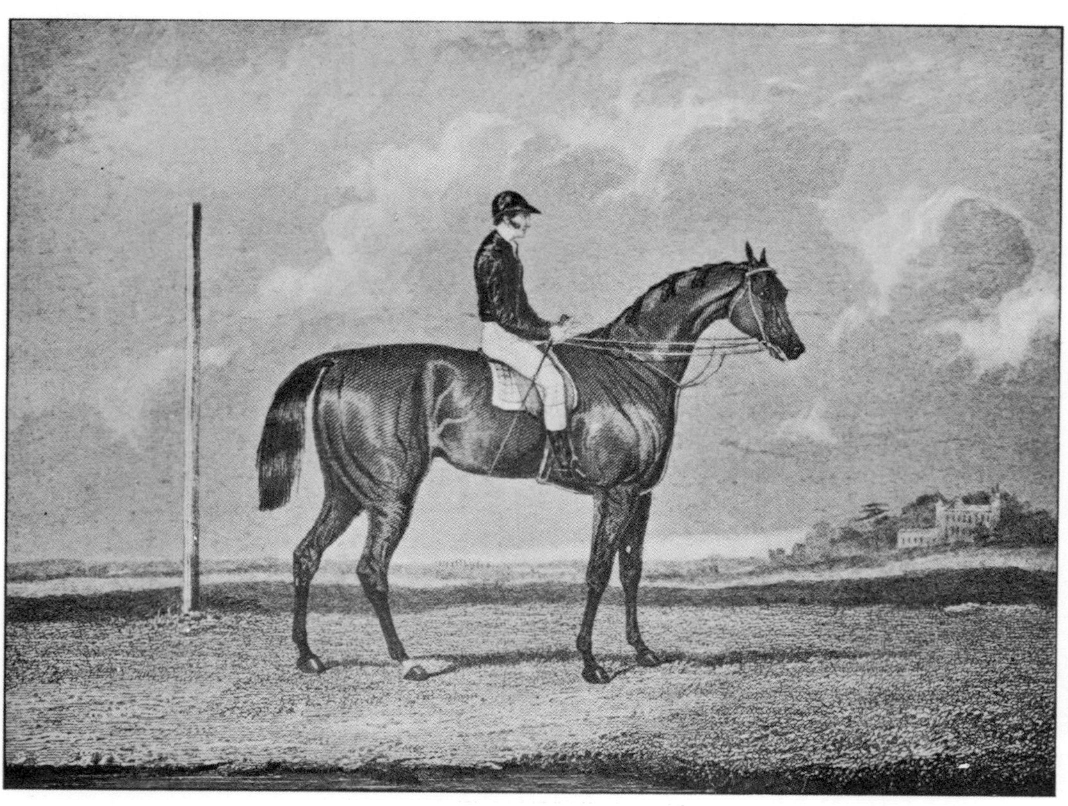

COTHERSTONE.   WINNER OF THE DERBY, 1843
By Hacker, after H. Alken

thing of the past and a report even stated that he was dead.   Mrs. Thornton in consequence received a number of letters of condolence to one of which the Colonel sent the following quaint reply :—

" PARIS, RUE DE LA PAIX,

" *December 25th, 1821.*

" My honest Brother Sportsman,

" This is Christmas-Day, dedicated by me, from my youth, to gaiety and reasonable hospitality, endeavouring to make all happy, according to the situation in which Providence has placed me.

" In health no man can be more hearty, but not quite stout in my knees and feet ; stomach invincible ; always in appetite ; eat three times a day—tea, muffins, and grated hung beef at nine—at two, roasted game or cockscombs, and about a pint of the finest white burgundy—dinner at five and then a bottle of wine—about three or four glasses of spirits and water, rather weak—then to bed ; *sleep better* than I ever did in my life.   Pretty well, you will say, for a dead man.   Rise at eight, breakfast at nine, so we go on—every night the finest dreams.   I expect some wild boar ; if it comes our friend B. may be sure of a part."

" P.S. Dec. 26,—I find by the Papers that I died, after a short illness, much lamented, &c., &c., at Paris.   However that may be, I gave a dinner yesterday to a dozen sportsmen : we had roast beef, plum pudding, Yorkshire goose pie, and sat up singing most gaily till two this morning. At twelve we had two broiled fowls, gizzards, &c. ; and finished a bottle of old rum, in punch.   No intoxication ; for I went to bed well and never rose better."

(SIGNED) " THORNTON, MARQUIS DE PONT."

His actual death, it may be mentioned, occurred in the spring of 1823.   He was at the time seventy-four years old.

Philip Reinagle, like his patron, also lived to a green old age, dying aged eighty-four, at Chelsea, in 1833.   As a sporting artist the accuracy of his draughtmanship is very remarkable, minute and careful attention being devoted to anatomical truth.   In addition to this he was a landscape painter of considerable talent, his sporting pictures being rendered doubly attractive by the real artistic feeling which is almost invariably displayed in their scenic accessories, certain of the landscape settings being of high merit. Richard Ramsay Reinagle, the painter's son, inherited his father's artistic gifts, and achieving success as a landscape painter, in due course became an Academician.   He was, however, eventually obliged to resign, having, contrary to rule, submitted for exhibition a picture at which another artist besides himself had worked.

Another sporting artist who painted a large number of horses, dogs, and sporting scenes was James Barenger, whose animals are drawn with a fidelity which would seem to be the result of personal observation.   As a young man he was fond of landscapes which allowed the introduction of deer, but he modified his style when he began to exhibit at the Royal Academy.

Amongst prints after Barenger which call for special notice are the following : *Pheasant* and *British Feathered Game*, a pair engraved by Charles Turner and published by Ackermann in 1810.   *The Earl of Derby's Staghounds*, engraved by R. Woodman, a print containing equestrian portraits of Lord Stanley, the Hon. C. Stanley, and Jonathan Griffin, the huntsman, who is the central figure. This was published in 1823 by T. Griffin, of Carshalton. The best of twenty-six pictures reproduced in the *Sporting Magazine* was *Doll*, a pointer, which was admirably engraved by John Scott. Barenger's pictures were highly appreciated in his own day, the best engravers being employed to reproduce them for the various publishers of sporting literature and prints, with whom this artist's productions were in considerable demand.

British Field Sports, Vol. III., by William Henry Scott, published in 1818, contains the following plates from works by Barenger, twelve of which were engraved by John Scott and the remaining five by J. Webb :—

  (1) *Pointers going out with Sportsmen.*
  (2) *Woodcock Shooting.*
  (3) *Sportsmen with Spaniels.*
  (4) *Greyhounds with Dead Hare.*
  (5) *Greyhounds with Sportsmen finding a Hare.*
  (6) *Duck Shooting.*
  (7) *Sportsmen with Spaniels.*
  (8) *Earth Stopping.*
  (9) *Pony and Dogs.*
 (10) *Hunting, going into Cover.*
 (11) *Hunting, the Chase.*
 (12) *Hunting, the Death.*
 (13) *Racing, the Finish.*
 (14) *Sligo, a Racehorse.*
 (15) *Cock-fighting.*
 (16) *Game Fowls*, and
 (17) *Fly Fishing.*

The *Sporting Repository*, Vol. VIII., published in 1822, by Thomas McLean, contained five plates engraved by T. Hunt from Barenger's pictures. These were :—

  (1) *Claret, a Hunter.*
  (2) *A Hawk.*
  (3) *A Herefordshire Ox.*
  (4) *Rubens, a Hunter*, and
  (5) *Merino Sheep.*

The portrait of *Rubens* was engraved for separate publication by C. Turner. The *Annals of Sporting* for the year 1824 contained two plates of special interest, these being the only examples of the artist's work which were engraved by his uncle, S. Barenger. "Topthorn" is depicted in the act of taking a leap of twenty-one feet over the Whissendine Brook.

A beautiful engraving after Barenger is the one by John Scott, representing "Doll," a pointer bred by the artist from a bitch belonging to W. Whitbread, Esq., of Much Hadham, Hertfordshire, a gentleman well known for his famous strain of pointers. Many of Barenger's works were engraved in large size.

A certain number of old coloured prints depict the rather brutal
sports which were popular as late as the early days of the nineteenth century. A series of seven oblong coloured plates representing bull-baiting, cock-fighting, and the like, were published about
the year 1823; another old coloured engraving not undeserving of
attention shows a dog-fight in the Westminster pit, whilst the
feats of " Billie " the rat-killing dog have also been commemorated
by the engraver. A coloured plate represents the canine celebrity
in question, as the legend sets forth, " killing 100 rats in five-and-
a-half minutes."

" Billie " attracted some attention in his day as the following
extract from the *Morning Herald* of October 22nd, 1822, will
demonstrate :

" The owner of the famous dog, Billie, of rat-killing notoriety,
has again undertaken that he shall perform the almost incredible
task of killing 100 rats in twelve minutes. This task he performed
before in eight-and-a-half minutes for a bet of 20 sovereigns. The
bet is 50, besides considerable other sums, which are pending upon
the issue. The match will take place on Thursday evening next, at
the Westminster Pit, when the rats are all to be turned loose in a
12 foot square. The floor of the pit is to be whitened, so that the
whole of the rats are to be visible to the dog, and to the amateurs
for whose accommodation galleries are already erected. Some
difference having arisen on the last match, as it was said that one
rat escaped, there are to be now an extra number provided to
prevent any disappointment. An eminent artist is now employed
taking the likeness of the dog and his master. They have each lost
an eye through their valorous exploits, in endeavouring to clear this
country of rats. We may also add that their esteem stands so high
that a most respectable picture frame maker has actually received
and executed an order for 114 of the most costly frames that can be
manufactured for so stylish an ornament, and that scarcely any of
the fancy or the sporting world, that will not have it exhibited in
their parlours. Billie is to be drawn with his silver collar on, and
his master with a brilliant star, presented to him by the amateurs
of rat-killing note."

Amongst prints which are connected with cock-fighting, the most
celebrated is of course Colonel Mordaunt's *Cock Match*, engraved
by Earlom, after Zoffany, the oriental setting of which imparts a
charm rather lacking in most pictures of this sort of combat. A
fine pair of portraits of fighting cocks, is *The Cock in Feather* and
The Trimmed Cock, by C. Turner, after B. Marshall; companion
prints to these by the same artist and engraver, are a *Black-breasted
Dark Red* and a *Streaky-breasted Red Dunn*. The title of the first
pair, it may be mentioned, is occasionally given as *Peace and War*.
Fine impressions of the four being worth some twenty guineas.

Benjamin Marshall, the painter of these pictures, was a
Leicestershire man, born in 1767, originally a portrait painter. *The
Death of the Fox*, by Sawrey Gilpin, which was exhibited in the
Royal Academy of 1793, made such an impression upon him that he

determined to devote his talents entirely to the painting of subjects connected with sport.

This form of art, it must be remembered, was at the time in question highly remunerative, there being a positive rage for pictures of race-horses, hunting scenes, and the like; Stubbs easily obtained a hundred for a likeness of some famous horse.

Introduced to Mr. Wheble by John Scott, Marshall's name begins to figure in the *Sporting Magazine* about 1796, as the painter of pictures which Scott engraved.

For Sir Henry Smith, Marshall painted the portraits of the famous pugilist, John Jackson, a portrait of almost the same size, representing Thomas Belcher, being executed for John Harrison, Esq. Both of these tributes to the champions of the ring, it may be added, were engraved in mezzotint by Charles Turner, proofs being now worth about five guineas apiece.

In 1812, Marshall took up his residence at Newmarket, where, in high favour with a large number of aristocratic patrons, he painted pictures of racehorses; amongst these may be mentioned *Filho da Puta*, and *Sir Joshua*, (together) engraved by W. Ward, who also executed *Hunters at Grass* after this artist. The latter is a fine print, and proofs of it are worth at least ten pounds. The engraver in question also executed *Two Dogs Fighting for a Stick*, after Marshall, a print worthy of attention; whilst R. Woodman produced an excellent engraving of Francis Dukinfield Astley, Esq. and his Harriers, of which a few impressions were struck in colour.

In 1825, Marshall once more returned to London, where he remained till his death, ten years later.

Two pictures by Marshall are particularly worthy of attention, these are *The Sportsman* and *A First-rate Shot*. The first of these is a portrait of Thomas Gosden, a celebrated sporting bookbinder, of St. Martin's Lane, which has been twice engraved, in small size by Maile, and in a larger form by Giller. The smaller engraving, a few impressions of which were executed in colour, was published by Gosden in 1824. It is a peculiarly attractive print.

A First-rate Shot, an engraving of which appeared in the *Sporting Magazine* for October, 1831, represents the famous sporting character George Osbaldeston.

Amongst sporting engravings now in great request, none are more highly valued than the best of those after James Pollard, who lived till the early sixties, his coaching scenes being especially attractive. The road, indeed, was Pollard's speciality, though it by no means monopolised his brush, which dealt besides with racing, hunting and fishing. A keen angler himself, and well acquainted with all the best angling round London, he painted a large number of fishing pictures. A set of four coloured prints after Pollard, *Fly Fishing*, *Bottom Fishing*, *Trolling for Pike*, and *Anglers packing up*, were published by T. Helme, in 1831.

James Pollard's father, Robert Pollard, was a Newcastle man who established himself in London as an engraver; his business was in Holloway, the title of the firm being R. Pollard & Son.

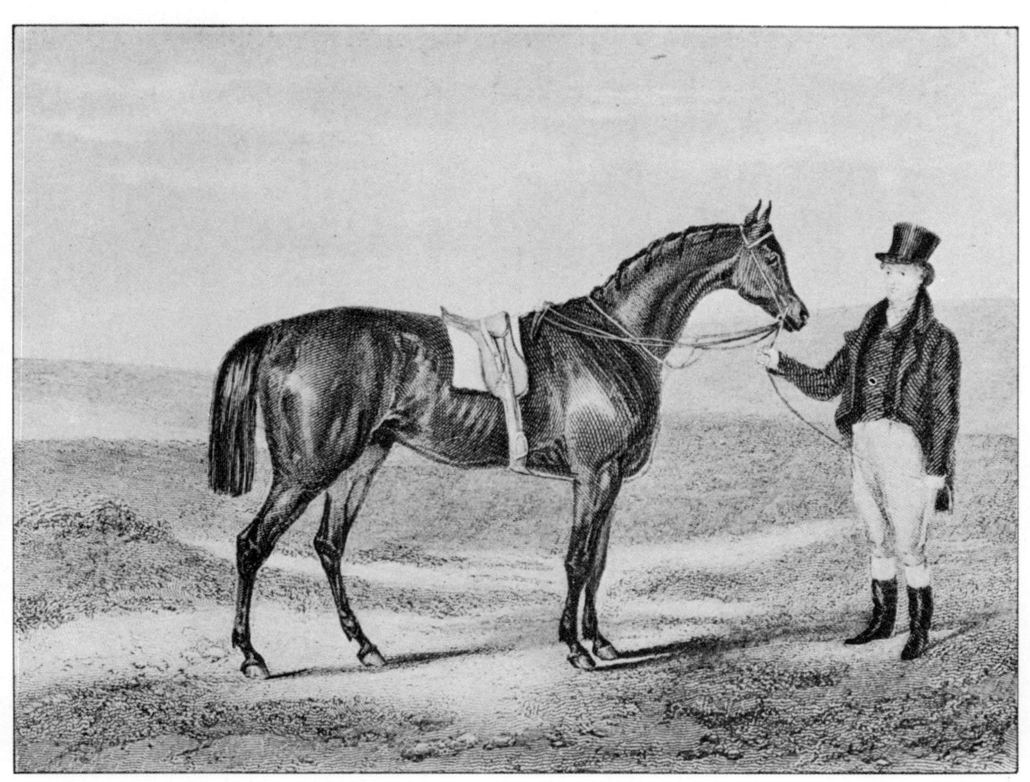

LITTLE WONDER. WINNER OF THE DERBY, 1840 *By Beckwith, after F. C. Turner*

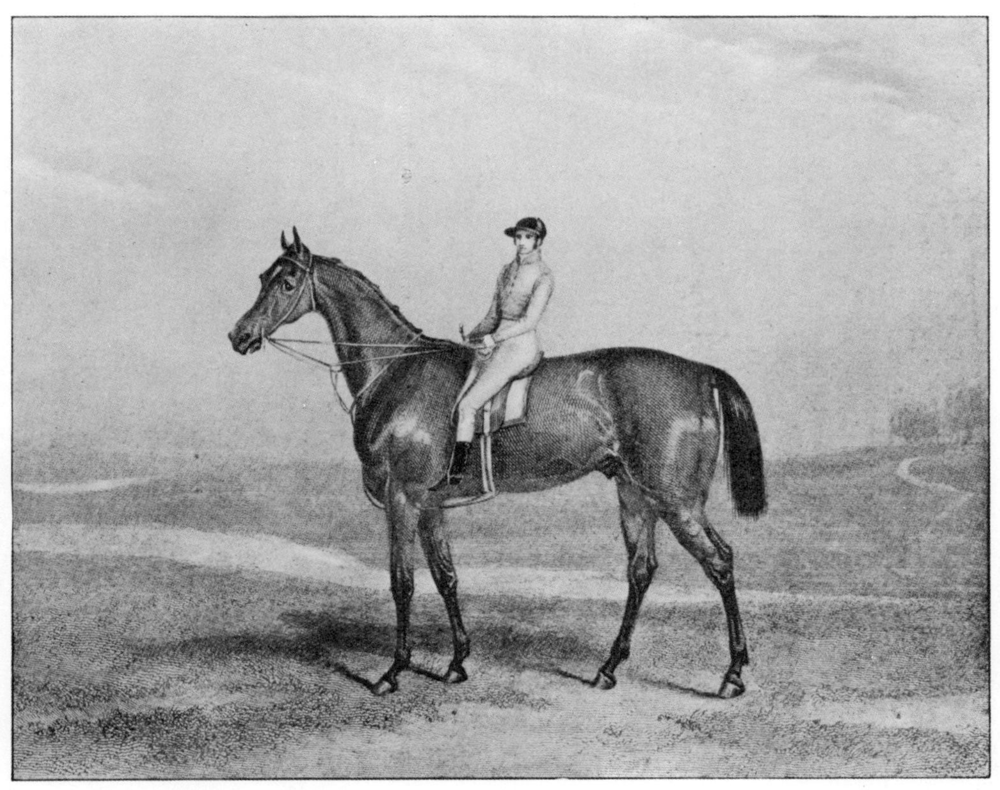

CORONATION. WINNER OF THE DERBY, 1841
By Beckwith, after F. C. Turner

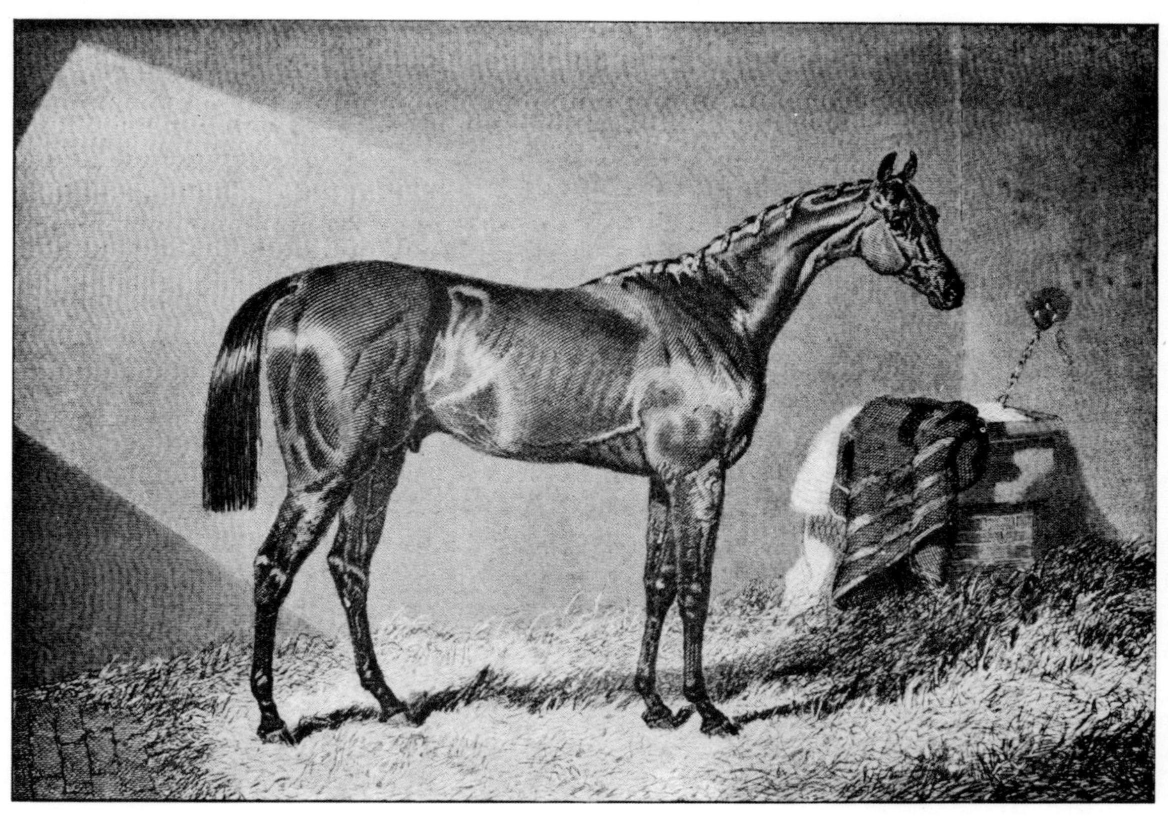

MERRY MONARCH. WINNER OF THE DERBY, 1845
By Hacker, after J. F. Herring

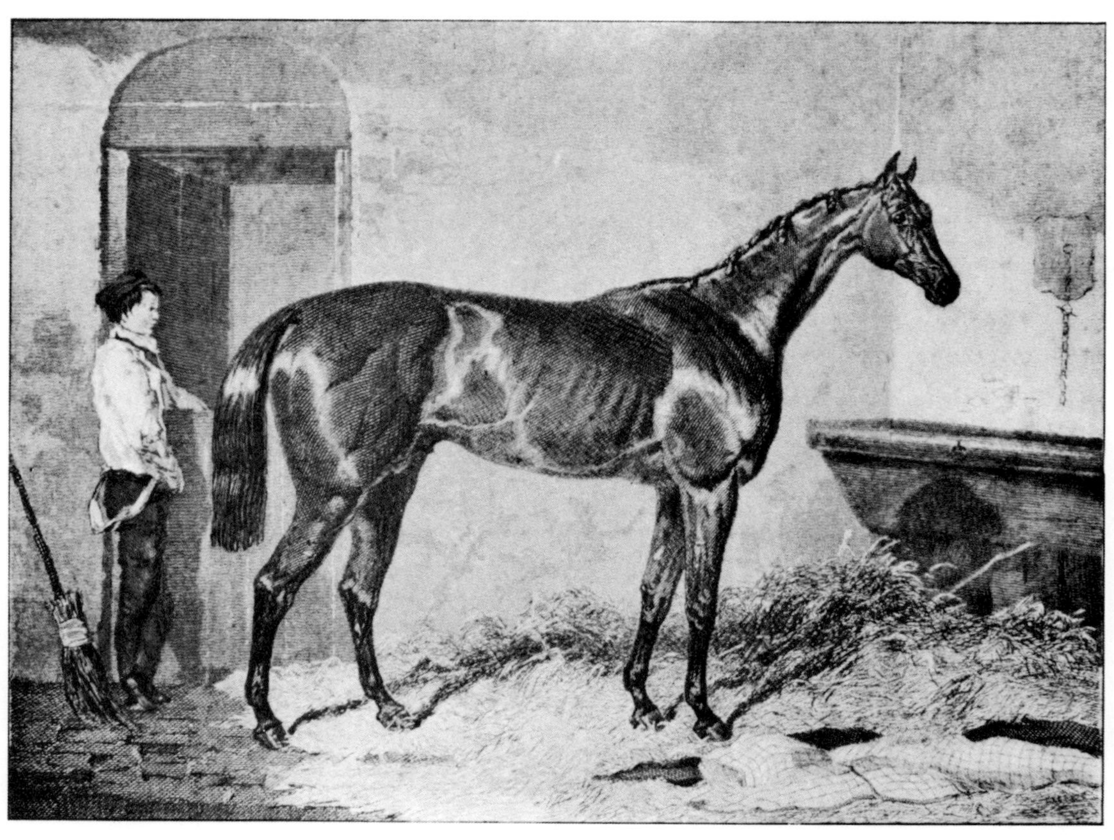

COSSACK. WINNER OF THE DERBY, 1847
By Hacker, after Harry Hall

Pollard's talents essentially lay in the vivacious delineation of sporting incidents. Though better known by engravings after his pictures, than by the pictures themselves, he was by no means devoid of cleverness in his own particular line. In 1821, he sent to the Academy, *North Country Mails at the Peacock, Islington*, a subject which he had found quite close to his own home, whilst in 1824, he was again represented by two coaching pictures, depicting incidents on the road.

One of the most attractive series of coloured prints after Pollard is that depicting the great steeplechase, which took place in the Vale of Aylesbury in 1836.

Plate 1 shows *The Start*; No. 2, *The Brook*, Mr. Galloway's The Amazon clearing it, and Jerry fairly in, Yellow Dwarf down on the landing side, and Cannon Ball scrambling out; No. 3, the horses coming over a big bank though underwood: Yellow Dwarf and Sailor are down and The Pony leads. No. 4 shows *The Finish*: Captain Lamb's Vivian, ridden by Captain Becker, wins; Mr. Elmore's Grimaldi, ridden by Mr. Seffert comes in second under the whip; and Mr. D. Baring's The Pony, Mr. Cooper up, is a good third. They were engraved by J. Harris, and published in 1836 by Ackermann & Co., 96 Strand. A good set, it may be added, fetches about £20.

The Royal Mail Leaving the G.P.O., St. Martin's-le-Grand, after Pollard, engraved by R. G. Reeve, printed in colours and published in 1836 by W. Soffe, 288 Strand, is also a valuable print which is worth some twelve pounds.

The London Fire Engines: the Noble Protectors of Life and Property, is a good example of Pollard's most spirited work. This picture was engraved, and printed in colours. It bears the inscription: " Dedicated to the Insurance Offices by their obedient servant, Thomas McLean, 26 Haymarket."

A Prospective View of Epsom Races is the title of a series of six plates, printed in colours and published by R. Ackermann. These represent: (1) *Saddling in the Warren*: Jem Bland occupies a prominent place in the foreground of this picture; (2) *The Betting Post;* (3) *Preparing to Start;* (4) *The Grand Stand, the Race;* (5) *The Race Over;* and (6) *Settling at Tattersall's*. The last plate is admirable; not only is it highly characteristic but it has all the interest of a page of Turf history, containing many sketches of well-known racing men taken from life.

Wings is the portrait of a race horse, bred in 1822 by Lord Grosvenor; Sam Chiffney, in yellow jacket and black cap, is in the saddle. On the right of the picture is the weighing room with jockeys going to scale. Engraved, printed in colours, and published by R. Pollard and Son, in June, 1825.

Other prints after Pollard are *His Majesty George IV. Travelling*; coloured print, engraved by W. Dubourg.

Fox Chase: View Halloa; engraved by R. Pollard.

The Merry Monarch; published and lithographed by Dean & Co.

Hyde Park Corner, by Rosenberg, in colours, which never fails to command a good price at sales, £30 being by no means an unusual figure.

On the Highgate Road, "*The Woodman;*" a fine colour print, by Charles Hunt. "The Woodman" on the Great North Road, between Highgate and Finchley was the house at which Flower and Milsom called just before the Muswell Hill murder for which they were hanged in 1896.

Highgate Tunnel, the companion print to the above; a coach, with passengers, coming under the tunnel, the horses and coach well foreshortened.

West Country Mail-Coach at the Gloucestershire Coffee House, Piccadilly. This engraving is by Rosenberg.

The Royal Mail; a coach passing a sportsman who carries a gun, and is accompanied by a setter and a pointer. E. Roviskere engraved this plate, which was published March 30th, 1829, by J. Wilson, of 7 Vere Street, Cavendish Square.

Stage Coach Passengers Seated at Breakfast and *The Coach in the Snow;* cottagers showing the delayed passengers hospitality. (Interiors). Both these engravings were published by R. Pollard and Son.

The St. Albans Tally-ho Stakes; two companion pictures of a great hurdle race run at Albans on May 22nd, 1834. A sweepstakes of five sovereigns each, with twenty added from the fund; each horse to carry eleven stone; gentlemen riders only. Run in two heats, each heat once round the course and a distance; two leaps to be taken in each heat over hurdles. Won by Mr. Coleman's Latitat. *Plate No. 1* shows the first leap of first heat. Mr. R. Oldaker with extended crop is galloping forward to cheer on Latitat, ridden by Mr. John Palmer, who is well into his stride again after taking a hurdle. Norman (Mr. F. P. Delme Ratcliffe up), Pompey (Mr. Mason), Splinter Bar (Mr. Richard Bevan), and Deceiver (Mr. T. Nestley) are taking the hurdle in a cluster. Thesis (Mr. Simmons) and Figurante (Captain Beecher) are coming up. *Plate 2* shows the second leap in the second heat, which was a very close race. Mr. Bevan was thrown, and Splinter Bar running up came in third without his rider. Latitat is again leading, Norman and Splinter Bar are over the hurdle, Deceiver and Figurante are clearing it, and Pompey and Thesis are coming up. These plates were engraved by G. and C. Hunt; size of plates, 17 inches by 12 inches; published by J. Moore, " at the Corner of West Street, Upper St. Martin's Lane."

Scenes on the Road, or *A Trip to Epsom and Back*, is the title of four plates. Engraved by J. Harris, printed in colours, and published May 30th, 1836, by R. Ackermann.

Plate 1 is *Hyde Park Corner;* No. 2, *The Lord Nelson Inn, Cheam;* No. 3, *The Cock, at Sutton;* and No. 4, *Kennington Gate.* Each picture bears a verse from a song in the musical farce, " Hit or Miss."

Easter Monday: Turning Out the Stag at Buckitt's Hill, Epping Forest. This plate is printed in colours.

Easter Monday: A View of Fairmead Bottom, Epping Forest. Also printed in colours, a companion to that last mentioned.

Stage Coach, with Opposition Coach in Sight; published in colours.

The Cambridge Telegraph starting from the White Horse, Fetter Lane. Engraved by G. Hunt, and published by J. Moore, of London.

Mail Coach in a Flood;—in a Drift of Snow; and—in a Thunderstorm, by Thomas Reeve, after Pollard. Three good coloured coaching prints, the most attractive of the three being the *Coach in a Flood,* which is reproduced.

Stage Coach Arriving, Changing Horses, and *Setting Off.* Another fine series engraved by Howell.

Stage Coaches with News of Peace and—*News of Reform,* in colours, also by Howell, are a pair which are in considerable request, often when in good condition fetching £20.

Besides these, there exist a number of other coloured coaching prints after this artist who made the Road his speciality. Within recent years coaching prints have been gradually rising in price, their attractive colouring and the spirited execution of a number of them, causing them to be in considerable request.

Stage coach journeys were naturally more prone to give rise to incident, and even sometimes to adventure, than the prosaic railway travelling which has now become part of civilised life. A coloured print after Pollard, of some value, portrays a disconcerting occurrence which much startled the passengers by the Exeter Mail. This is entitled *Lioness attacking the Exeter Coach.*

The Exeter Mail Coach on its way to London, was, one Sunday night attacked at Winterslow Hut, seven miles from Salisbury, in a most extraordinary manner. At the moment when the coachman pulled up to deliver his bags, one of the leaders was suddenly seized by a ferocious animal. This produced a great confusion and alarm; two passengers who were inside the mail got out, ran into the house and locked themselves up in a room above stairs; the horses kicked and plunged violently, and it was with difficulty the coachman could prevent the carriage from being overturned. With considerable consternation, the coachman and guard eventually perceived by the light of the lamps, that the animal which had seized the horse, was a huge lioness. As luck would have it, however, it was just at that moment a large mastiff dog came up and attacked her fiercely, on which she quitted the horse and turned upon him. The dog fled, but was pursued and killed by the lioness within about forty yards of the place. The beast, it was afterwards discovered, had escaped from a caravan that was standing on the roadside, belonging to a menagerie on its way to Salisbury fair. An alarm being given, the keepers pursued and hunted the lioness into a hovel under a granary, which served for keeping agricultural implements, and by half-past eight they had secured her so effectually, by barricading the place, as to prevent her escape. The lioness attacked the horse in front, and springing at his throat, fastened the talons of her fore feet on each side of his neck, close to the head, while the talons of her hind feet were forced into his chest. In this situation she hung, while the blood was seen gushing forth as if a vein had been opened by a lancet.

The ferocious animal missed the throat and the jugular vein, but the horse was terribly torn. Notwithstanding the agitation and excitement produced by this incident, a fresh horse was procured, and the mail drove on, after having been detained only three quarters of an hour.

Occasionally also, unpleasant passengers caused delay on the road. In 1812 a passenger in a stage-coach, which ran daily from Chichester to Brighton, was seized near Shoreham, with a violent fit of insanity, and bit a lady who was in the coach with him, in a most shocking manner about the face and arms. The coachman and outside passengers, hearing her screams, got down, and with much difficulty rescued her from the jaws of the maniac. Two gentlemen then got inside, and pinioning his arms, prevented him from doing further mischief.

A more amusing instance of an undesirable fare, was the case of a passenger of enormous bulk.

On one occasion a gentleman of elephantine proportions made his appearance in Huddersfield, and went to a proprietor of one of the coaches to take a passage for Manchester, but, owing to his enormous size, he was refused, unless he would consent to be taken as lumber, at 9d. per stone, hinting at the same time the advantage of being split in two. The gentleman was not to be disheartened by this disappointment, but adopted the plan of sending the ostler of one of the inns to take a place for him, which he did, and in the morning wisely took the precaution of fixing himself in the coach, with the assistance of the bystanders, from whence he was not to be removed easily. Thus placed, he was taken to his destination. The consequence was, that on his return, he was compelled to adopt a similar process, to the no small disappointment of the proprietors, who had to convey three gentlemen who had previously taken their places, in a chaise, as there was no room beside this gentleman, who weighed about thirty-six stone.

It can easily be realised that the huge individual, who so annoyed the coach proprietor, was very much out of place at a time when the proprietors of coaches were in the habit of filling these conveyances with a larger number of passengers than was allowed by Act of Parliament. The constant evasions of the regulations relating to Stage Coaches, in carrying more persons than they were allowed to do, and the many accidents which happened in consequence, aroused great irritation on the part of the public. The section of the Act relating to this ran as follows :—

" By the 50 G. 3. C. 48 it is enacted, that any coach or other carriage of four or more wheels employed as a Stage Coach in Great Britain, and drawn by four or more horses, shall be allowed to carry ten outside passengers, and no more, exclusive of the coachman, but including the guard; that one passenger only may sit with the coachman, three on the front of the roof, and the other six behind, but none on the luggage, or place allotted for it; and all such carriages drawn by two or three horses, shall be allowed

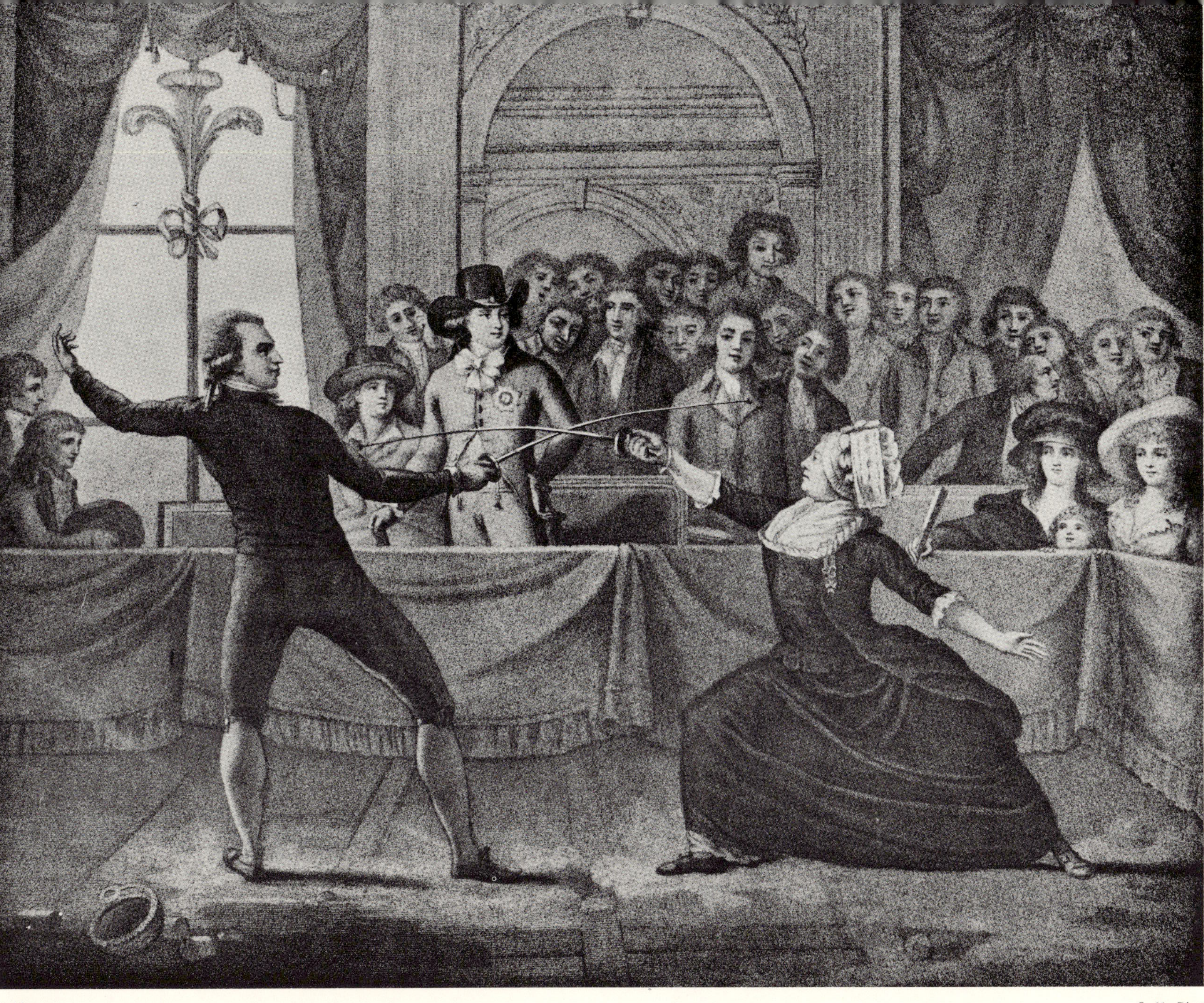

Robineau

J. M. Picot

FENCING MATCH BETWEEN MADEMOISELLE LA CHEVALIÈRE D'EON DE BEAUMONT AND MONSIEUR DE SAINT GEORGE, 1787
By permission of A. Moreton Mandeville, Esq.

55

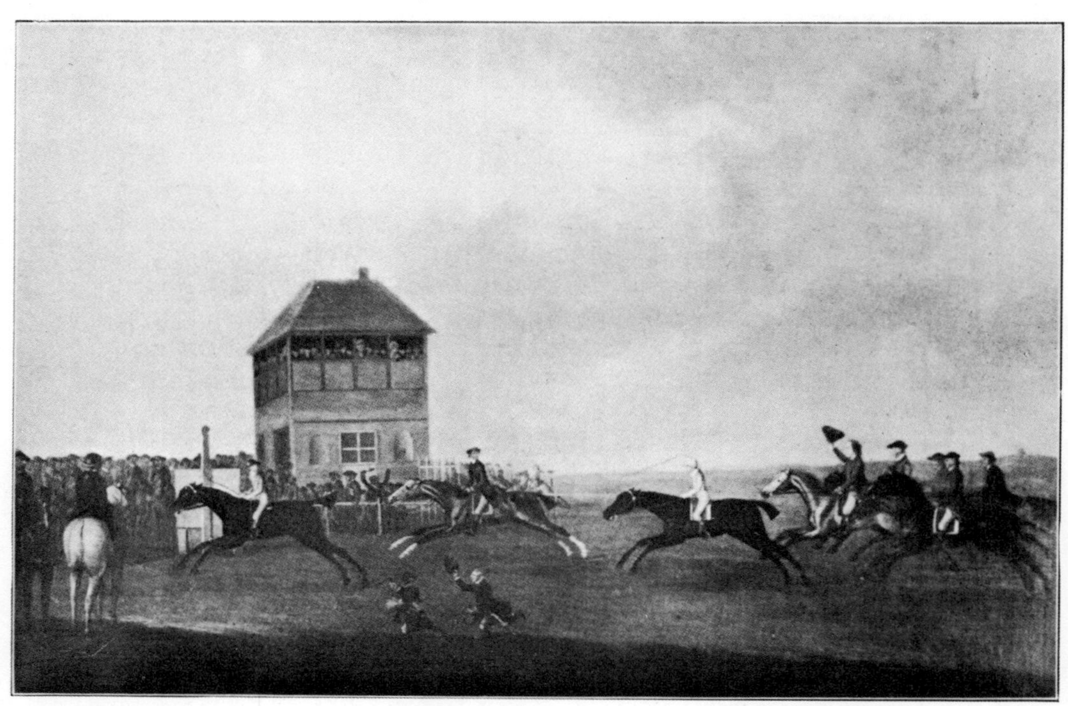

OIL PAINTING
By Francis Sartorius

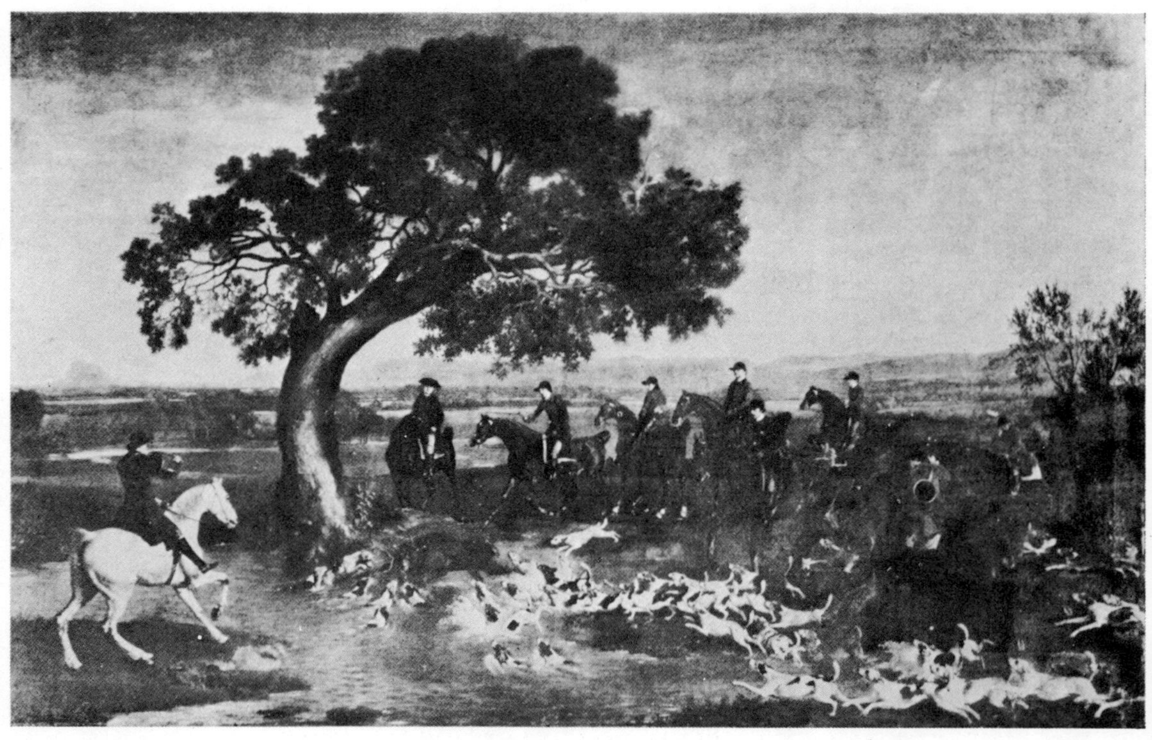

THE GROSVENOR HUNT
By Stubbs

five outside passengers, exclusive of the coachman; and that all Stages called long or double-bodied coaches, shall be allowed eight outside passengers only, exclusive of the coachman, but including the guard; no child under seven years to be counted one of the number; two such to be counted as one grown person, and so in proportion. No person paying as an outside passenger to sit as an inside, unless by consent of one inside passenger at least, and next to whom such outside passenger shall be placed. But where the carriage is sufficiently commodious, and is licensed for that purpose, four may ride on the front, provided the whole shall not exceed ten.

" No luggage to be carried on the roof of any carriage drawn by four or more horses shall exceed two feet, or if drawn by two or three horses eighteen inches above the roof. Penalty on the driver so offending, or, if the driver cannot be found, on the owner, £5 for every inch above the height allowed; or £10 if the driver is the owner; and, in default of payment, commitment for two months or till paid.

" Driver leaving his horses without having some one to hold the reins, or otherwise neglecting his duty, penalty 10s. to £5.

" Passengers may require the toll-collectors to count the number of passengers. Driver refusing to stop, penalty £5 and forfeit beside double the penalty already laid on extra passengers. Award half to the passenger and half to the toll collector. Toll collector refusing to count, penalty £5. Passenger evading examination by descending before he comes to a turnpike and reascending afterwards, penalty £10.

" Coachman permitting other persons to drive, penalty from £5 to £10.

" Guard wantonly firing his arms, penalty £5.

"The Magistrate may mitigate penalties, but not less than one half, with reasonable costs. Award, when not otherwise specified, half to the informer, half to the trustees of the road.

" Persons receiving money to connive at offences against this Act, penalty £50, or in default, commitment from one to three months. Prosecutions to be commenced within fourteen days of the offence."

The spirit of opposition in stage-coach proprietors was frequently carried to a great pitch. Instances occurred of proprietors reducing their prices till they actually carried passengers for nothing, and on some occasions they even treated people with a dinner and a bottle of wine, while in one case there was actually a fight for a coach. The " Royal Leeds Union," in 1812, used to put up at the White Horse Inn, in Fetter Lane; but in consequence of a dispute between the proprietors of that inn and those in the country, the latter determined to discontinue to let it run to the White Horse, and ordered it to be driven to the Angel Inn, in Angel Street, St. Martin's-le-grand. This so enraged the proprietors of the White Horse Inn, that they determined to bring the coach to their Inn by force, and for that purpose employed some prizefighters, coachmen, guards, etc., who were sent in December, in post chaises from London to Barnet, being the last stage previous to the coach's arrival in town. The coach arrived at Barnet between one and two o'clock and found the change of horses to take it to the Angel Inn were in readiness, as well as a set of horses to take it to the White Horse Inn whereupon a general fight took place between the partizans of the two Inns, as to which horses should be put to. It lasted for a considerable time, during which several black eyes and bloody noses were given, and teeth were knocked out. Jay, a well-known prize-fighter, had a black eye given him, and a tooth knocked out. It being discovered who Jay was, and that Powers, another of his fraternity, was engaged in the affray on the part of the White Horse Inn, the coachman and guard belonging to the Angel Inn declared it in vain to continue the contest, and in consequence hostilities ceased, and the White Horse Inn party carried off the coach, but not without experiencing many difficulties, some of the passengers refusing to proceed with it. The coach was driven to the White Horse Inn. A few days later it left London from the same Inn, but when it got to Hatfield such was the spirit of opposition there that it could not procure a change of horses, and it was actually obliged to return to London. By the activity of Adkins and Pearkes, the Bow-street Officers, Jay and Powers, the prize-fighters, George Elliot and John Merchant, coachmen, Charles Turner and Robert Cook, guards, James Buckingham and Stephen Goodwin, horsekeepers of the White Horse Inn party, were taken into custody, and held to bail, for a violent assault on James Williams and John Boyle, the coachman and guard belonging to the Angel Inn.

So keen did the competition between coaches become, that in December, 1821, a paragraph appeared in the Dock Paper informing the public that " in consequence of opposition among the coach-proprietors, the fares from thence to this city and London had been reduced to a few shillings; " and as a further inducement to travellers, stated that on Sunday the Safety Coach would leave Weakly's Hotel, at *any* or no *fare*, just as the passengers chose ?—that breakfast would be provided at Weakly's in the morning ; lunch at Goss's, Seven Stars, Totnes, in the forenoon ; and dinner and wine at Congdon's Hotel, Exeter, on the arrival of the coach, *without any charge !* In compliance with this notice, Mr. Congdon, provided a very handsome dinner, over which was exhibited a placard to the following effect :—" J.C. will feel obliged by the parties partaking of this. N.B.—All free – shall be glad to see our friends again to-morrow."

At times robberies of a serious nature took place in connection with coaches. In February, 1821, the Bath Mail-coach drew up to the Gloucester Coffee-house, in Piccadilly, as was customary, when the man employed at the coach office, known by the name of the " runner," set about packing the parcels, belonging to the passengers and others, when finding that he could not pack a large band box, there not being room for it, he took it into the office, but on his way was intercepted by a stranger, and asked some questions, no doubt asked for the purpose of delay.   When he returned to the coach, and opened the door, he found the other door had been opened and left so, and immediately missed a parcel, which proved to be of very considerable value, as it contained Bank notes to the amount of £14,000, belonging to the Devizes Bank, and strange to tell, one of the Proprietors was going with it to take care of it. The robber escaped undiscovered, no doubt with the man in league with him who stopped the porter or " runner " to ask him a trifling question to delay time.

Perhaps the most curious circumstance connected with the annals of coaching is the true story of a man's life being saved owing to a coach passing over him.   A labouring man returning home near Berkhamstead from a frolic during the severest night's frost of the winter, in 1830, fell on the turnpike road and remained insensible, without power to move, till half-past eleven at night, when he was effectually roused by a " friendly hint " from the hind wheel of the Birmingham mail, which grazed his head, and passed obliquely over his body.   The man was severely injured, and was taken inside the mail to Berkhamstead, but no bones were broken, and he was soon as well as ever, having escaped from inevitable death by frost, in consequence of being run over by the mail.

Another singular circumstance in connection with the road occurred in July, 1804, when a certain driver of one of the northern mail coaches, who used, as he rode along, to exert his athletic strength by breaking large branches off trees, noticed a huge oak, a branch of which, of an uncommon thickness, projected over part of the road.   Proud of his former *achievements*, and thinking himself possessed of more than Herculean strength, he laid hold of the branch with his brawny hands; when lo! the sturdy oak, not yielding as he expected, the coach drove on, and left the *astonished* guard dangling in the air ! who, quitting his hold, fell to the ground, and unfortunately broke his arm.

Some of the old coachmen must have travelled enormous distances during their lives.   Such a one was old Dan Sellers, who drove the Oxford and Bath mail for 35 years from Oxford to Cirencester every morning, and returned to Oxford every evening, a daily journey of 74 miles.   He altogether travelled more than 942,760 miles, the yearly journey exceeding the circumference of the globe.

Though the competition between coach proprietors was, as has been said, very great, misfortune not infrequently overtook this sort of business.   An advertisement appeared in a Bath paper of 1826, put in by some of the unlucky shareholders in an unlucky concern known as " The Stage Coach Company."   At the head of the advertisement in question was a print of a coach and four reversed, or, in the language of the road, *overturned*.

With the coming of the railroad several prints made their appearance, contrasting the dangers of travelling by rail behind an engine with the pleasures of a journey behind a spanking team.

Of this sort is the print, by Cooper Henderson, which shows the passengers on a coach very unconcernedly viewing an accident to a train which has fallen over an embankment.

In 1828 some enterprising English coach-masters endeavoured to establish a coach between Calais and Paris, to perform the journey in 24 hours, which would be at the rate of seven miles an hour; but the absurd restrictions imposed by the French Government as to the breadth of wheels, weight of carriage, etc., prevented the prosecution of the undertaking. With a view to ensure safety, the French Government required that public carriages should be of a weight, and have their wheels of a breadth, such as to put rapidity of travelling quite out of the question. The desired safety, however, was not always attained by these regulations, for the overturn of French diligences was frequently reported, for the most part attended with destruction of life or serious injury.

The first experiment of stage coaches travelling upon railways was made with great success between Darlington and Stockton. The railway from Witton to Stockton, a distance of 25 miles, was formed for the conveyance of coals; and so great was the advantage of this kind of road in lowering the expense of carriage, that coals which formerly sold at 18s. per ton in Stockton, were sold there for 8s. 6d. The railway passed through Darlington, which is at a distance of twelve miles from Stockton, and two coaches travelled the road daily, conveying a very great number of passengers at the rate of a penny per mile each. These vehicles were the bodies of old six-inside coaches, placed upon new and lower wheels fitted for the railway; they were drawn by a single horse, which often drew from 20 to 30 passengers at the rate of ten miles an hour, with quite as much ease as a horse moving in a gig, the traces being generally loose the animal's principal effort being to maintain his speed.

A great engraver of sporting scenes was John Scott, who was born in 1774. Like James Pollard's father, John Scott was born at Newcastle-on-Tyne from which city he came to London, entering the business of Robert Pollard, afterwards attracting the attention of Mr. John Wheble who secured his services for the *Sporting Magazine*.

John Scott is of course best known by his engravings, having indeed been the founder of a school which made a particular feature of reproductions of sporting incidents and animal life. In addition to this, however, it must not be forgotten that, possessing artistic qualities of the highest possible character, he was the designer of many charming compositions; so great indeed was his talent that certain of the engravings executed by him are improvements upon the pictures from which they were taken. An adept in conveying the peculiar texture to be found in the coats of animals and the animation seen in the eyes of dogs, his plates are invariably distinguished by a boldness which clearly displays the sure confidence of the hand which wielded the graver. So much attention and care did he devote to his work that the

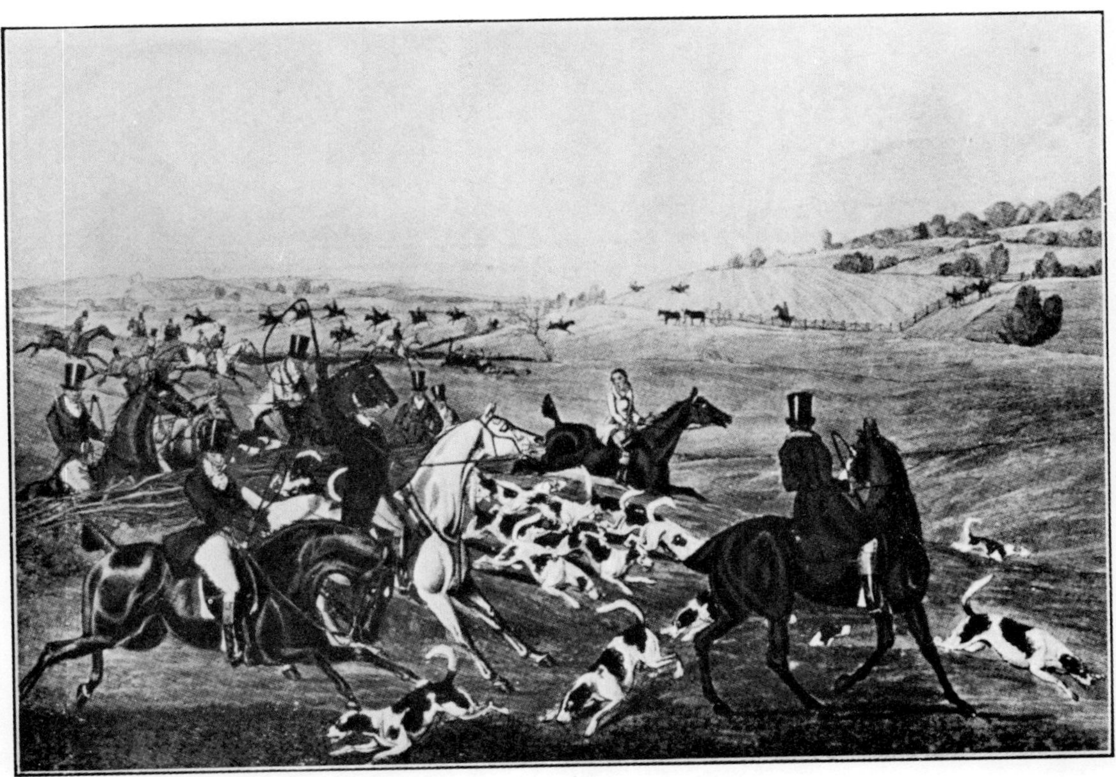

THE CHECK
By permission of A. Moreton Mandeville, Esq.

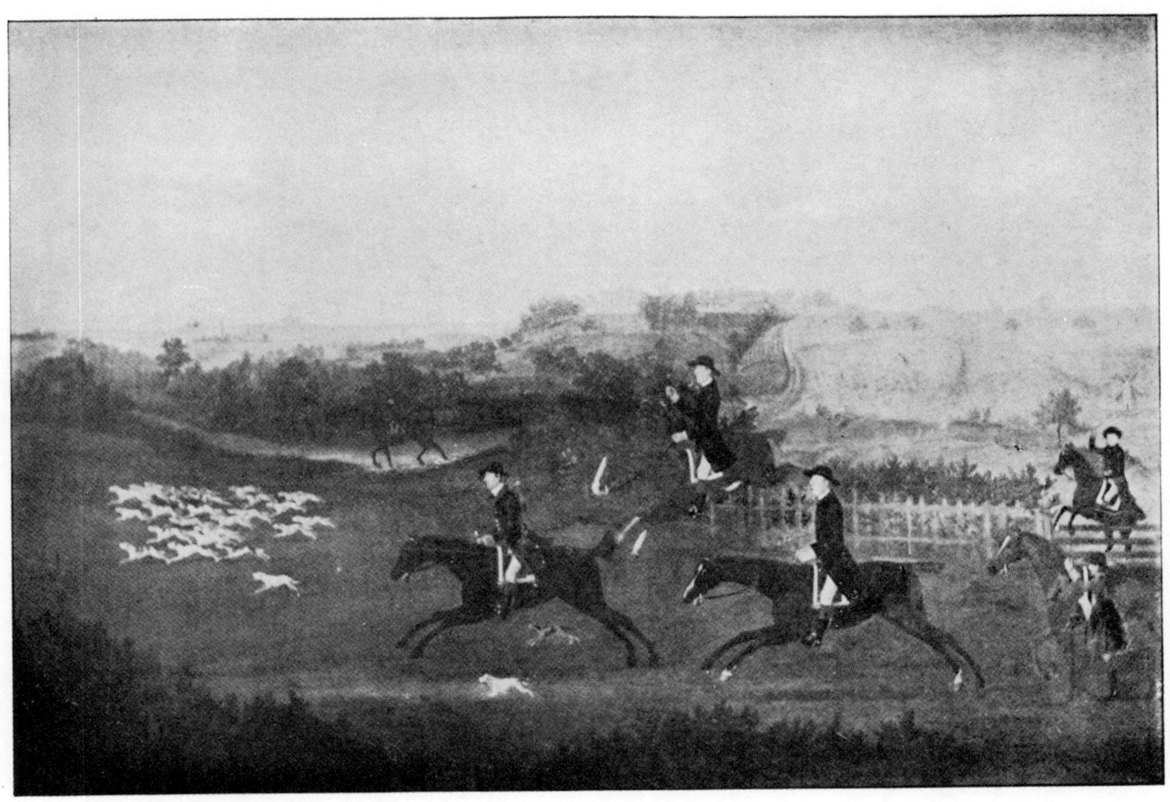

THE BROTHERS FERMOR HUNTING IN AYNHO PARK
By F. Sartorius (1754)
In the possession of W. C. Cartwright, Esq.

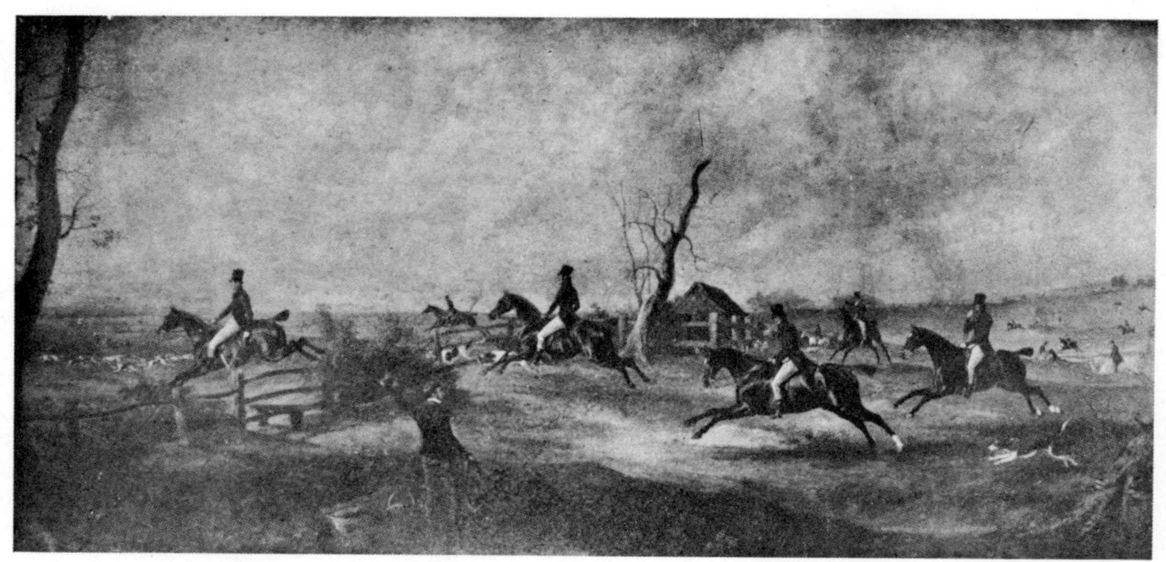

THE CHESHIRE HUNT
By T. Ferneley

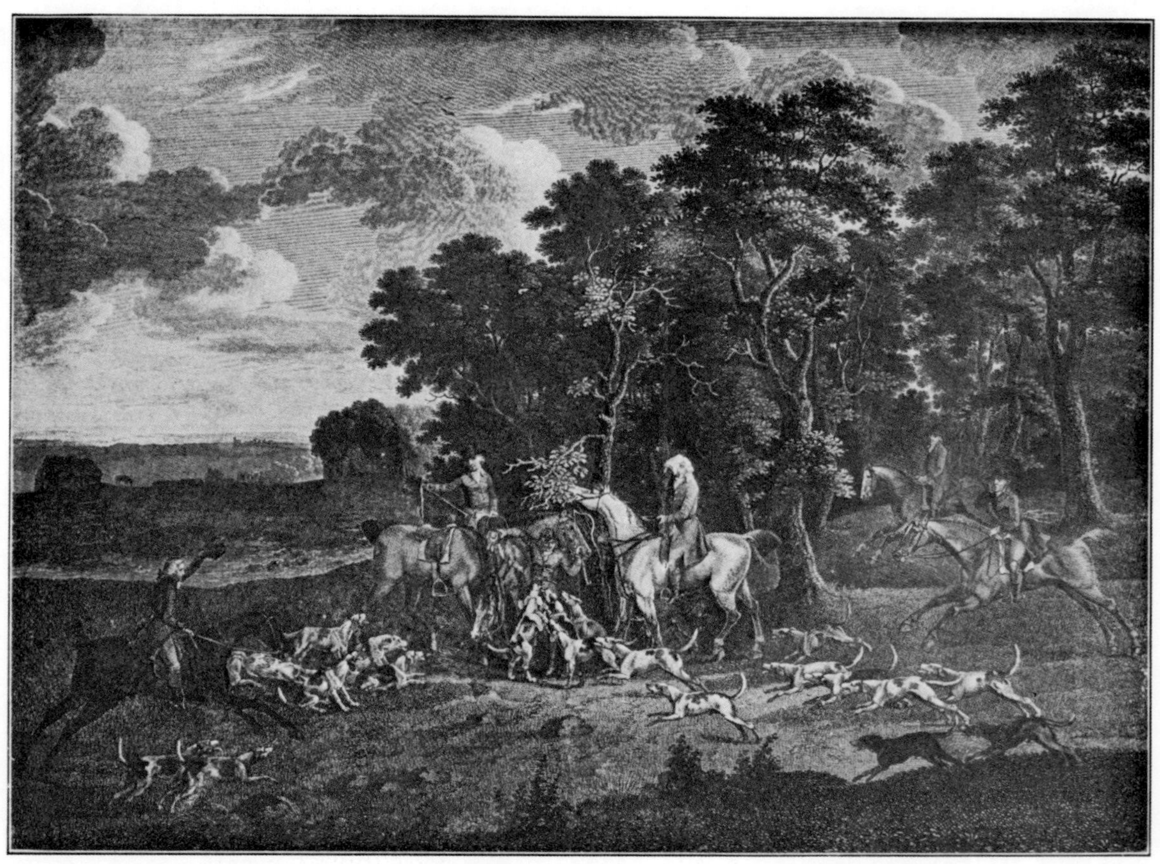

" THE DEATH "
    By J. N. Sartorius.   Landscape by Peltro.   Figures Engraved by Neagle

large prints of *The Death of the Fox*, after Sawrey Gilpin, and *The Fox breaking Cover*, after Reinagle, were no less than six years in his hands. These were published in May, 1811, when the Society of Arts presented Scott with their large Gold Medal " for having completed two such works which do so much honour to his country and himself."

Many not interested in sporting subjects cannot fail to have from time to time seen a set of curious little designs representing different field sports. These were originally patterns for silver buttons, and were published by J. H. Burn in 1821. The original drawings by Abraham Cooper, R.A., were engraved by Scott on a silver plate, from which the buttons were then cut and sold for shooting coats. A complete set is, needless to say, almost unobtainable at the present day, though Sir Walter Gilbey (that high authority on all matters connected with sporting pictures and prints) possesses the whole fourteen.

Amongst the best known engravings of John Scott are the plates which he executed for Daniels' Rural Sports, many of which are beautiful works of art. The *Sportsman's Repository*, published in 1820, also contained a series of prints by this engraver, who contributed some fine work to two Editions of the " Complete Angler."

Nine engravings in Tegg's Edition of *The Chase*, by Somerville, were executed by Scott after designs by J. N. Sartorius, whilst the beautiful frontispiece which embellished the Essay on Hunting, published by Jeffrey, was both drawn and engraved by him.

Scott died in 1827, aged 53, his illness, it is said, being the result of intense application and study, notwithstanding which, his last years were embittered by pecuniary worry of a harassing kind.

An animal painter, who produced a number of works, many of which have been engraved, was Henry Bernard Chalon, who came of old French Huguenot stock. Born in 1770, he became an exhibitor at the Royal Academy when twenty-two years old, being appointed animal painter to the Duchess of York, in 1795, an honorary distinction which in after years was also conferred upon him by King William the Fourth. Amongst this artist's works, *The Passions of the Horse*, seven large pictures engraved and published by Jackson, must not be forgotten.

In the *Sporting Magazine* is an engraving after a picture by Chalon of a famous fighting dog, owned by Lord Camelford, which dog is said to have killed three celebrated dogs in his time, and was never beaten. Other plates after Chalon in the same publication, are *Flora*, a famous hunter, belonging to Lord Darlington whose great achievement was a leap of 23 feet 3 inches; *Streamer*, a red grey-hound bred by Mr. George Lane Fox, of Bramham Park, and owned by the Rev. F. Best, which won the cup at the Malton Coursing meeting in 1821; *Vanity*, a blue and white greyhound bitch, also the property of Mr. Best, which won the cup at Malton in the following year. The *Dwarf Beagles*, whose portraits appeared in the *Magazine* in 1831, were from the pack of Colonel

Thornton, who bred them. These beagles were of the smallest breed and were noted for their beauty. *Bracer*, whose picture appeared in the *New Sporting Magazine* in 1836, was a famous hound in the Linlithgow and Stirlingshire pack. The plate was taken from a part of a large picture of Mr. W. R. Ramsay, of Barnton, the Master, and his hounds.

Amongst a great number of engravings after Chalon, the following must not be forgotten :—Eight engravings in mezzotint, by W. Ward, A.R.A.—(1) *Pavilion*, a racehorse with Chiffney in the saddle, published by Boydell & Co., 90, Cheapside, London, 1st March, 1803 ; (2) *Coursing*, a portrait of the greyhound Snowball, published by Random & Sneath, 1807 ; (3) *Violante*, a racehorse with Buckle in the saddle, published by Boydell & Co., 1st March, 1808 ; (4) *Quiz*, a race-horse, jockey, saddle on arm, entering the weighing-room, published by R. Ackermann & Co., 1st September, 1808 ; (5) *Costive*, one of the best foxhounds in Lord Darlington's Raby pack. An etching from this work by H. R. Cook, was also published in the *Sporting Magazine*, of 1810 ; (6) *A Setter*, belonging to the Marquis of Ely ; (7) *The Raby Pack*, portraits of the hounds on the flags with huntsman and feeder ; and (8) *Bulldogs*, namely, Wasp, Child and Billy, three famous dogs belonging to Mr. Henry Baynton, published by Random & Sneath, 1809. This picture was also engraved by Duncan for the *New Sporting Magazine*, in 1835. Billy was originally purchased by Lord Camelford, and from whose possession it passed into that of Mr. Boynton, member of a Yorkshire family.

Chalon's portrait of *Brainworm*, a race-horse, was engraved by J. C. Easling and published by R. Ackermann. His portraits of the racehorses *Morelli* and *Vandyke*, were engraved by William Say as companion pictures. The portraits of the Prince of Wales' horses, *Orville* and *Sir David*, exhibited in the Royal Academy of 1808, were engraved by William Ward, and published by Colnaghi & Co., of 23, Cockspur Street, the former on 25th March, 1809, the latter on the 12th August in the same year. The portrait of *Barbarossa*, also shown at the Royal Academy of 1808, was engraved by William Ward, and published by C. Random, at the Sporting Gallery, 5, Hart Street, Bloomsbury Square, on 2nd December, 1809. His portrait of *Selim* was also engraved by W. Ward, and published by Random & Sneath, The Sporting Gallery, 5, Hart Street, Bloomsbury Square, on 25th March, 1809.

Chalon died in 1849, from the effects of a severe accident which had befallen him three years before.

Seventeen years after Chalon, in 1787, was born Abraham Cooper, who, though showing signs of artistic gifts when quite a child, did not take up painting as a profession till his twenty-second year. Obtaining an introduction to Benjamin Marshall, R.A., he received much guidance and useful advice, which he turned to excellent account. Cooper, it may be added, was a most prolific painter. Between the years 1812 and 1869 he sent no fewer than 332 pictures to the Royal Academy, a number of which were scenes connected with the civil wars, and battle pieces in which an old white charger almost invariably figured.

A good example of sporting portraiture executed by Abraham Cooper is the picture of Thomas Waring of Chelsfield, engraved by W. B. Scott. Mr. Waring is shown on his favourite hunter, Peter, with five couples of hounds close by. Of this portrait Nimrod wrote :—

> " Mr. Waring, as Master of Harriers, hunts the country between Farningham and Sevenoaks, in Kent. The horse upon which he is mounted may be called a pattern-card for the purpose for which he is wanted. From that great obliquity of shoulder he must be a good and safe fencer, and from the setting-on of his head and his apparently placid disposition, it is no wonder he is a favourite. His hounds, as Mr. Cooper has represented them, are thoroughbred harriers, without a cross of foxhound, not rounded in the ear and conveying to us the idea of being well calculated to hunt."

Of racehorses and hunters Cooper painted a great number of portraits. Many hunting groups were also executed by him.

An all-round sportsman himself, who rode well to hounds, this artist possessed a practical knowledge of field sports, the result of which is clearly to be discovered in his pictures.

An excellent appreciation of Mr. Cooper's talents and work appeared in volume cxxxiv. of the *Sporting Magazine*.

"Whether racing, hunting, shooting or fishing, you have only to look at them to see that they are done by a thorough sportsman, and are sure to bring back some pleasant recollection of the past— either when you were at Newmarket and had a pony on something of Lord George's—you remember John Day sitting with his hands on both thighs, the horse with his nostrils extended, and remarked the dilated eye on his going back to weigh just as Mr. Cooper had depicted him; how Todd, when Mr. Coombe hunted the Berkeley country, capped on the hounds in the Woodlands when the meet was at Halton, and the fox broke away in a line for Wendover. You had a glorious five-and-thirty minutes—only two up and your-self, the others on the wrong side of the wood. You felt half inclined to write to the editor for the addresses of the owners of the hunters and hacks, and have them at any price."

Amongst English sporting artists no name is more familiar than that of Henry Alken, whose work is justly held in very high esteem.

The family of Alken, of Danish origin, only came to this country about the year 1772, having been obliged to fly from Denmark on account of political disturbances, in which some of its members were involved. The refugees at first settled in Suffolk, but after-wards took up their residence in London.

The original name of the Alken family would appear to have been " Seffrien," a patronymic which was exchanged for that of Alken (a little village in North Jutland), at the time of the migration into England.

Henry Alken is said to have at one time been huntsman, stud groom, or trainer to the Duke of Beaufort of the day, but there is no proof that this was the case, and the story must be dismissed as a mere legend. When seventeen years of age the young man sent a miniature portrait of "Miss Gubbins" to the Royal Academy Exhibition. This was in 1801, and the miniature in question was his sole exhibit at the Academy. It is probable that his dislike of criticism was the cause of his not again sending any of his work. Beginning as a portrait painter—a line unsuited to his natural talents—Henry Alken abandoned miniature painting, and took to depicting sporting subjects under the name of "Ben Tally O."

At the beginning of his career, Henry Alken was undoubtedly influenced by his uncle, Samuel Alken the delineator of a number of hunting scenes, many of which are well drawn and interesting. This artist also painted a series of shooting pictures which were engraved by J. Pollard. His dogs, it may be remarked, are generally exceedingly good. At one time an engraver in aquatint, Samuel Alken seems subsequently to have entirely devoted himself to sporting subjects, painting in oil and water colours, attaining considerable proficiency in both methods. A careful comparison of the work of Henry Alken with that of his uncle, will demonstrate the influence which the latter exercised upon his relative's style, the delicacy of touch which the one seems to have acquired from the other, being especially striking.

Henry Alken was a man of considerable artistic attainments, his small pencil drawings in particular betraying much delicacy of execution. Essentially an artist of the country, he was admirably equipped to delineate hunting scenes, the engravings of which are in considerable request at the present day. The leading firms which published his work, were Rudolph Ackermann, Thomas Maclean and S. & J. Fuller.

At the age of thirty-two, Alken, who had previously signed his productions "Ben Tally O," executed the *Beauties and Defects of the Figure of the Horse comparatively delineated,* to which he affixed his own name. These eighteen plates with an illustrated title page were published by S. and J. Fuller in 1816. It may be added that his anatomical studies for this series greatly facilitated his renderings of the various coaching and hunting scenes which have rendered his name famous.

In 1819, *How to Qualify for a Meltonian,* a set of six plates accompanied by some humorous directions to hunting men, was once again signed "Ben Tally O."

Eight oil paintings were executed by Henry Alken for Mr. Magniac, of Colworth. This fine series was entitled *The Leicestershire Steeple-chase,* and in it appear most of the best-known Leicestershire hunting men and horses of 1829, in which year, on March 12th, the steeple-chase was run. In 1833, Alken painted *The Quorn Hunt*—eight scenes, engraved by Lewis, and printed in colours. These served to illustrate *Fox-hunting,* published by Ackermann. This set also contains many portraits. Another series of pictures was Alken's *Sporting Anecdotes,* of which perhaps the best-known is *The Hunting Sweep,* which was engraved by the painter himself. This sweep was a celebrated and popular character, who hunted with the

Duke of Beaufort's hounds.   Another of this series was *The Sporting Bishop*, mentioned by Nimrod in one of his Hunting Tours.

A certain Bishop had, on his elevation to the Bench, made over a pack of foxhounds, which had been his delight, to his brother. Some time later the Bishop, out riding, chanced to come upon the fox and the hounds at fault.   Carried away by excitement, the high dignitary of the Church at once gave one of the view-halloos for which he had been famous.   The huntsman, listening for a moment, soon recognised his old master's voice.   "That's Gospel, by G—!" said he.

Whether there was any truth or not in the report that Alken had originally been a huntsman or stud-groom, it is certain that he knew a great deal about horses, and was intimately acquainted with hunting in all its phases.   The accuracy of his compositions is a sufficient demonstration of this.   It may safely be averred, that hardly any artist ever displayed such an aptitude for depicting the various phases and incidents of a run, in which it was often his practice to include the portrait of some follower of hounds, well-known as a sporting character.   As a rule, individual portraiture was not made the sole aim of his works, an exception to this must be mentioned in the case of the equestrian likeness of the Marquis of Anglesea, which was engraved by H. Meyer.

A most prolific artist, it is hardly possible to make any adequate mention of even a small portion of Henry Alken's work.   He was perhaps the most popular of any English sporting painter, and prints from his paintings are to be found all over the country. Who is there who does not know *The Night Riders of Nacton, The Chase and the Road,* and many other similar compositions?

An especially attractive series of four engravings after Henry Alken, engraved by Harris, were published by Rudolph Ackermann in 1844.   These were—

    (1) *The Meet.*

Delightful scene
When all around is gay—men, horses, hounds,
And in each smiling countenance appears
Fresh blooming health, and universal joy.

The meet is at the Cross Roads, where the finger-post, pointing to "Melton Mowbray" tells the locality.   There, surrounded by the hounds, stand the huntsman and his two whips.   The rough-rider of the county lays down the law for the benefit of the rural Boniface.   The country squire—my lord in chariot and four—and the sporting parson are coming down the hill, the chawbacons are tucking up their skirts for a run, and all is expectation and exciting hope.

    (2) *A Change, and We're Away!*

Hark!   What loud shouts
Re-echo through the groves!—he breaks away:
Shrill horns proclaim his flight.   Each straggling hound
Strains o'er the lawn to reach the distant pack;
'Tis triumph all—and joy.

The hounds have gone away, somewhat straggling perhaps, but the huntsman on his grey is well up with them. The parson has got a capital lead, and is taking the rails in style. The thistle-whipper in green too, is well handicapped—the squire is going at the rails in a quiet workmanlike manner, and the crowd are emerging from the cover here, there, and everywhere. The game's alive.

(3) *A Shift of the Scene*.

The brook stares us in the face. The huntsman's grey is landed—not very well—but on the right side. The squire is pulling himself out as he best may, having been left, like Moses, in the bulrushes. The parson goes like a man, clear over his head, the thistle-whipper has lost start, and the rest of the field, in various positions, but only thirteen in sight, look very determined to make the best of a bad thing.

(4) *Whohoop !*

In bolder notes
Each sounding horn proclaims the felon dead.

The hounds are clamouring for their due, the parson is evidently entitled to the brush, and we may add, that the thistle-whipper is nowhere to be seen.

Occasionally Alken would himself engrave his own designs. "British Proverbs," published by Maclean in 1824, contains six plates, which are his work. Some of the plates which he contributed to "Nimrod's Life of a Sportsman "—there were thirty-six coloured illustrations in all—were also etched by the artist, who executed a number of illustrations for sporting books of his day. The " Life of John Mytton," his " Life and Death," and the " Jorrock's Jaunts and Jollities," all owed a good deal of their success to the talents of Alken, who was, besides, a frequent contributor to the *Sporting Magazine*, *New Sporting Magazine*, and *Sporting Review*.

Some of the artist's finest work it should be mentioned was contained in the " National Sports of Great Britain," a volume in royal folio, published by Maclean, in 1821. In this are fifty large plates engraved by T. Clarke, after Alken, printed in colours, the accompanying descriptions of the various field sports being in English and French.

"The National Sports of Great Britain " was originally published at £10, but of late years it has greatly increased in value, not infrequently fetching seven or eight times that sum. A great many of Alken's productions were soft ground etchings coloured by hand, and a number of plates are more often to be met with in their uncoloured state. His " Sporting Notions," a set always extremely popular, has been reproduced in a number of different forms, and collectors wishing to obtain genuine examples above all suspicion should take care to exercise a very large degree of caution.

In character, Henry Alken was somewhat eccentric and fond of leading a secluded life. Exceedingly independent in manner, his usual method of introducing himself to anyone with whom he might have business to do, was a curt " I am Henry Alken." His appearance, if somewhat shabby, was picturesque in the extreme. A coat of vernal green, embellished with large brass buttons, breeches of brown cloth with gaiters to match, together with a broad-brimmed, low-crowned hat, formed his usual equipment—his portrait, bearing no date, the work of M. Gauci, was published by G. S. Tregear.

Henry Alken died in April, 1851, in the sixty-eighth year of his age, and was buried in Highgate cemetery. Though fairly affluent during most of his life, his circumstances at the time of his death were anything but prosperous, indeed he was buried at his daughter's expense.

Henry Alken's son, Henry Gordon Alken, possessed something of his father's talents, which, however, he used for a somewhat unedifying purpose, executing pictures in imitation of the elder Alken's style, which he was in the habit of passing off upon those who could be induced to purchase them. From an artistic point of view these are, for the most part, inferior, though not altogether devoid of cleverness. The imitations in question were executed in water colour, oil, and pencil, being signed Henry Alken, or simply H. A. Had this artist chosen to devote himself to a more legitimate sphere of art, there is reason to believe that he would have made a name for himself. Content to earn a somewhat precarious livelihood as a mere copyist the designs which he produced are but feeble counterfeits which careful examination cannot fail to detect. Henry Gordon Alken died some sixteen years ago, aged 82, being in receipt of parochial relief at the time of his death.

Samuel Alken (uncle of Henry Alken) was born in 1750, and as has before been said, largely influenced his nephew in his manner of painting. He did not at first devote himself to painting sporting subjects, but when he took to that particular line, he executed an enormous amount of hunting scenes. One of the best of these is *Hunters at Covert-side,* engraved by J. Pollard, and published in 1820 by T. Knight. The horses in this composition belonged to Colonel Thornton. A pleasing series of pictures, also engraved by J. Pollard, is a set of four : *Partridge Shooting, Pheasant Shooting, Woodcock Shooting,* and *Grouse Shooting.* Another series is *Fox Hunting, Hare Hunting, Stag Hunting,* and *Coursing.* These were engraved by T. Sutherland, and published sixteen years after Samuel Alken's death, by Laird, of Leadenhall Street.

Samuel Alken possessed a decided talent for depicting hunting scenes, and his work is as a rule an accurate representation of the horse and hound of his day. He especially excelled in painting dogs. This artist, it may be added, died about the year 1825.

A sporting artist, whose work was only second in popularity to that of Henry Alken, was Dean Wolstenholme, senior. Born in Yorkshire in 1757, this artist was originally a man of independent means, whose time was largely devoted to sport. Originally he painted only for amusement, occasionally presenting his friends with portraits of favourite horses or hounds. Ruined by lawsuits, however, he determined to make painting his profession, thereby verifying the prediction of Sir Joshua Reynolds, who had early observed the great talent of Wolstenholme, and predicted that he would in time develop into a serious painter. Though more than forty years of age, Dean Wolstenholme came up to London in 1800, and took up his abode in East Street, Red Lion Square, where he commenced to paint for a livelihood. His first contribution to the Academy in 1803 was *Coursing*, and he continued to execute many works during the next twenty-five years.

Dean Wolstenholme painted a good many sets of hunting, coursing, and shooting pictures. *Fox-hunting,* four scenes, printed in colours, and published by Ackermann, form an excellent set; and a shooting series, engraved by Himeley, is also very good. A large number of Wolstenholme's pictures, it may be added, were inspired by hunting songs. Several sets or series of hunting, coursing, and shooting scenes, being engraved by Sutherland and Bromley. One such set represents *Foxhunting*, in four scenes; these were engraved by Sutherland, printed in colours and published by Ackermann. *Shooting*, was the title of another series of four clever pictures, which represented respectively (1), *Going Out;* (2), *Game Found;* (3), *Dogs Bringing the Game;* and (4), *Refreshing*. These were engraved by Himeley. Others worthy of special mention are *The High-mettled Racer Sold to the Hounds* and *The Joys of Coursing. The Death of Tom Moody* and *Reynard seeking Refuge in the Church,* were companion works. These two pictures were engraved by his son, Dean Wolstenholme, junr., and were published by R. Ackermann.

After the year 1826, pictures signed Dean Wolstenholme, may be ascribed to his son, " Dean Wolstenholme, junior." There are certain differences in the work of father and son, which should be carefully noted as a means of identification. The elder artist loved to paint a gloomy sky, whereas the younger almost invariably depicted a bright and sunny one. The son's backgrounds were very carefully executed from nature, whereas the father was not in the habit of devoting particular attention to them. Leafless oaks constantly occur in Wolstenholme junior's landscapes, and his sketch-books were filled with studies of trees, afterwards to be utilised in pictures. If the points mentioned above are noted, there is less chance of confusing the earlier pictures of the younger Wolstenholme with the later ones of his father.

Dean Wolstenholme, junior, who was born in 1798; as a young man, studied engraving, and was in consequence able to engrave both his own and his father's pictures. In after years he lamented that he had not devoted himself entirely to painting, and declared that his labours at engraving had prevented him from fully developing his powers as a painter. Amongst his best works are his Brewery pictures, which represented the horses of certain celebrated firms.

The first of these " Brewery Pictures " was Messrs. Truman, Hanbury and Buxton's *Black Eagle Brewery;* this was exhibited in the Royal Academy of 1822. *A View of the Hour Glass Brewery,*

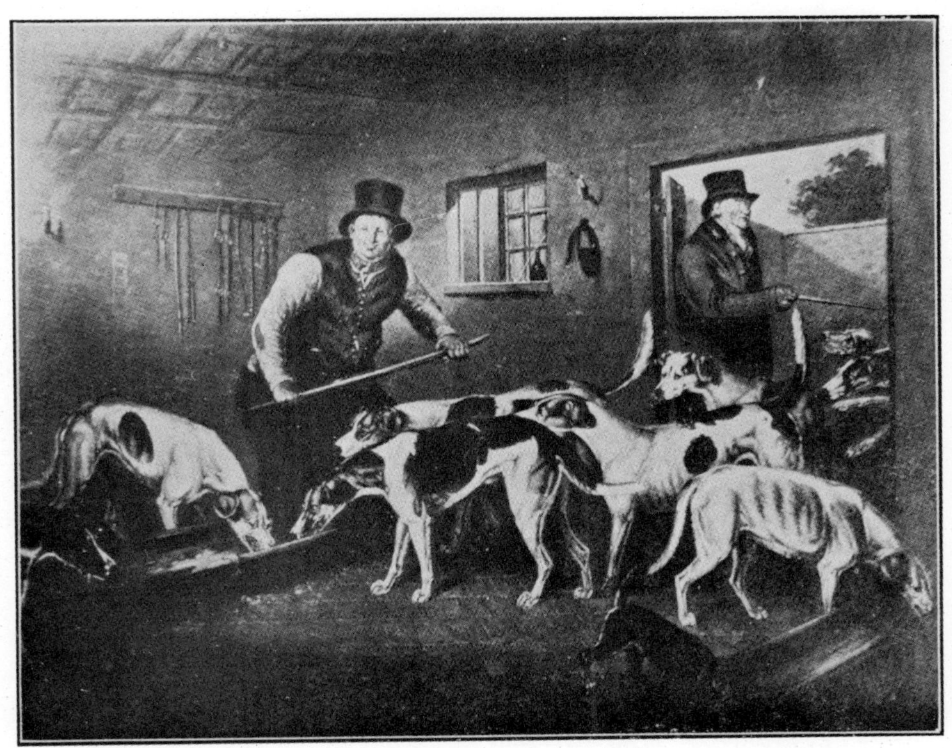

THE RABY PACK.   *By W. Ward after H. B. Chalon*
By permission of A. Moreton Maudeville, Esq.

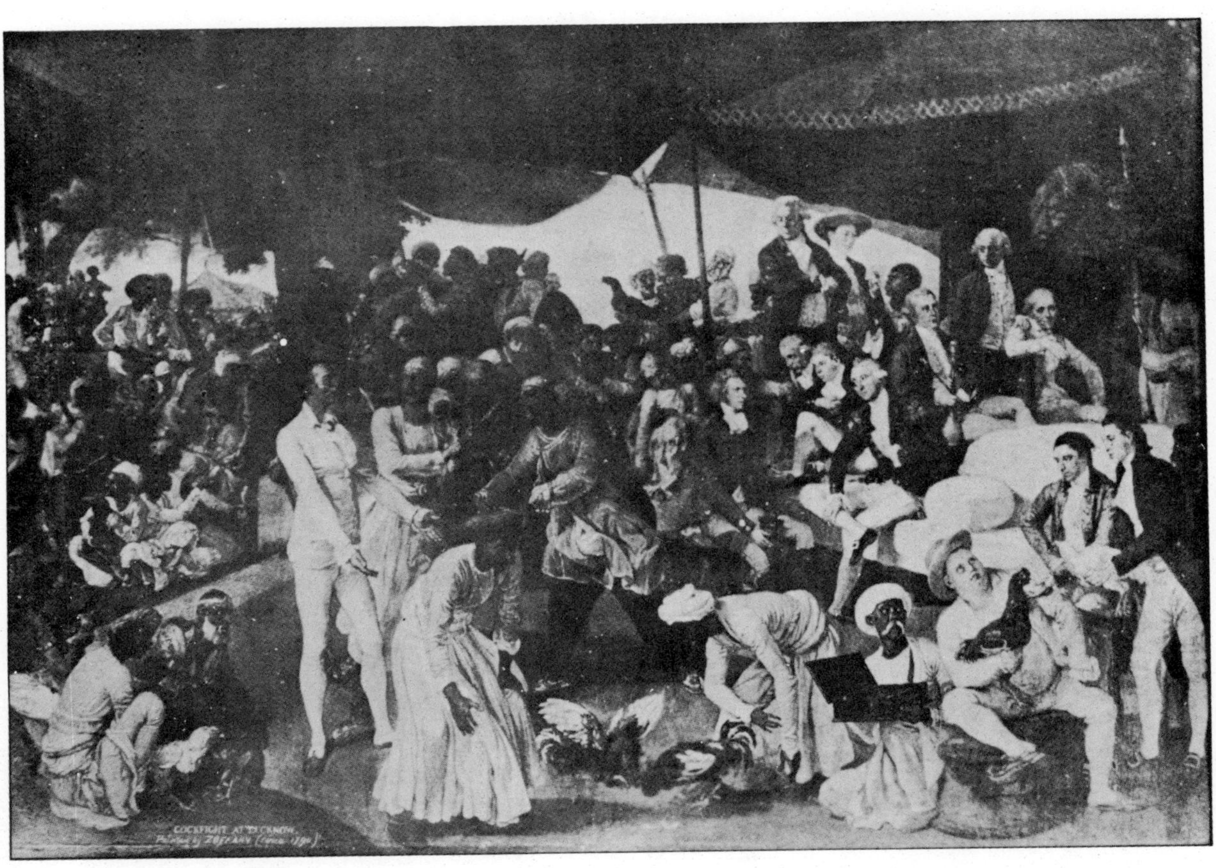

COCKFIGHTING.   *By Zoffany*

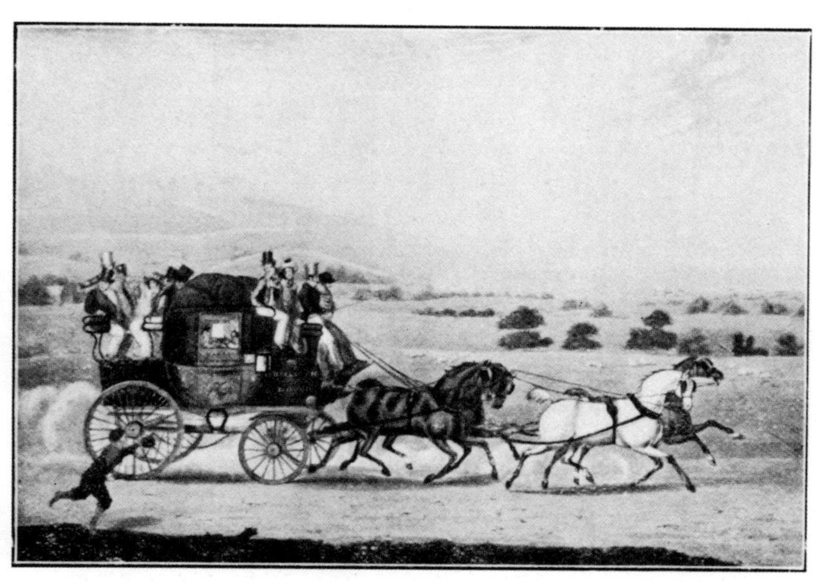

THE " EAGLE " PARIS AND DOVER COACH
Designed by G. Tregeen.   Engraved by Alken
By permission of A. Moreton Mandeville, Esq.

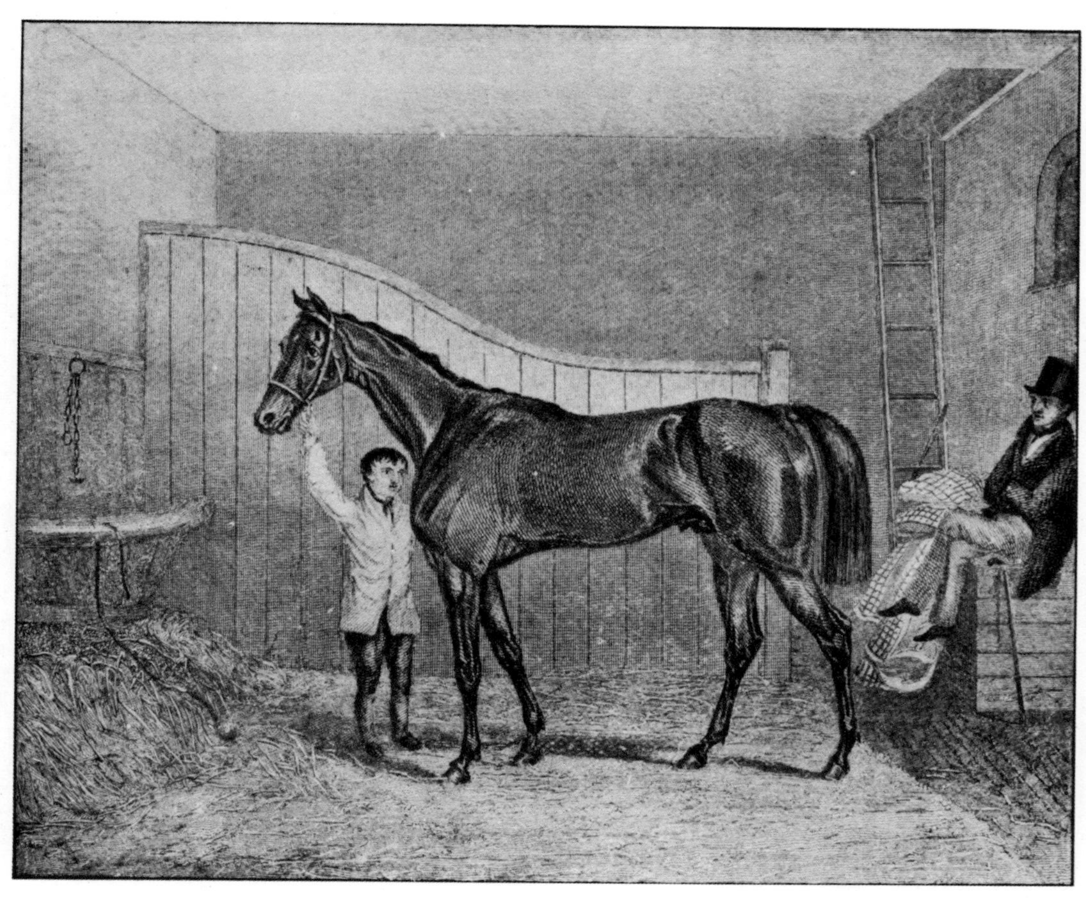

BLOOMSBURY.   WINNER OF THE DERBY, 1839
By Beckwith, after F. C. Turner

in Thames Street, belonging to Messrs. Calvert & Co., was one of his contributions to the gallery of the British Institution in the following year. The last of the series was *Messrs. Barclay, Perkins & Co's. Brewery, in Park Street, Southwark,* painted in 1840. All of these pictures he subsequently engraved.

Two well-known and popular pictures by the younger Wolstenholme were *The Burial of Tom Moody,* and *The Shade of Tom Moody.* The old huntsman in question made a dying request that at his grave side six earth stoppers should "give three rattling view halloos" in farewell, and his wish was respected. The copper plates of these works, which were engraved by the artist himself, are still in existence. A series of four pictures of the Essex Hunt afford striking evidence of this artist's skill in grouping numerous figures in appropriate landscape. These pictures are entitled (1) *The Meet at Matching Green;* (2) *Drawing the Covert of Man Wood;* (3) *Fox Crossing from Leading Roothing;* and (4) *The Death.* The figures in these pictures — men, horses and hounds — are all portraits; they were painted in the time of Mr. Henry J. Conyers, who succeeded his father in the Mastership, in 1818. This set was engraved by the artist.

Dean Wolstenholme the younger, it should be added, did not entirely confine himself to the delineation of sporting subjects. *Love in a Tub,* and *The Widow Bewitched* were two of his works which achieved considerable popularity, and were engraved. A great pigeon fancier he brought the variety known as the "Almond Tumbler" to a high state of perfection. A number of prize birds were painted by him, some of the portraits being engraved in life size. Fourteen of these, printed in colours, which are in the print room at the British Museum, show Wolstenholme's skill in rendering the peculiar metallic sheen of the pigeon's plumage. He was the inventor of a process of colour printing, afterwards patented by Leighton Brothers. This artist, it may be added, lived to the great age of eighty-four, the last twenty years of his life having been passed at Hampstead, the country surrounding which formed the background for much of his later work.

John F. Herring, the well-known animal painter, who was born in 1795, for two years drove the Wakefield and Lincoln coach Nelson, afterwards acting for a short time as coachman of the Doncaster and Halifax Mail. In his spare hours he appears to have painted sign boards, coach panels, and portraits of horses, his talents gaining for him the name of the artist-coachman. In 1818 he seems to have definitely given up the reins, for in that year he exhibited the *Portrait of a Dog* at the Academy. This was really the beginning of Herring's artistic career, and for thirty-three years afterwards he painted a number of portraits of racehorses, a complete collection of which would practically constitute a pictorial history of the Turf during the period in question.

The following are some of the numerous portraits of celebrated racehorses executed by this artist : *Touchstone,* who started twenty-one times, won nine races, including the St. Leger, 1834; walked over for seven, and lost five; *Queen of Trumps*, winner of the Oaks and St. Leger, 1835; *Elis,* winner of numerous races, ending with the St. Leger, 1836; *Bay Middleton*, winner of the Two Thousand and Derby, 1836; *Cyprian*, winner of the Oaks, 1836; *Phosphorus*, winner of the Derby, 1837; *Miss Letty*, winner of the Oaks, 1837; *Don John*, winner of the St. Leger, 1838; *Crucifix*, winner of the One Thousand, Two Thousand, and Oaks, 1840; *Coronation*, winner of the Derby, 1841; *Ghuznee,* winner of the Oaks, 1841; *Nutwith*, winner of the St. Leger, 1843; *Orlando*, winner of the Derby, 1844; *Faugh-a-Ballagh*, winner of the Two Thousand and Cesarewitch, 1844; *Merry Monarch*, winner of the Derby, 1845; *The Baron*, winner of the St. Leger and Cesarewitch, 1845; *Pyrrhus 1st*, winner of the Derby, 1846; *Mendicant* winner of the One Thousand and Oaks, 1846; *Sir Tatton Sykes*, winner of the St. Leger and Cesarewitch, 1846. *Camarine*, whose portrait Herring painted, was a remarkable mare. Foaled in 1828, she ran in neither the Derby nor the Oaks of her year, but had a highly successful turf career, beating among others, in 1831, Spaniel, winner of that year's Derby; Oxygen, winner of the Oaks of that year; and in 1832 she beat Rowton, winner of the St. Leger of 1829.

In his later years Herring devoted his energies largely to the painting of rural scenes, the execution of which betrays great delicacy and finish, his farmyard pictures being especially remarkable. For Queen Victoria, who paid this artist great attention, he painted the portraits of three Arabs—*Bagdad*, a charger of the Prince Consort's, *Korsaid*, and *Said*, a horse on which the royal children had received their first lessons in horsemanship. He died near Tunbridge Wells, in 1865.

Another artist who shared with Herring the distinction of being a fashionable and celebrated painter of racehorses was Charles Hancock, born in the same year, 1795. Between 1835 and 1843 he painted :—

Queen of Trumps, winner of the Oaks and St. Leger, 1835, and one of the celebrated winning mares. This picture was engraved and published in colours by Rudolph Ackermann: the plate is a large size, the same as that from the portrait of *Mundig*.

Mundig, winner of the Derby, 1835, for John Bowes, Esq. Scott is the jockey in the saddle. This portrait was engraved in large size, printed in colours, and published by Rudolph Ackermann, of Regent Street, in September, 1835. Richard Parr also engraved a small plate from this portrait.

Glencoe, bred by the Earl of Jersey in 1831: winner of the Royal Cup at Ascot in 1835. Painted in 1836, and engraved by E. Duncan; it was published in colours, by Rudolph Ackermann, in 1836.

Don John, bred in 1835 by Lord Chesterfield; winner of the St. Leger, 1838. This portrait was engraved by E. Duncan, and published in colours, by Rudolph Ackermann, in 1838.

Bay Middleton, winner of the Two Thousand and Derby, 1836. Engraved by E. Duncan; published in colours by Rudolph Ackermann in 1836.

Coronation, bred by Mr. Rawlinson; winner of the Derby, 1841. This picture was engraved in small size by E. Paterson.

Satirist, bred by Lord Westminster; winner of the St. Leger, 1841.

Attila, bred by Colonel Hancox; winner of the Derby, 1842.

Our Nell, bred by Mr. Dawson; winner of the Oaks, 1842.

Blue Bonnet, winner of the St. Leger, 1842.

Cotherstone, bred by John Bowes, Esq.; winner of the Two Thousand and Derby, 1843.

Nutwith, bred by Captain Wrather; winner of the St. Leger, 1843.

Faugh-a-Ballagh, bred in Ireland, and purchased in 1842 by E. J. Irwin, Esq.; winner of the St. Leger and Cesarewitch, 1844.

In 1835, Hancock painted *Tally-ho!* the picture of a fox breaking covert. This was engraved by Beckwith and Duncan, and was published by Rudolph Ackermann.

In 1836 he painted a portrait of "George Baker, Esq., on his Favourite old Mare." This was engraved by W. Giller, and published by Ackermann. "Mr. Baker, of Elenore Hall, in the County of Durham," said the *New Sporting Magazine,* "has been a gentleman jockey, an owner of racehorses, a master of foxhounds, a Member of Parliament, an amateur in the fine arts—in short, he is a thoroughbred British sportsman."

Hancock's services were also in request as an illustrator of books. *The Sportsman's Annual* (royal folio), published in 1836, by A. H. Baily and Co., of Cornhill, and R. B. King, of Monument Yard, London, contains plates from pictures by Sir Edwin Landseer, Abraham Cooper, R.A., and Charles Hancock. Hancock is represented in this book by his pictures of a Foxhound and a Bloodhound, drawn on stone and engraved by Thomas Fairland.

Sporting, illustrative of British field sports, edited by Nimrod, also a royal folio, and published by A. H. Baily and Co., contains plates from pictures by T. Gainsborough, R.A., Sir Edwin Landseer, R.A., Abraham Cooper, R.A., J. F. Lewis, and William Barraud. Hancock's five pictures in this work are *The Warreners,* engraved by R. Parr; *The Gamekeeper,* engraved by W. A. Scott; *Rat Hunting,* engraved by T. S. Engleheart; *Thorngrove* and *Sir Hercules,* two racehorses, engraved by H. Beckwith; and *Deerstalking,* engraved by W. Greatbach.

Hancock's career as a painter was from 1819 to 1847. The date of his death is unknown, but it would appear to have been about 1855.

Five years before this died William Barraud, who, though not an artist of very striking abilities, produced some very good pictures of sport and sportsmen, together with a number of portraits of famous horses and dogs. His younger brother, Henry Barraud, who died as late as 1874, is perhaps best known by the engravings of *We praise Thee, O God,* which in their day achieved a widespread popularity. The three youths in the picture were the artist's own son, his nephew, and a friend. Other well-known pictures by this artist were *Lord's Cricket Ground,* and *The London Season.*

We now come to almost the last of the sporting artists who flourished well within living memory. This was Charles Cooper Henderson, who, born in 1803, died only thirty-one years ago, having linked the days of the mail-coach with those of the railway train.

In consequence of his marriage, in 1829, to a Miss By, Cooper Henderson's father disinherited him, though there seems to have been no reason, except caprice, for taking such a course. Thrown upon his own resources, the young man adopted painting sporting pictures as a means of livelihood, living on the money earned by his own talents till 1850, when the death of his mother rendered him independent. Coaching scenes and incidents of the road were the subjects which most attracted Henderson, many of whose pictures have been rendered familiar through their engravings. Besides this, he occasionally painted in a different style, an example of this being the *Berkeley Hunt*. A number of his compositions represent travelling scenes in France, he having obtained a thorough knowledge of the horses, trappings, and vehicles employed across the channel, during a prolonged tour, taken as a young man, with his father. Cooper Henderson's elder brother, John Henderson, was a great collector and, as will be remembered, he bequeathed the most valuable portion of his treasures to the nation.

With the death of Cooper Henderson, terminated the old school of sporting artists, the engravings of whose works form such attractive ornaments to the smoking room and country house. The school in question finally ended just about the time that the various processes of reproduction now in vogue caused the decay of the old-fashioned engraver, who, in his time, had reproduced so many sporting scenes as well as pictures of horses and hounds. Though mechanical reproduction has been brought to great perfection, it can never convey the same impressions as were produced by many of the sporting prints so ably executed in the past by men who imparted a real spirit of actuality and life into the work upon which they were engaged.

Those desirous of obtaining full details of the lives of British Sporting Artists will find a wealth of interesting information in "Animal Painters of England," by Sir Walter Gilbey, Bart., a work which has been of great assistance to the present writer in the completion of his task.

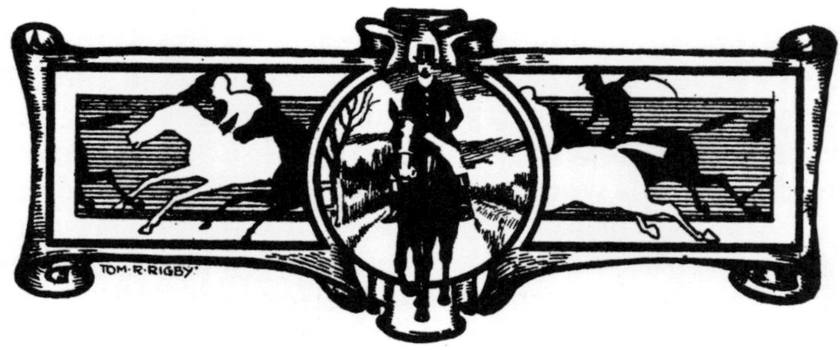

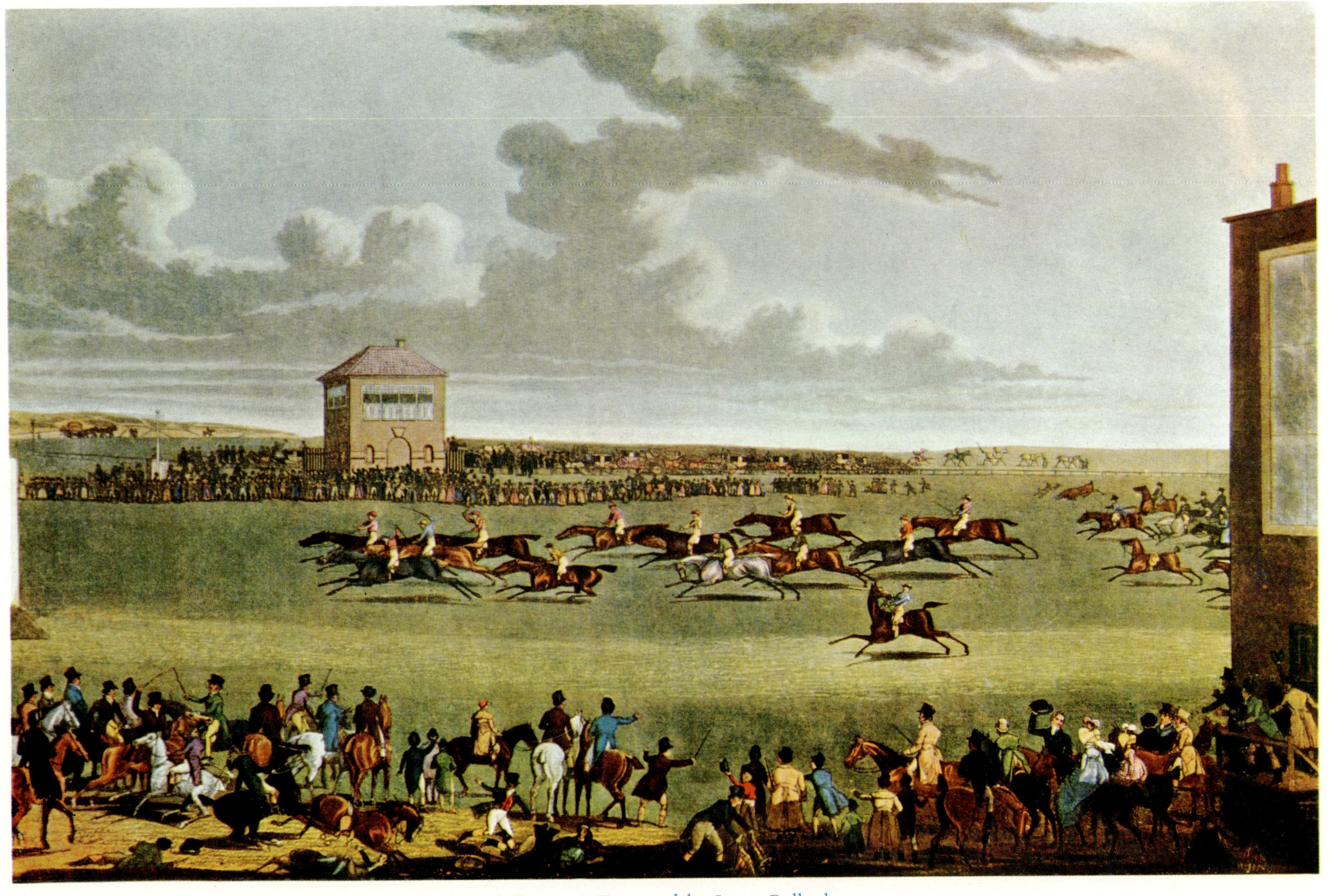

Drawn & Engraved by James Pollard
NEWMARKET RACES
London. Published by J. MOORE at his Looking-Glafs & Picture-Frame Manufactory. 1 West Street. St. Martin's Lane

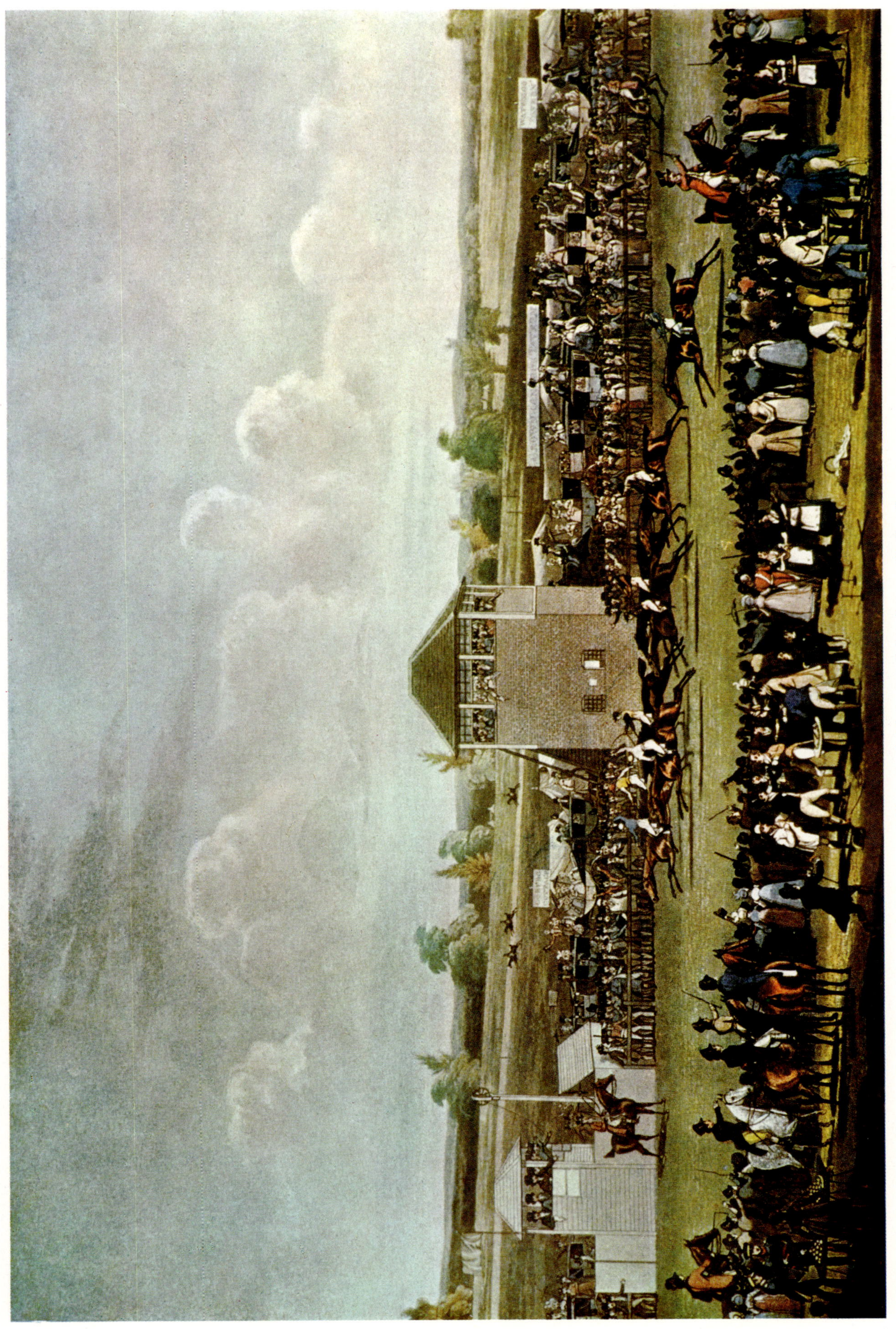

Drawn & Engraved by James Pollard
ASCOT HEATH RACES
London. Published by J. MOORE at his Looking-Glafs & Picture-Frame Manufactory, 1 West Street. St. Martin's Lane

Painted by J. POLLARD

London Published Novbr 1st. 1836 by Thos McLEAN. 26 Haymarket
Goodwood Grand Stand
PREPARING TO START

Engraved by R. G. REEVE

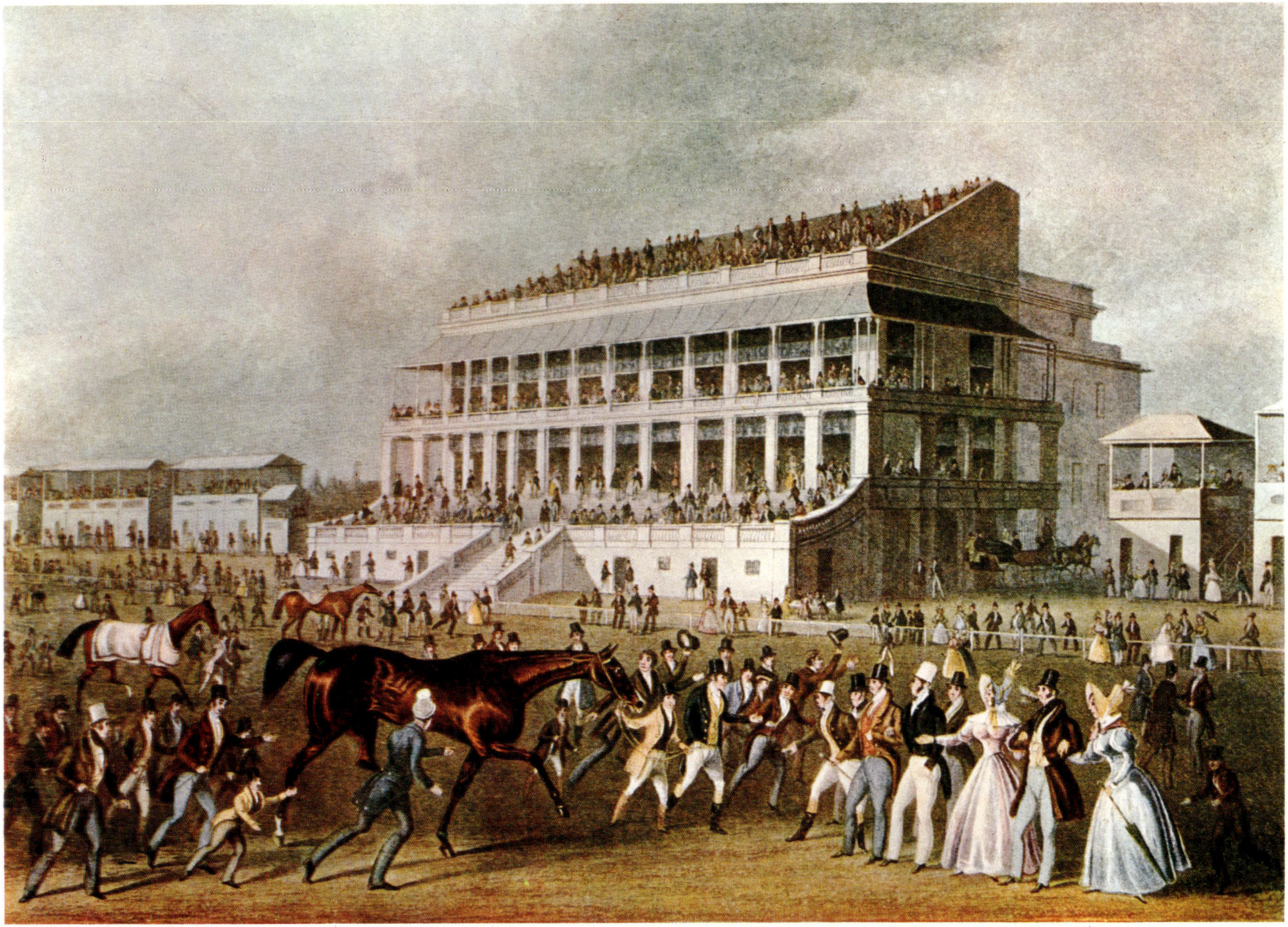

Painted by J. POLLARD

London Published by Thos McLEAN. 26 Haymarket. Novr. 1st 1836

Engraved by R. G. REEVE

Epsom Grand Stand

THE WINNER OF THE DERBY RACE

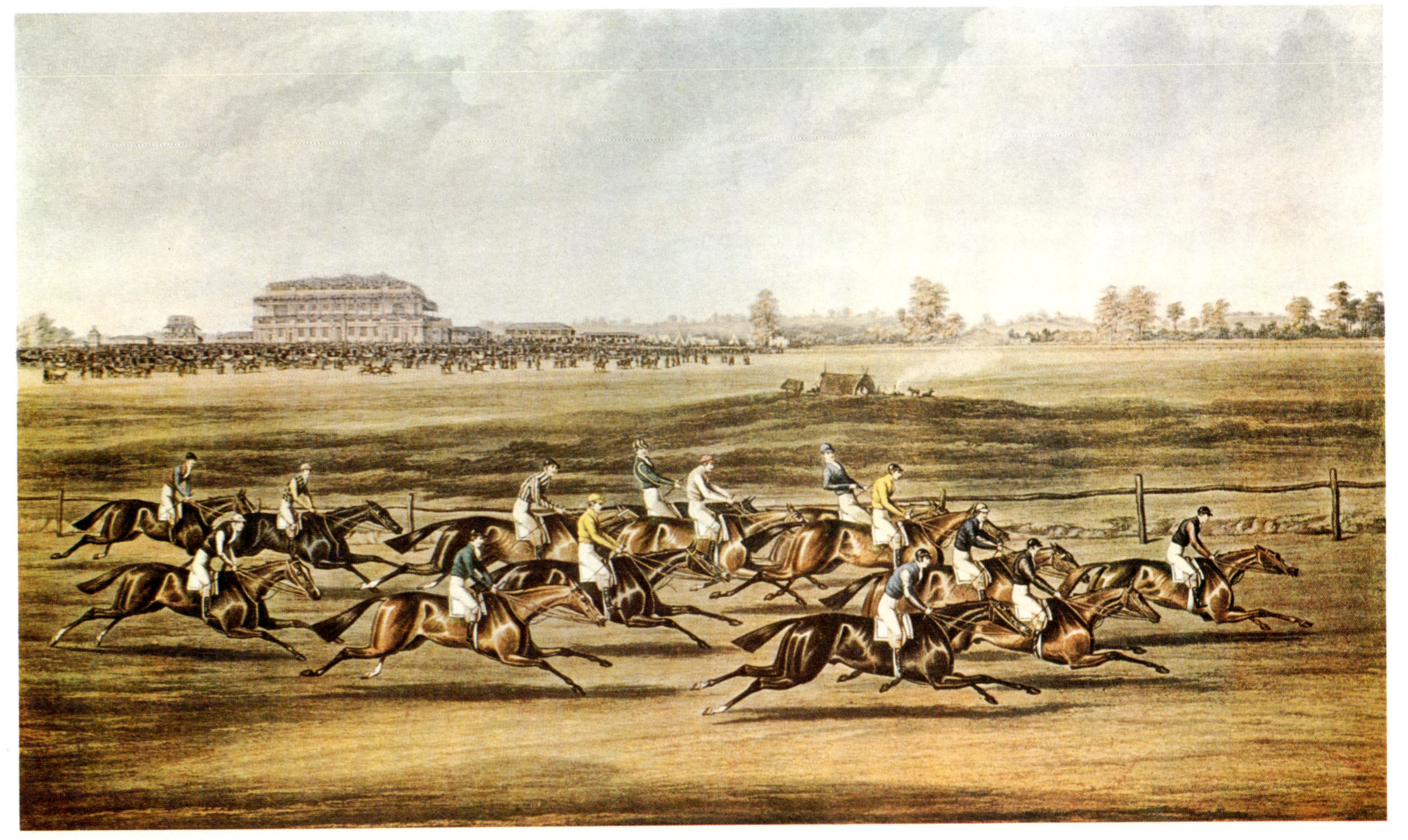

PAINTED BY JAS. POLLARD LONDON PUBLISHED MAY 24th 1837. BY ACKERMANN & Co 96 STRAND ENGRAVED BY J. HARRIS

RACE FOR THE GREAT St. LEGER STAKES, 1836.

Approbation—Off in good Style.

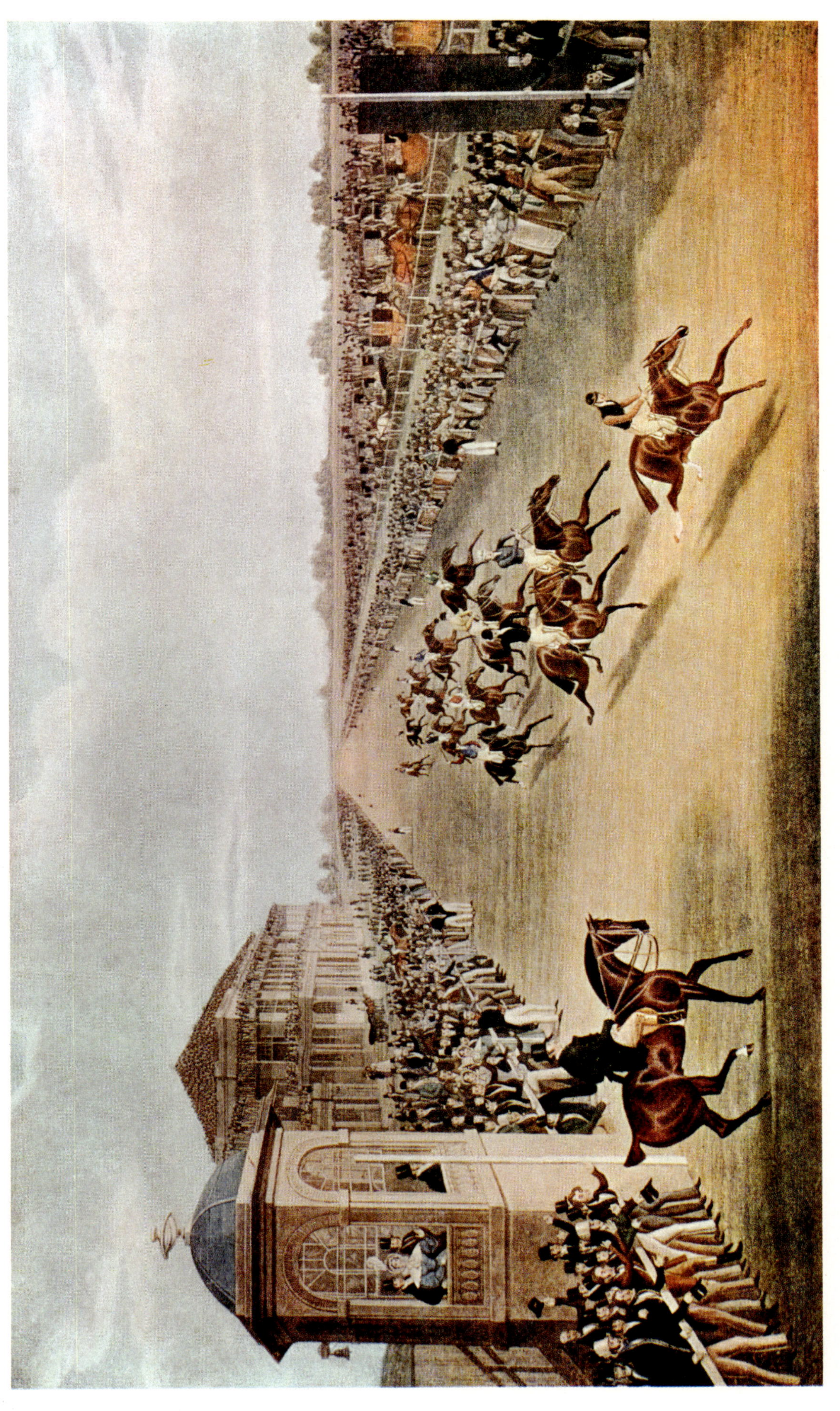

PAINTED BY J POLLARD   LONDON. PUBLISHED MAY 24th 1837 BY ACKERMANN & Co 96 STRAND   ENGRAVED BY J HARRIS

RACE FOR THE GREAT St. LEGER STAKES, 1836.

Anticipation—Who is the Winner?

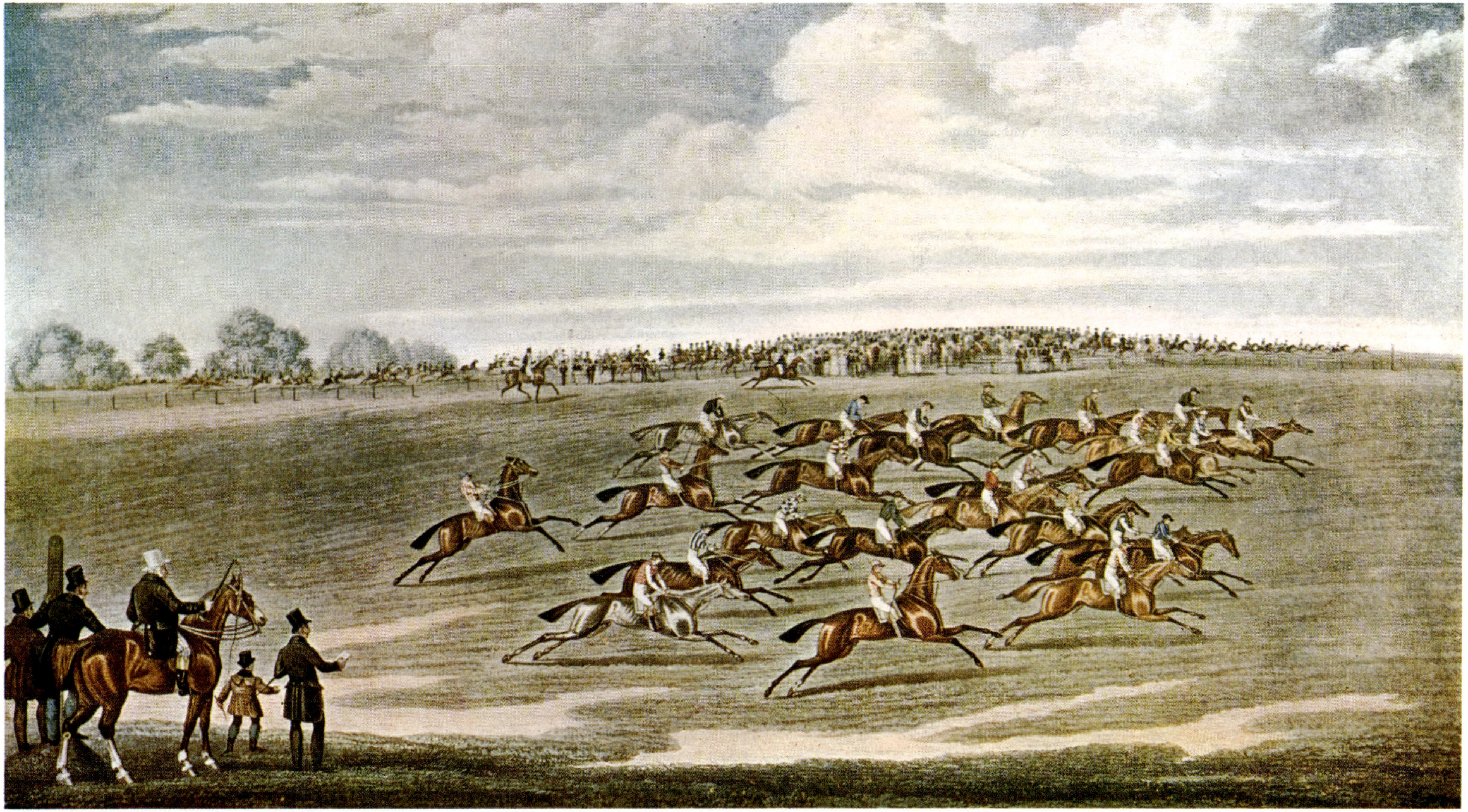

J. Pollard, delin.

EPSOM RACES.

Smart & Hunt. sculpt.

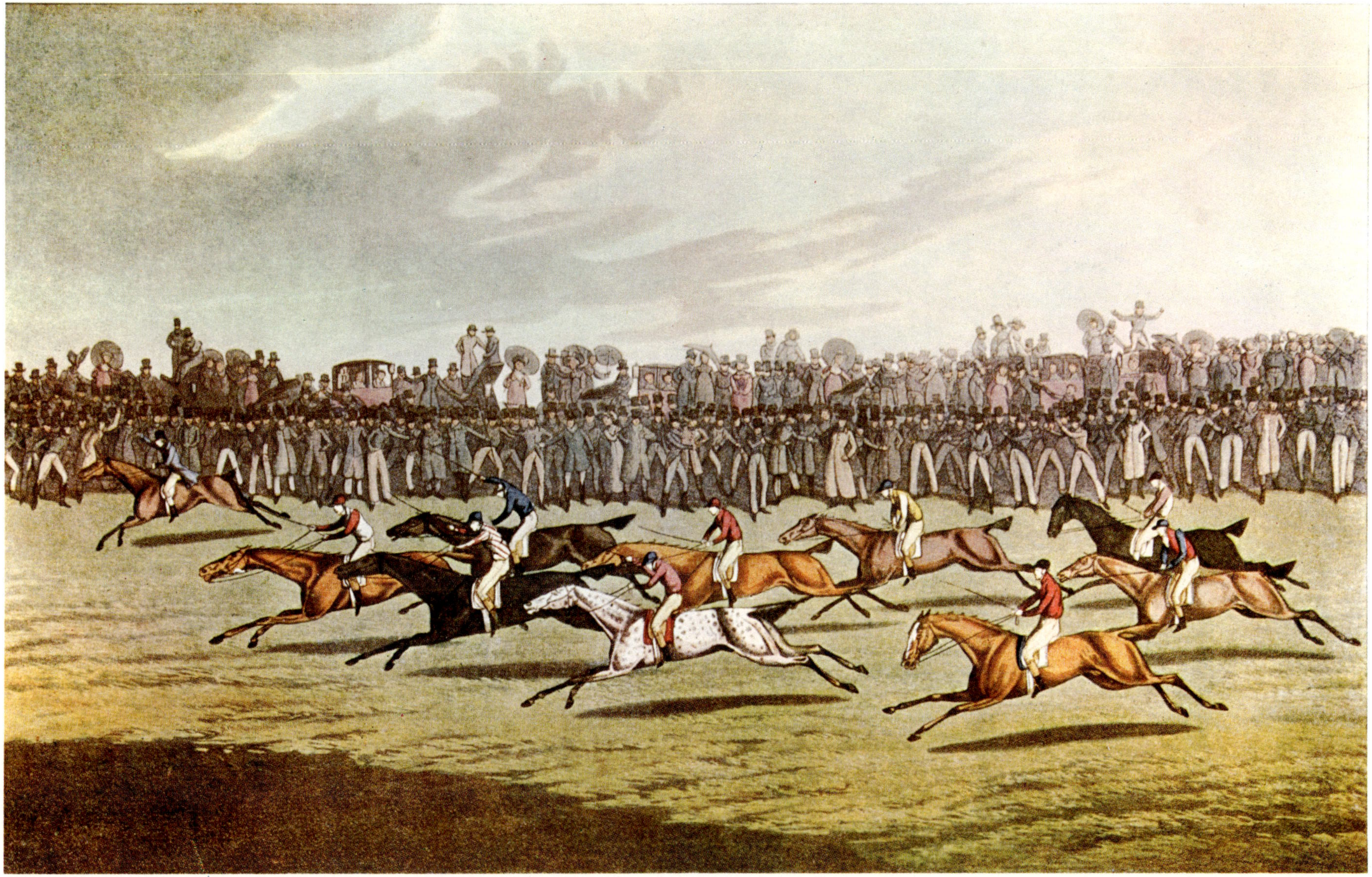

H Alken delt.

London, Published by T. McLean, Jany. 1, 1820
RACING.

I. Clark sculpt.

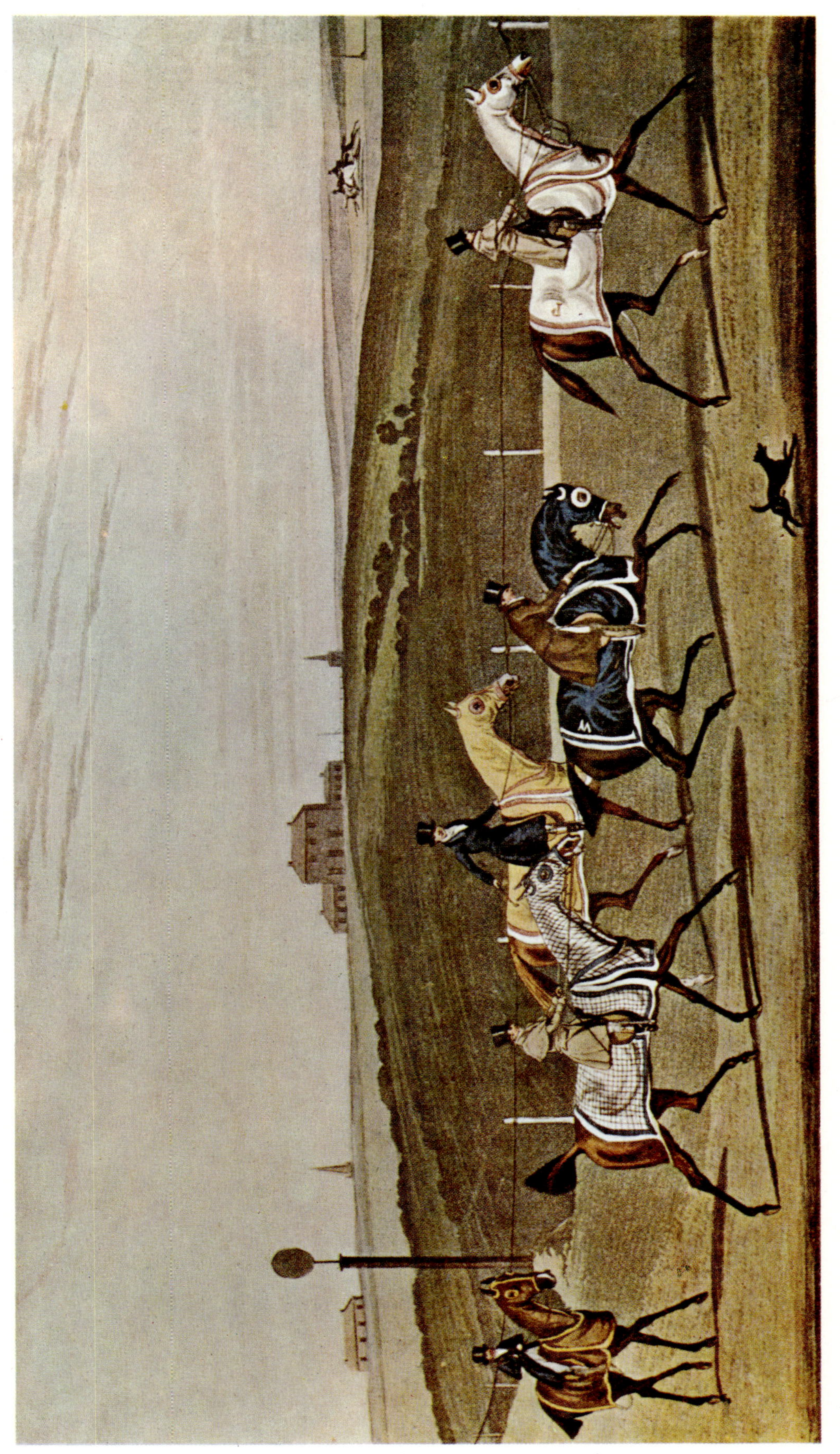

TRAINING
Engraved by G. Hunt
After J. Pollard

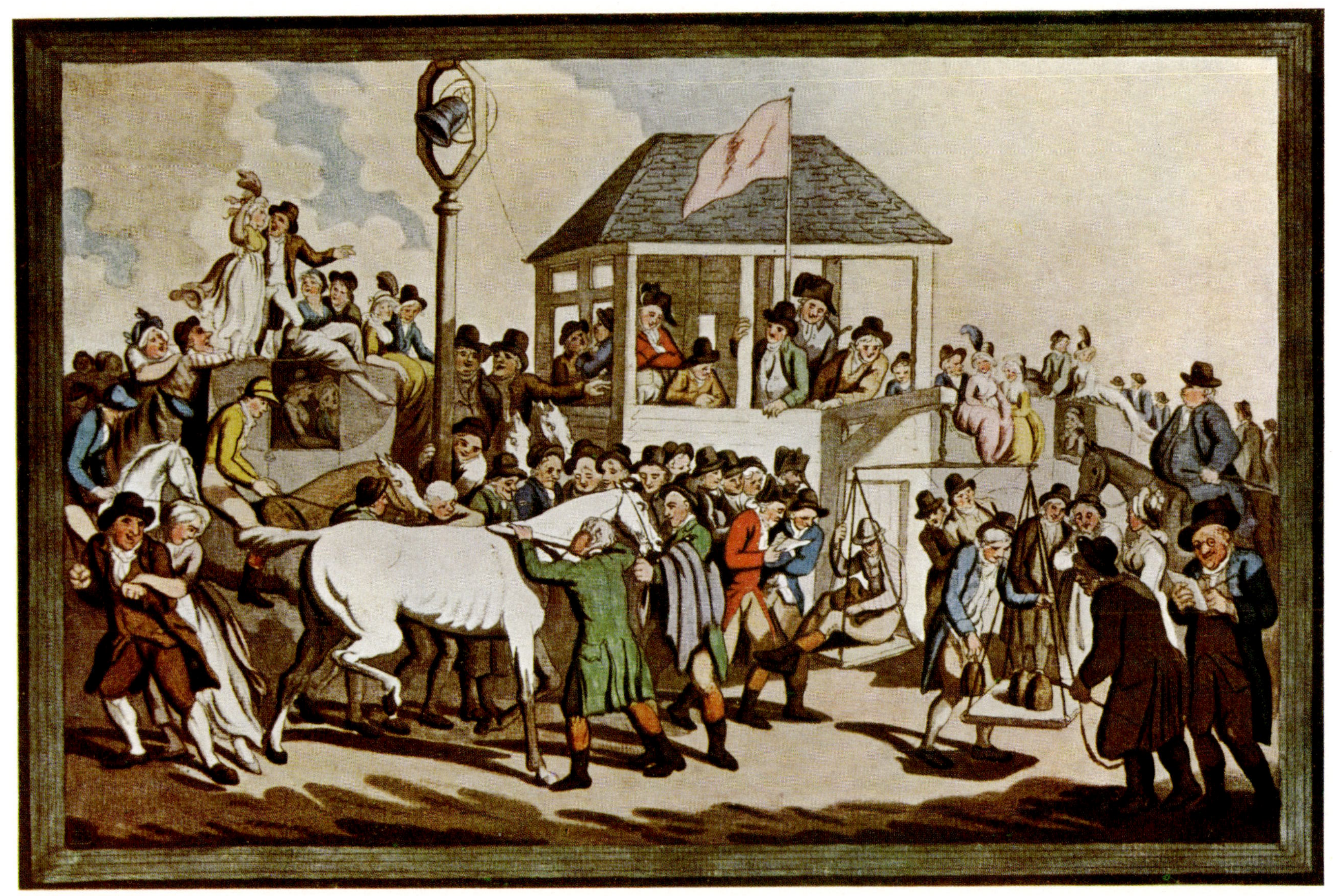

WEIGHING
From a set of six racing scenes
By Rowlandson

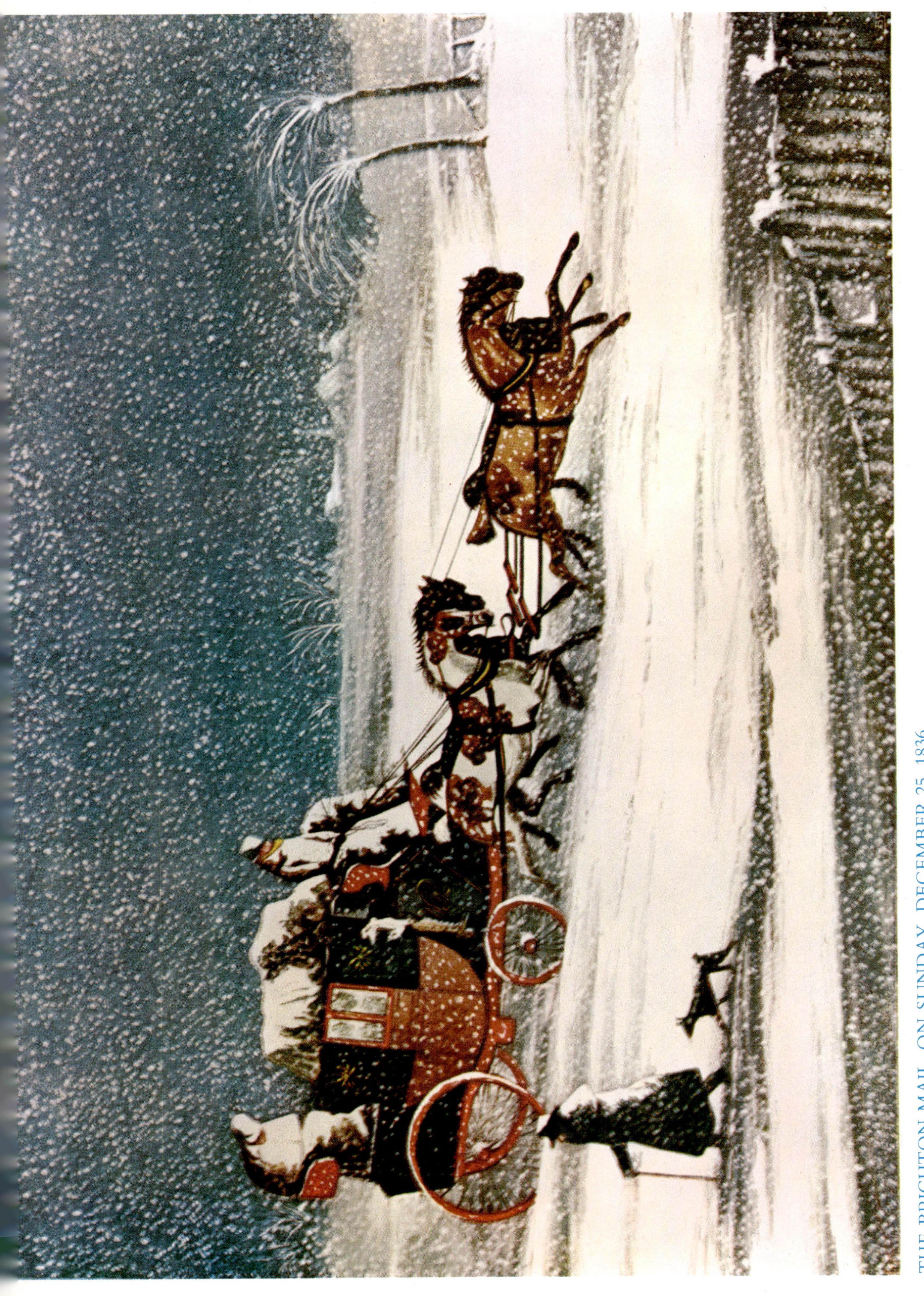

THE BRIGHTON MAIL, ON SUNDAY, DECEMBER 25, 1836
Drawn by H. Alken
Published by R Havell, 77 Oxford Street

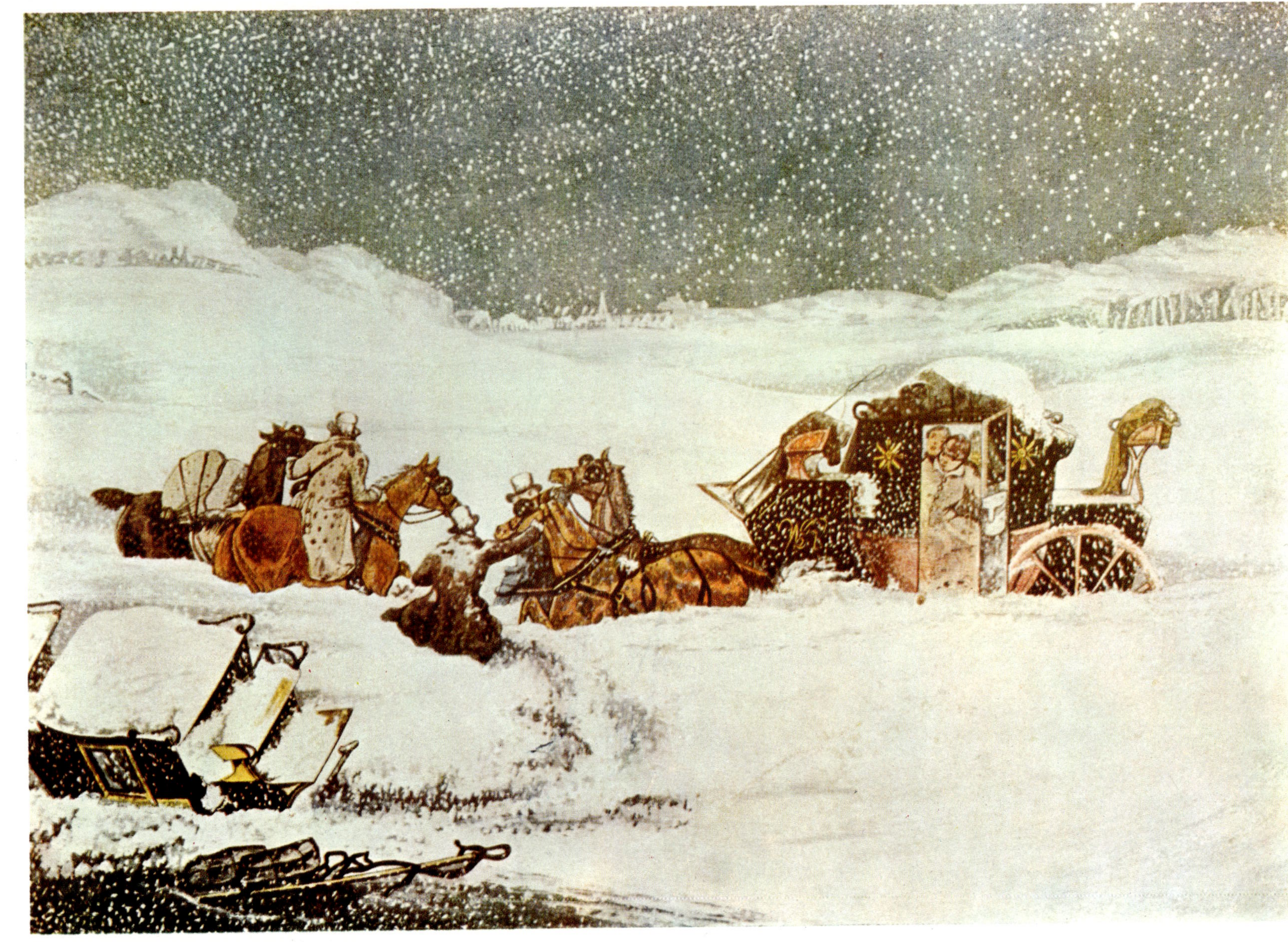

THE BIRMINGHAM MAIL NEAR AYLESBURY
The Guard Banbury proceeding with the bags
Drawn by H. Alken
Engraved by R. Havell

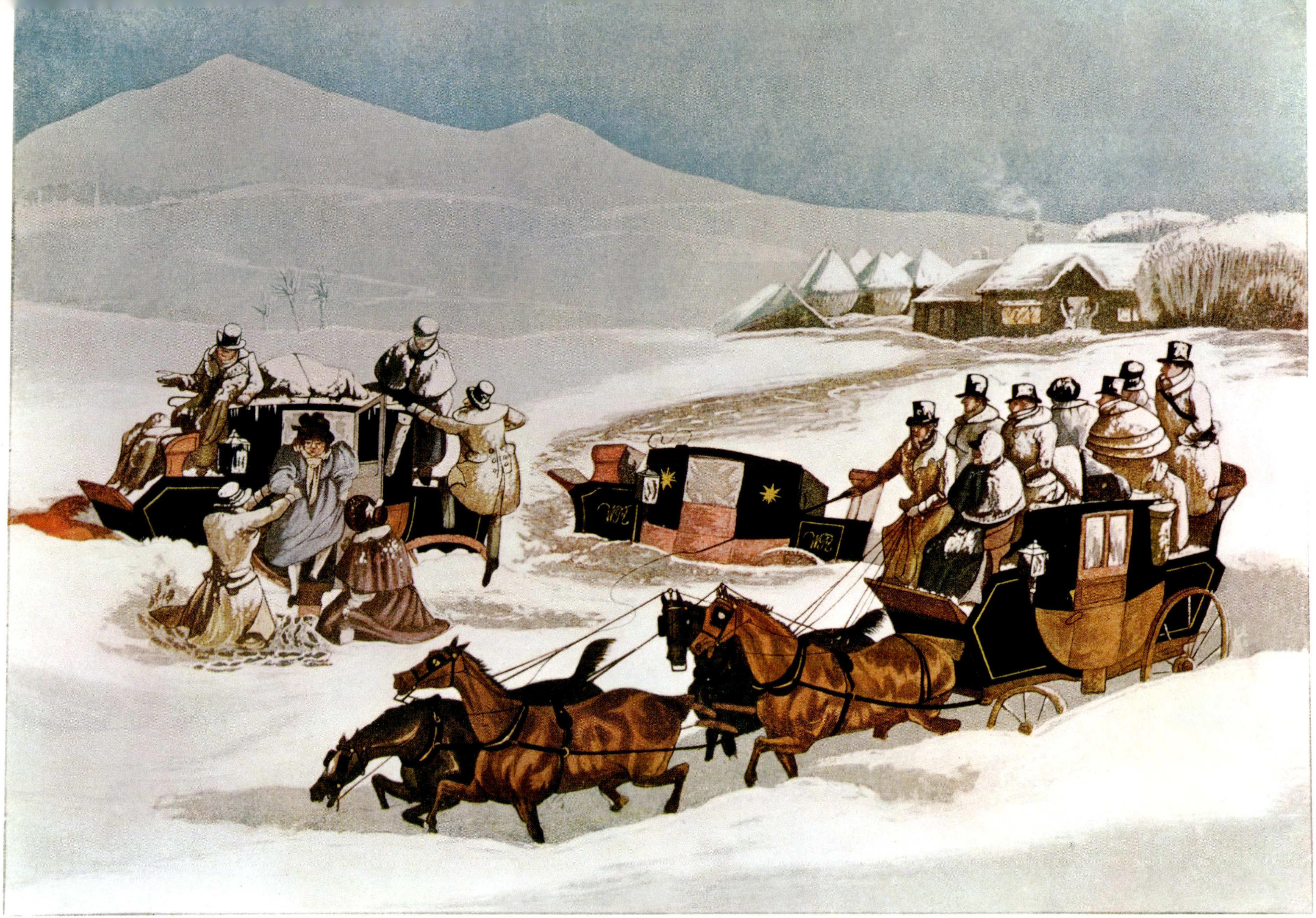

Drawn by H. Alken

THE BRUCE PASSING THE PEVERIL AND MANCHESTER MAIL

Engd. by R. Havell

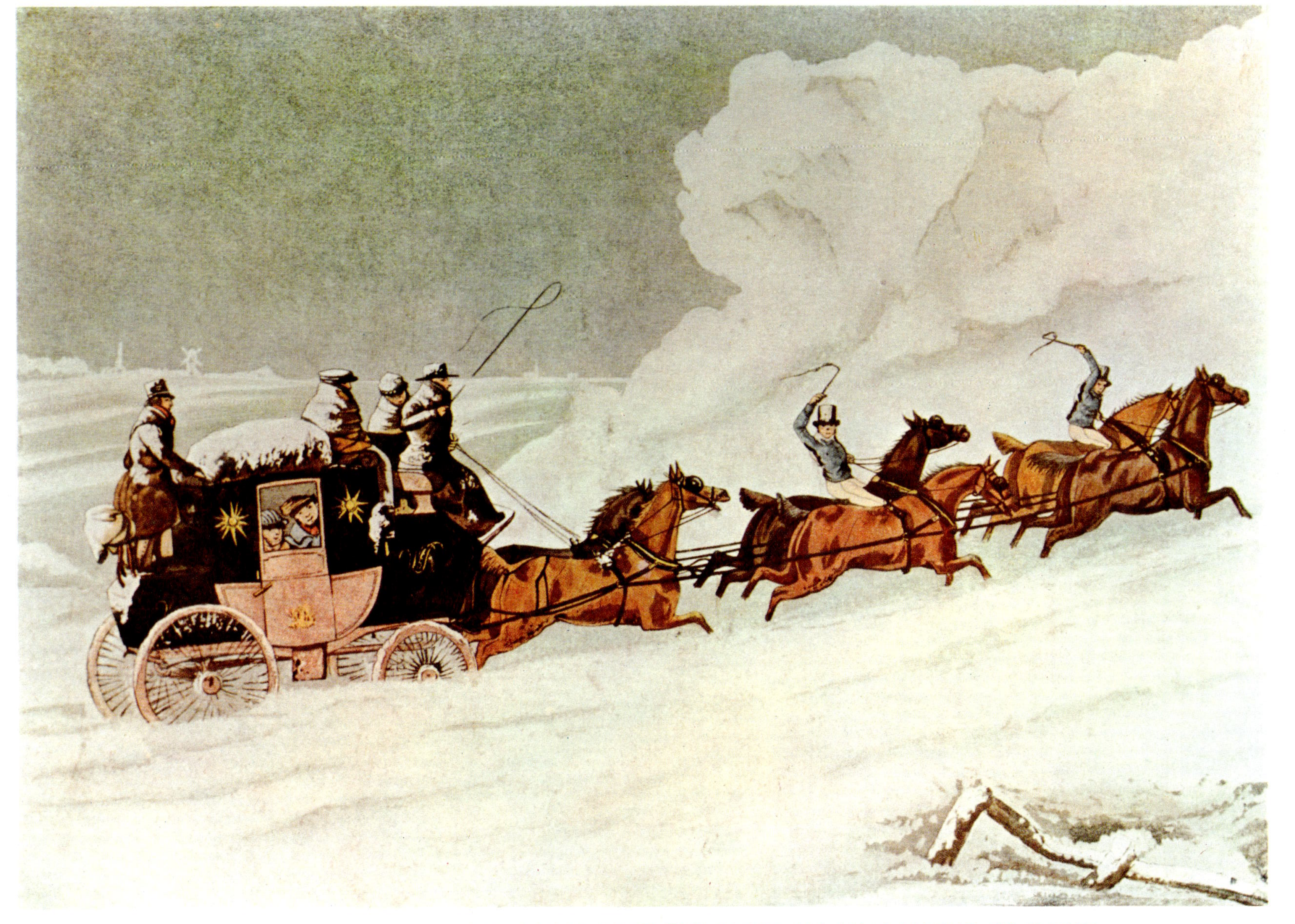

THE DEVONPORT MAIL NEAR AMESBURY, GOING POST THROUGH AN AVALANCHE OF SNOW
Drawn by H. Alken
Engraved by R. Havell

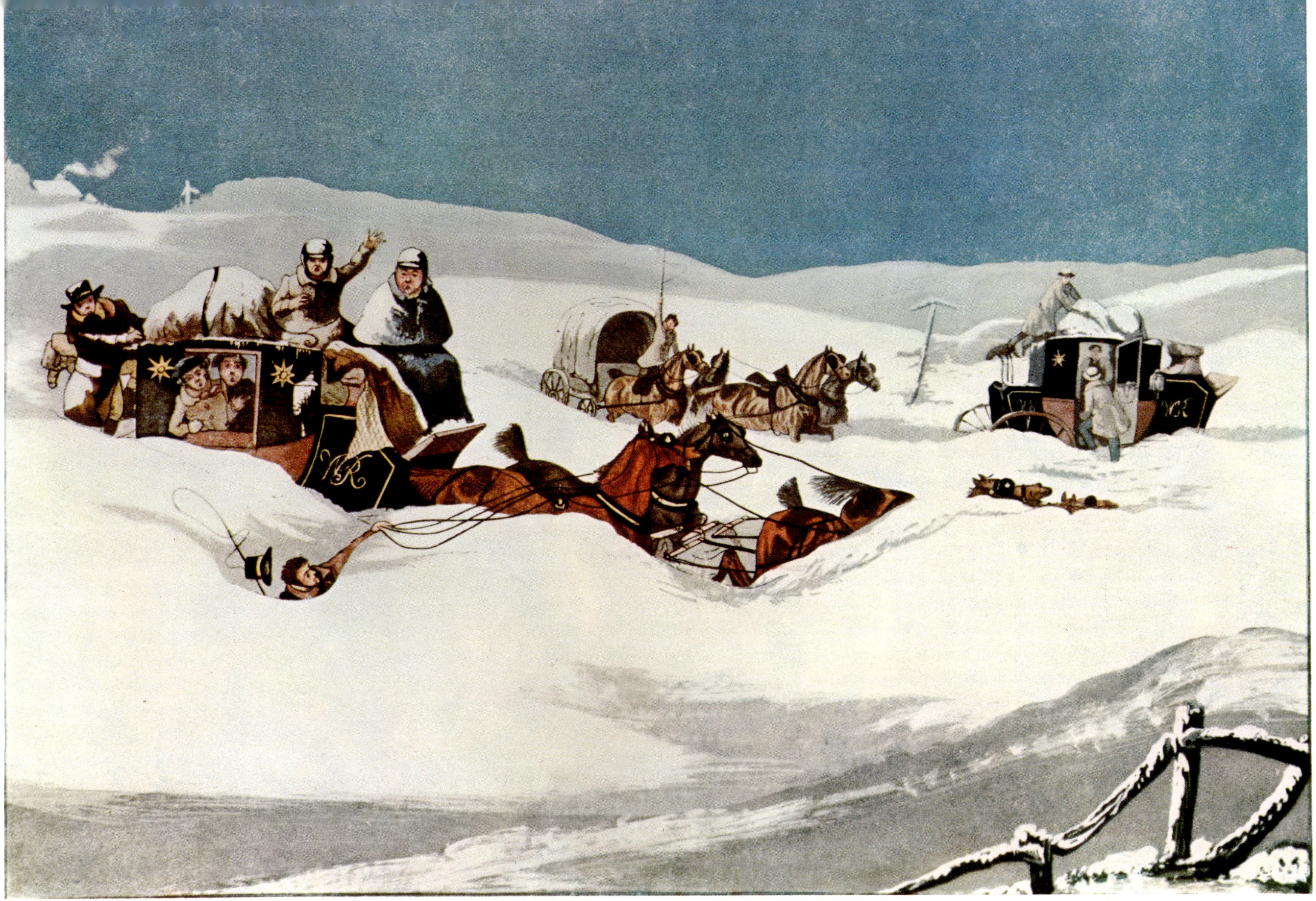

Drawn by H. Alken

Engraved by R. Havell

THE HOLYHEAD AND CHESTER MAILS,
At Hockley Hill, near Dunstable
Pubd. Feby. 6th 1837 by R. Havell 77 Oxford St

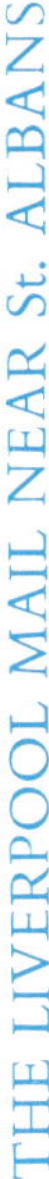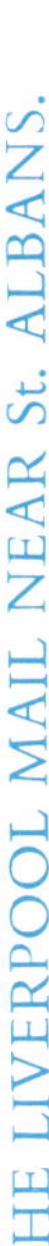

Drawn by H Alken
THE LIVERPOOL MAIL NEAR St. ALBANS.
Engraved by R Havell

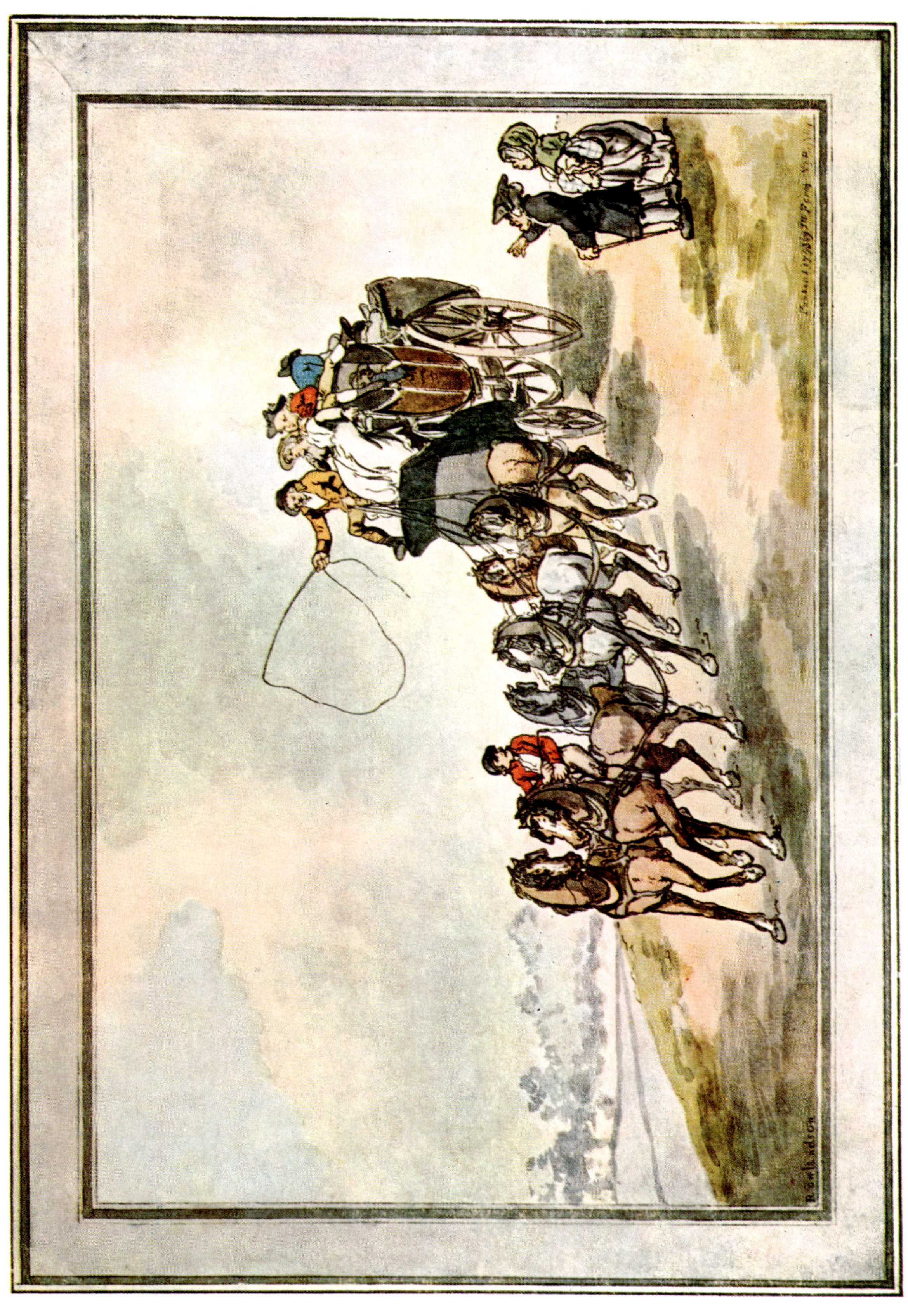

COACH AND SIX
From a Water Colour Drawing
By T. Rowlandson

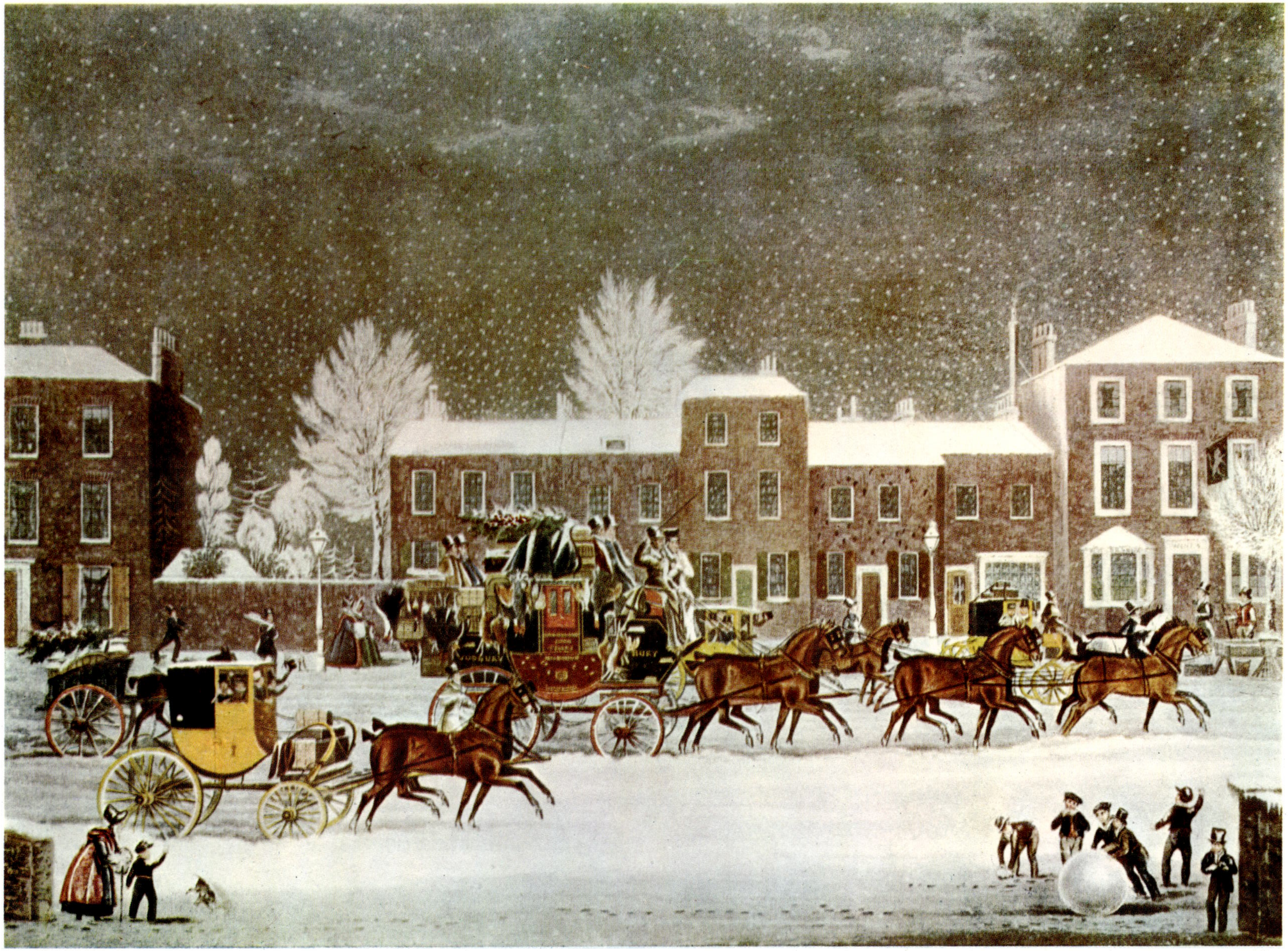

Painted by James Pollard

APPROACH TO CHRISTMAS.

Engraved by George Hunt

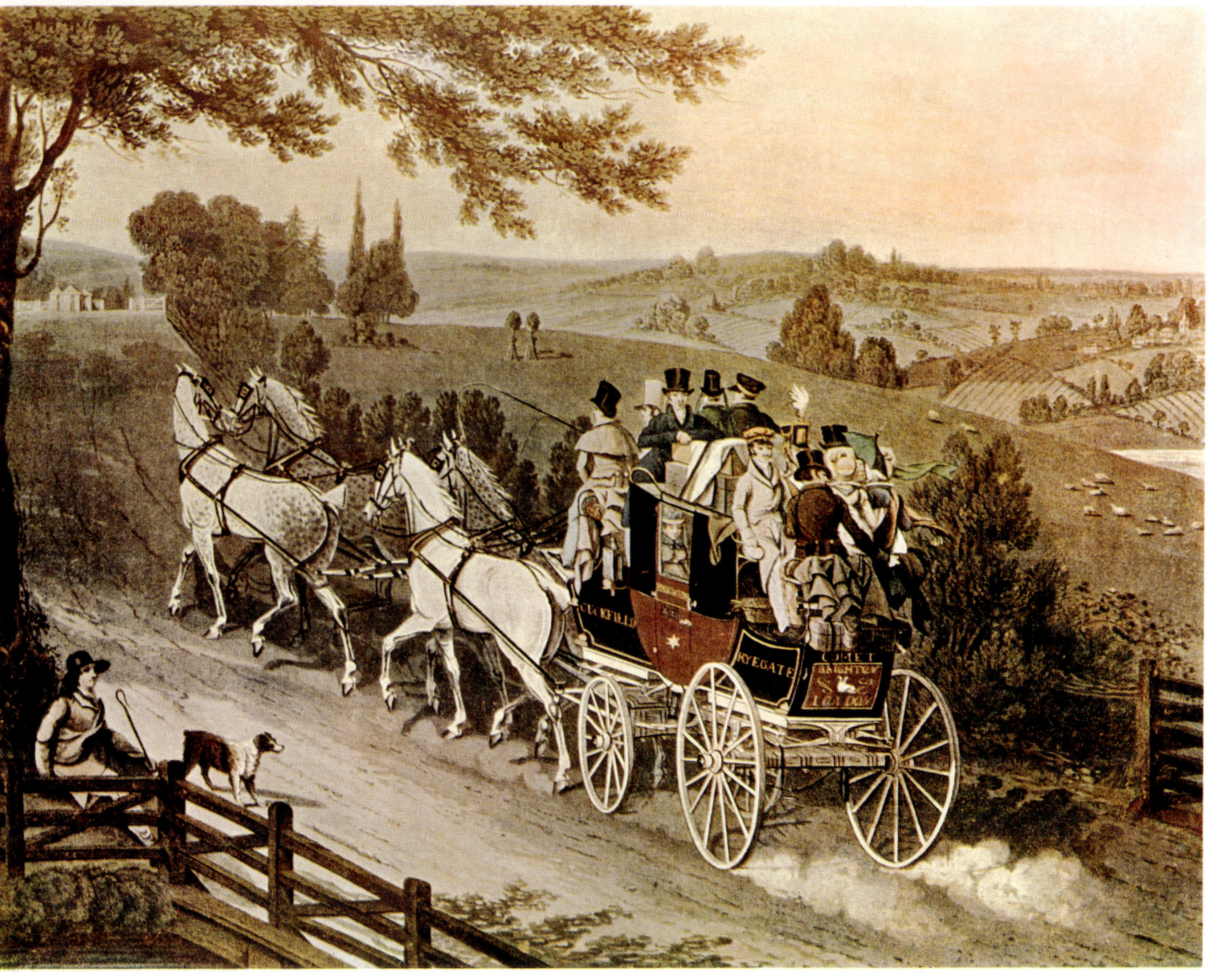

Painted by J Pollard   London Published Nov 1 1822 by Jon. Watson 7 Vere Street Bond Street   Engraved by Dubourg

STAGE COACH.

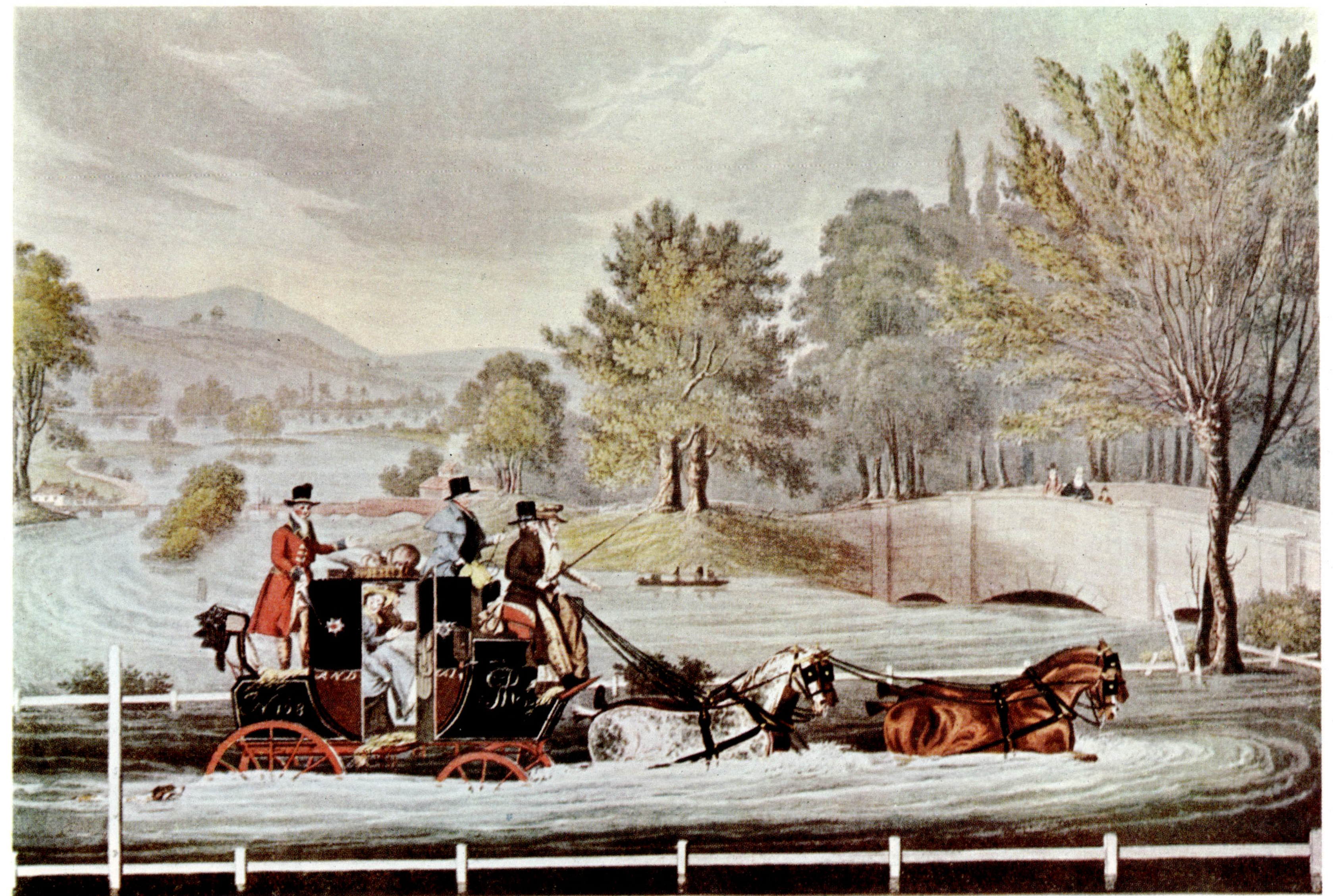

MAIL COACH IN A FLOOD
Painted by James Pollard
Engraved by F. Rosenbourg

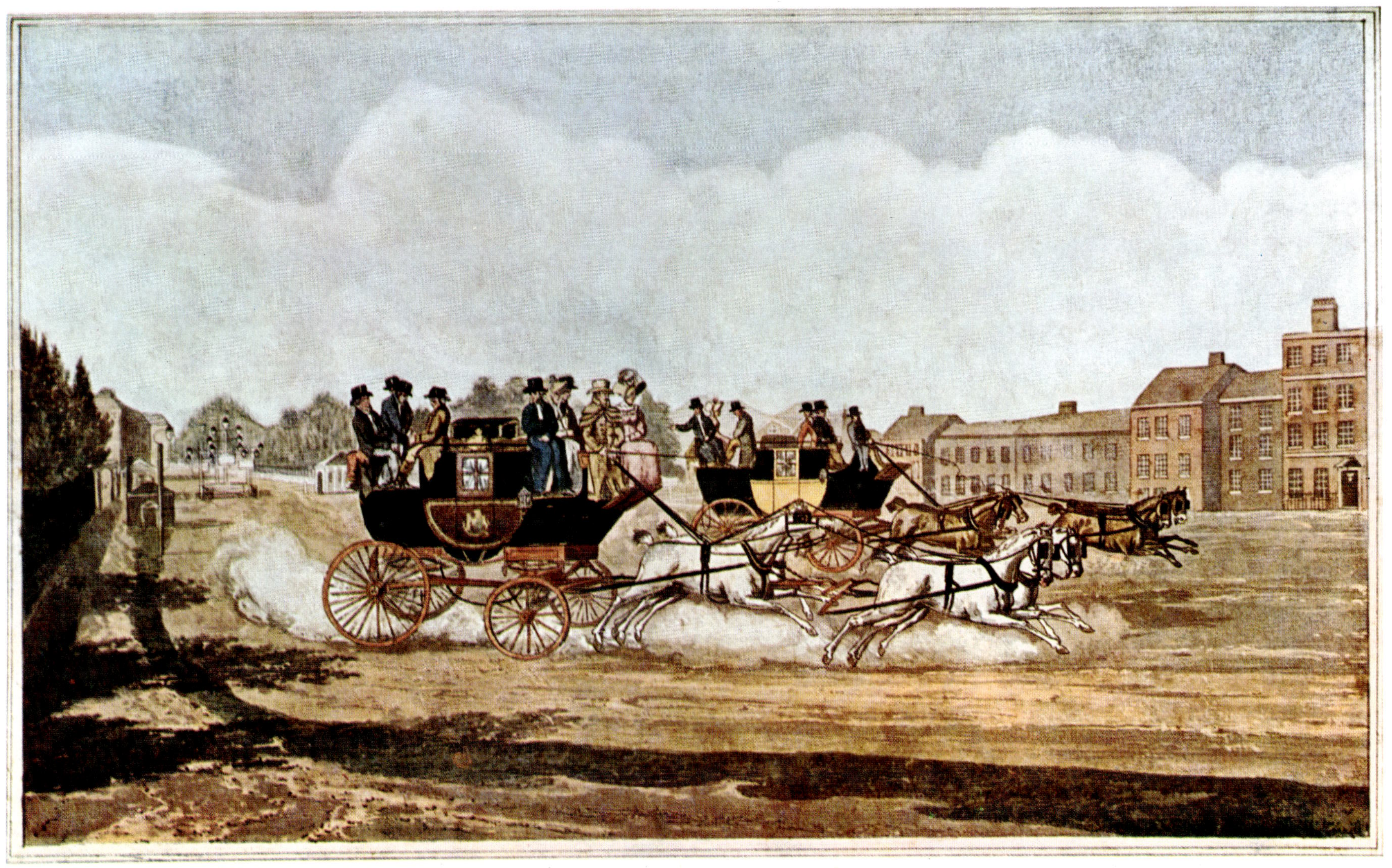

THE OXFORD AND OPPOSITION COACHES
W. Havell

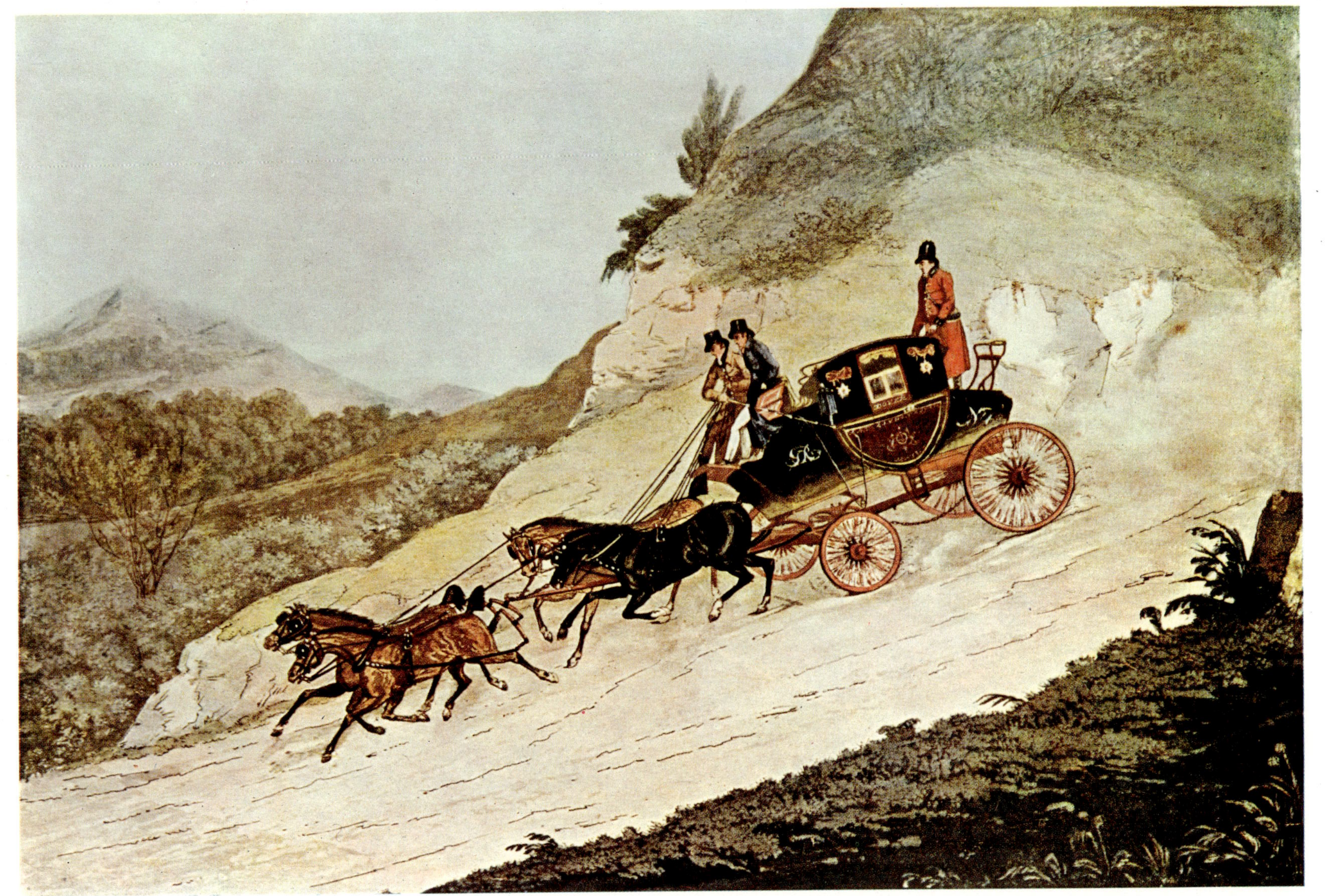

ROYAL MAIL COACH
Painted by James Pollard
Engraved by R. Havell

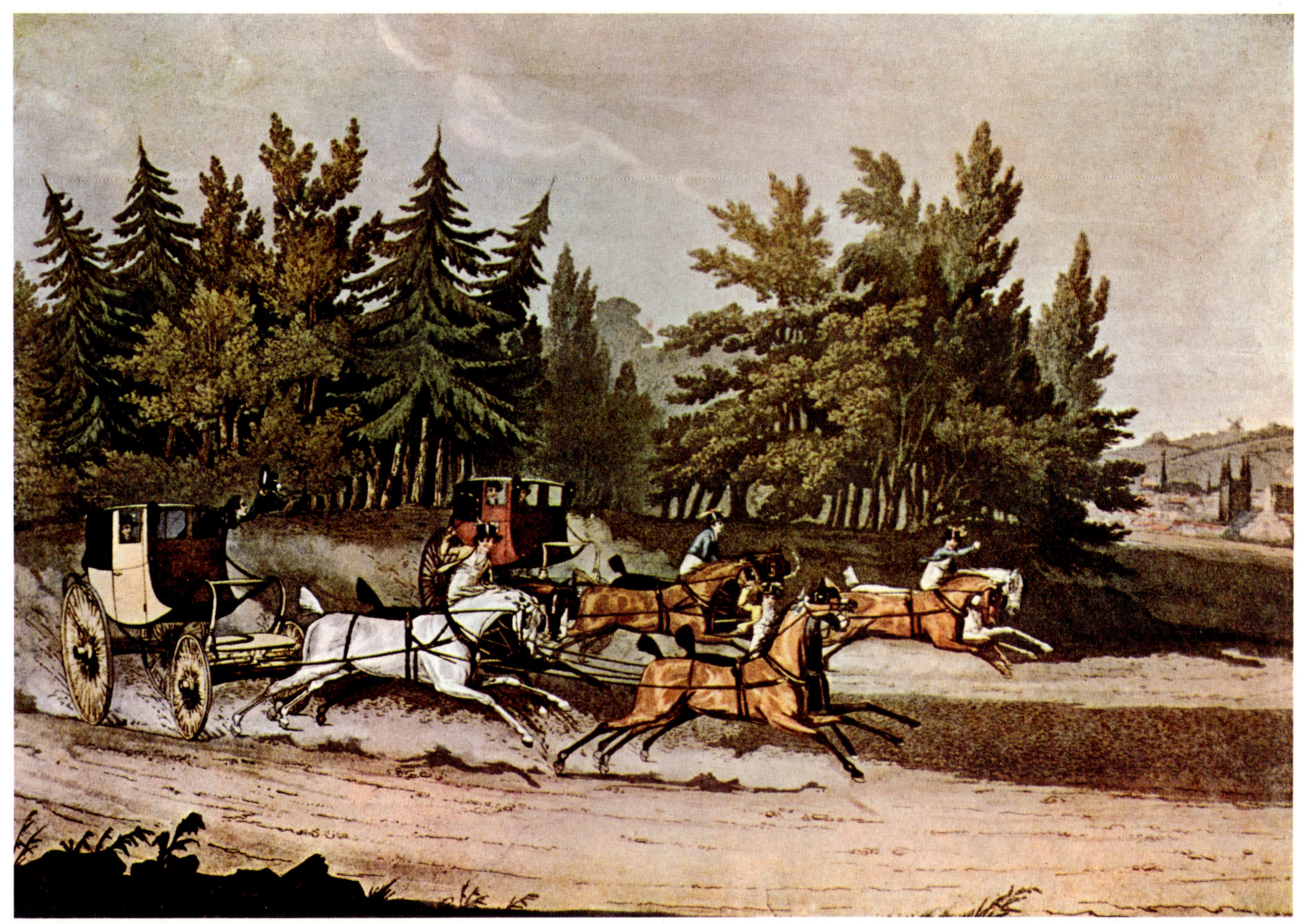

THE LAST HOUR OF A CONTESTED ELECTION FOR M.P.
Painted by Jas. Pollard
Engraved by R. Havell

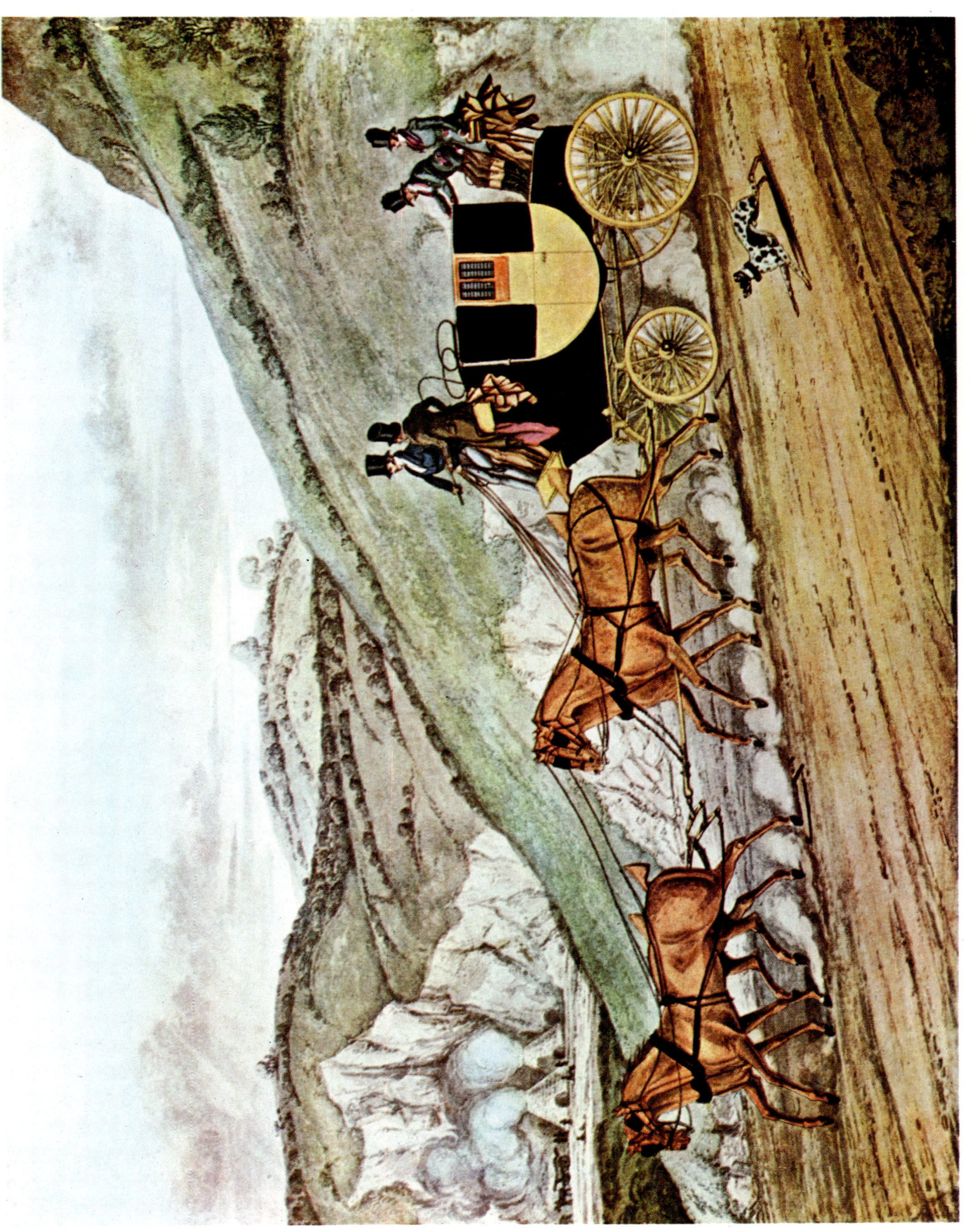

FOUR IN HAND
Painted by James Pollard
Engraved by J. Gleadah

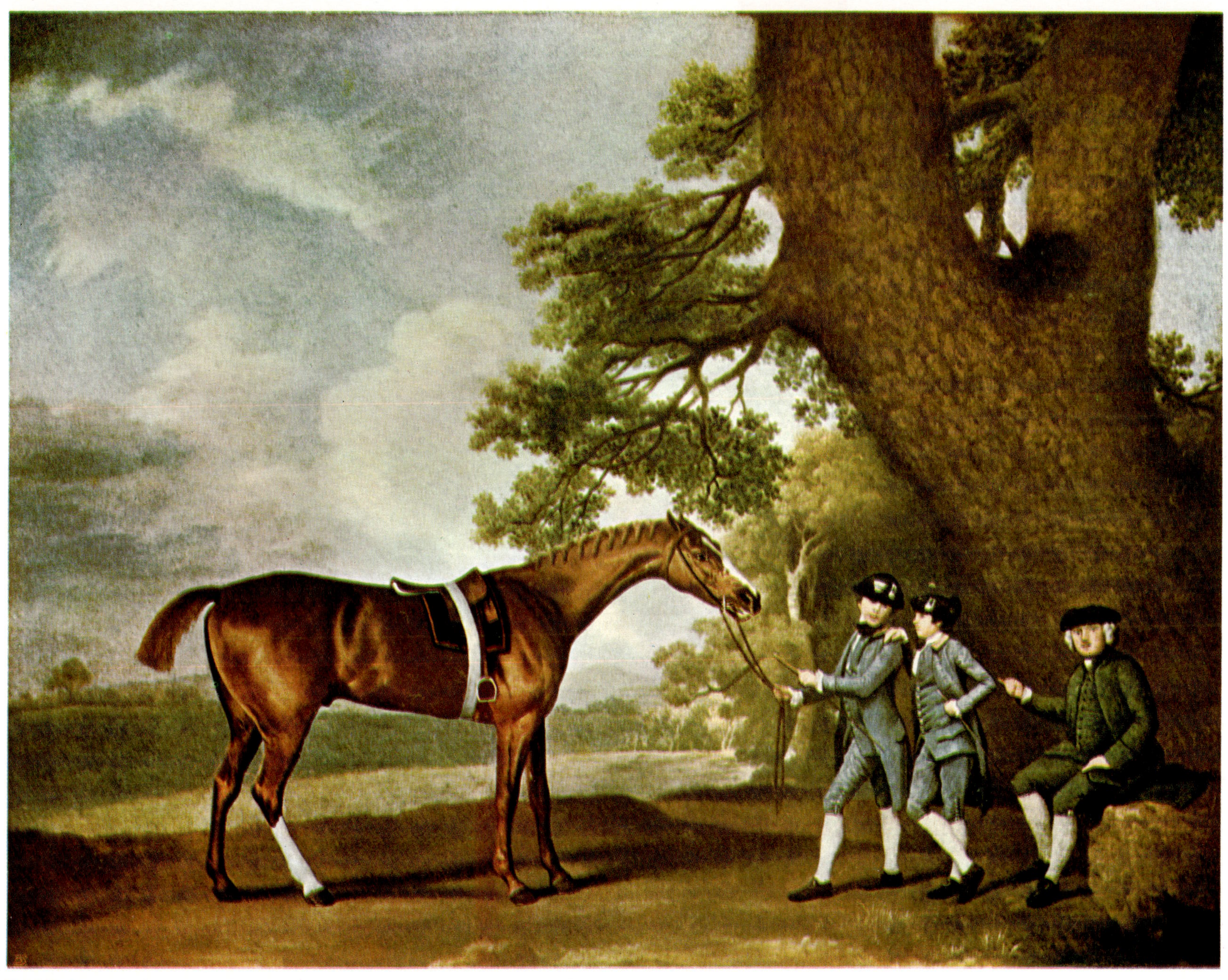

ECLIPSE
By George Stubbs, R.A.

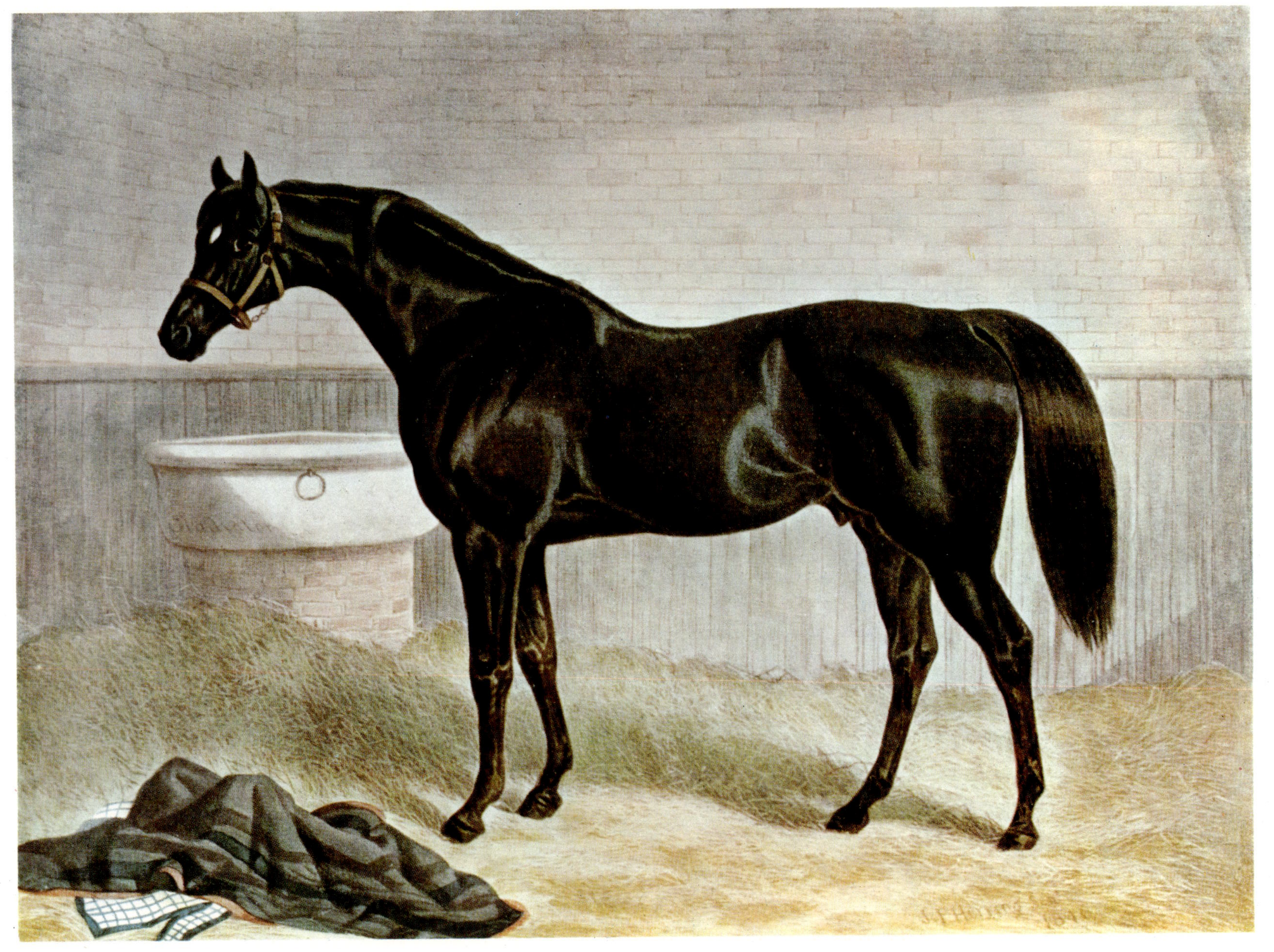

GLADIATOR
Painted by J. F. Herring, Sen.
Engraved by J. R. Mackrell

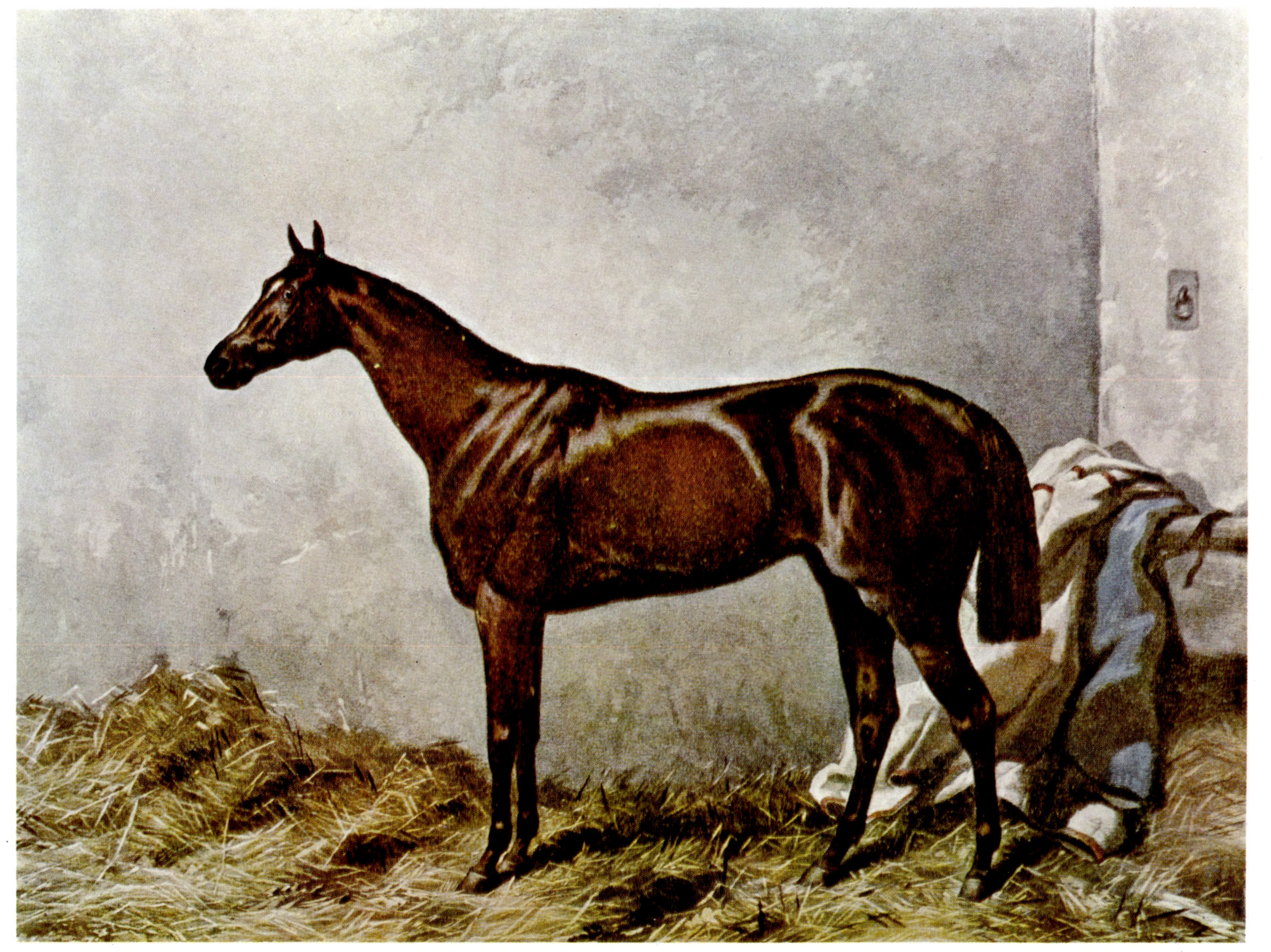

HERMIT
Winner of the Derby Stakes at Epsom, 1867
Painted by Harry Hall   Engraved by W. Summers

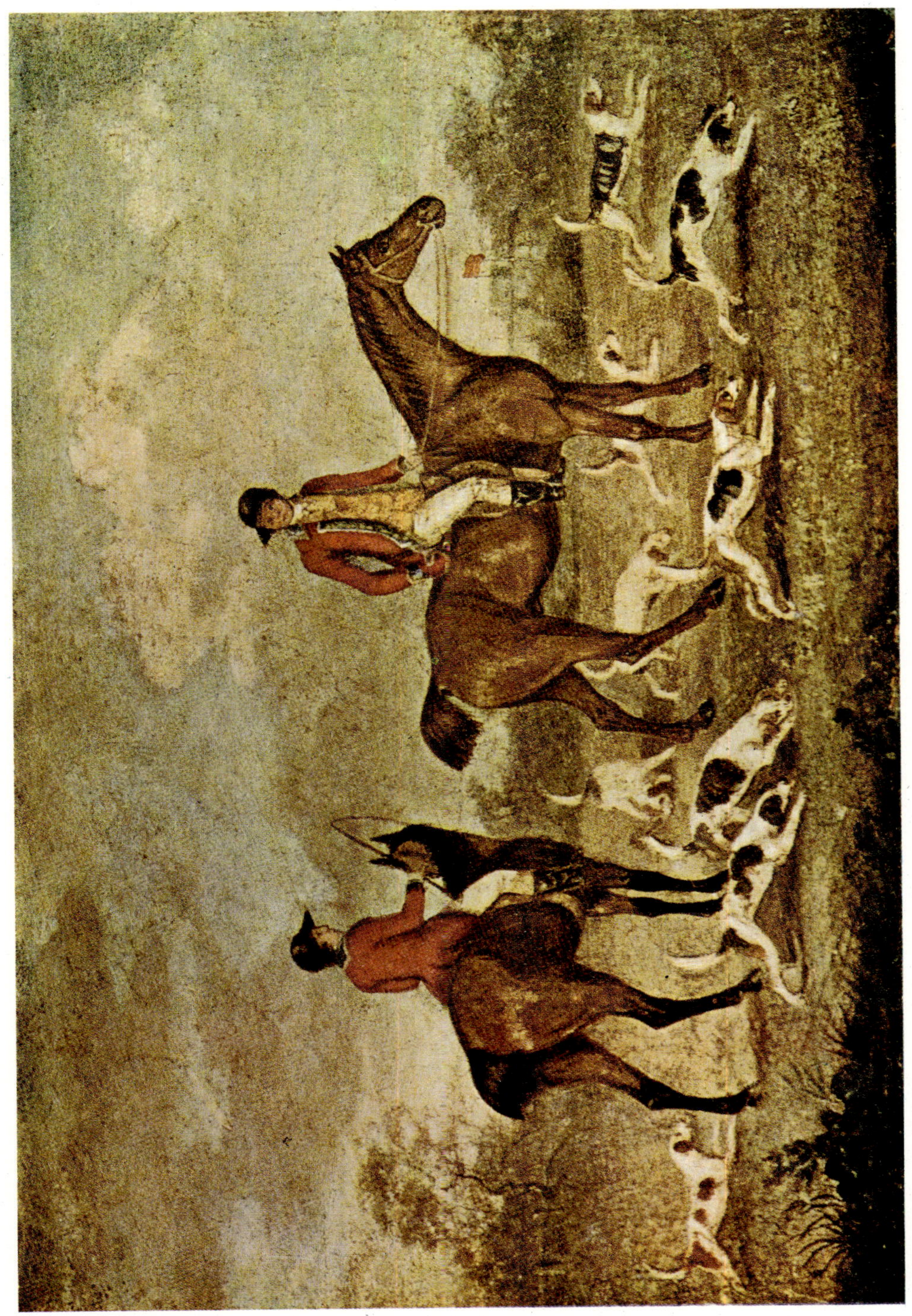

HUNTING SCENE
By Ben. Marshall

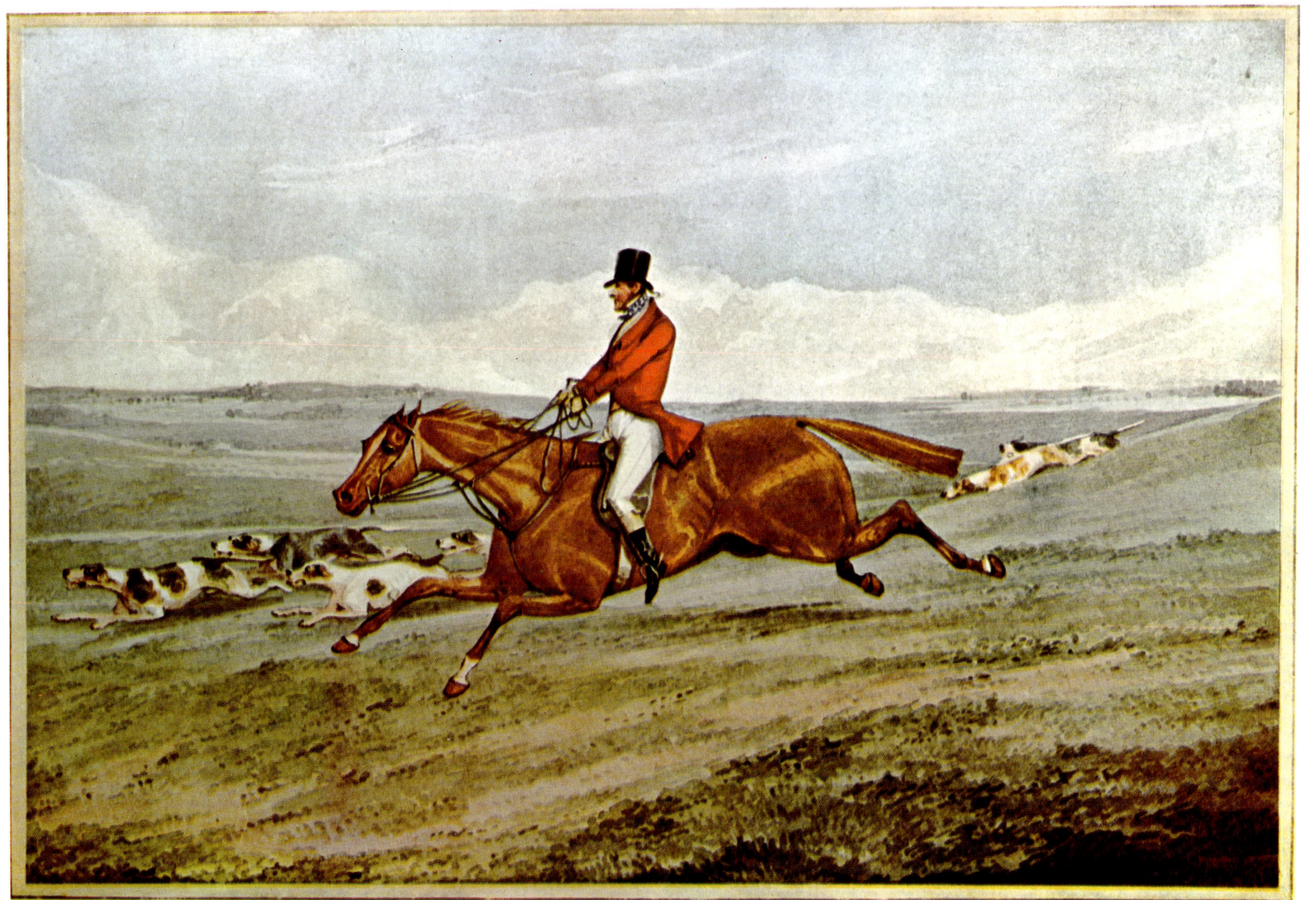

FOX HUNTING: "TAKING THE LEAD"
From an Original Drawing
By Henry Alken

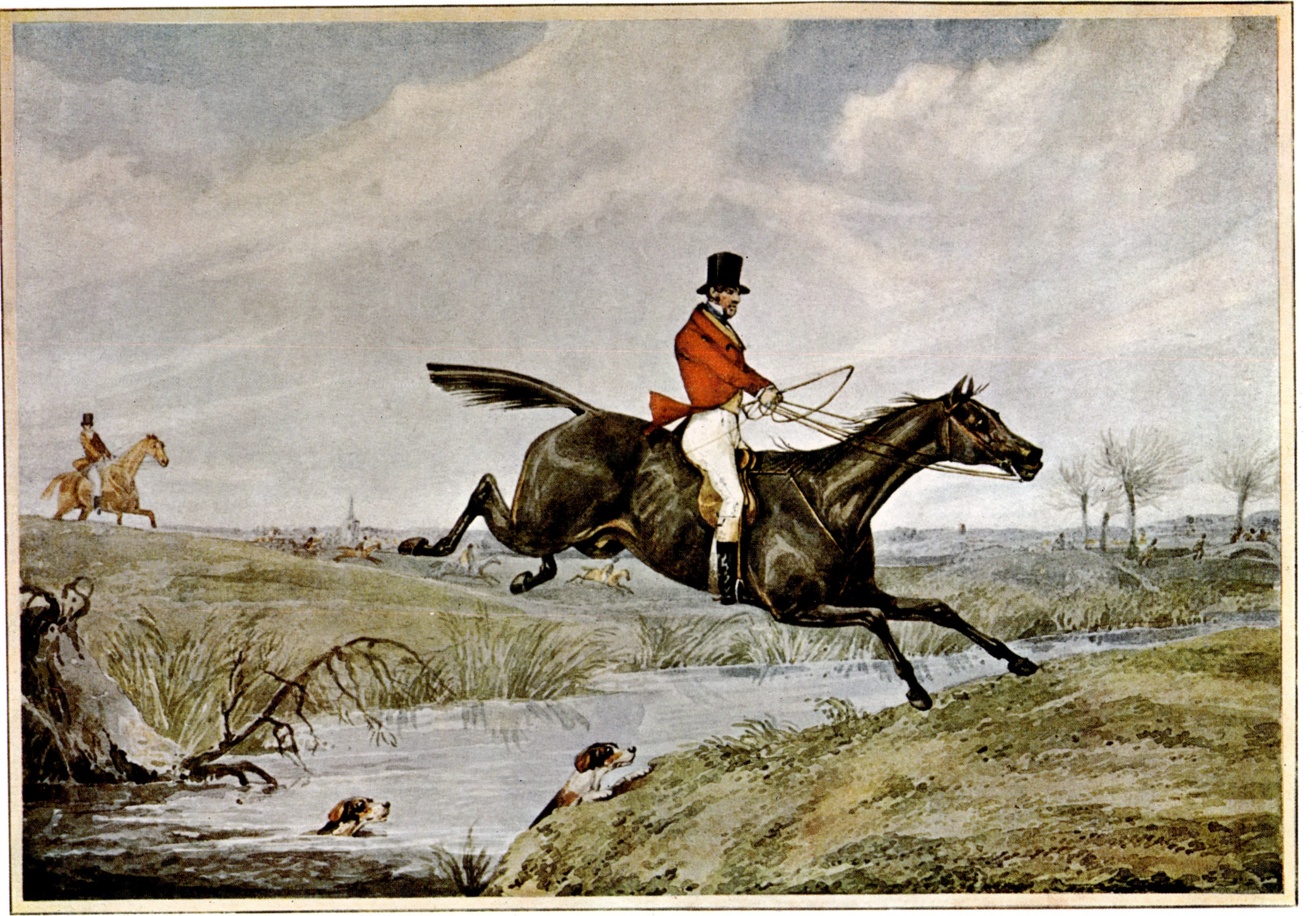

FOX HUNTING: "LEAPING THE BROOK"
From an Original Drawing
By Henry Alken

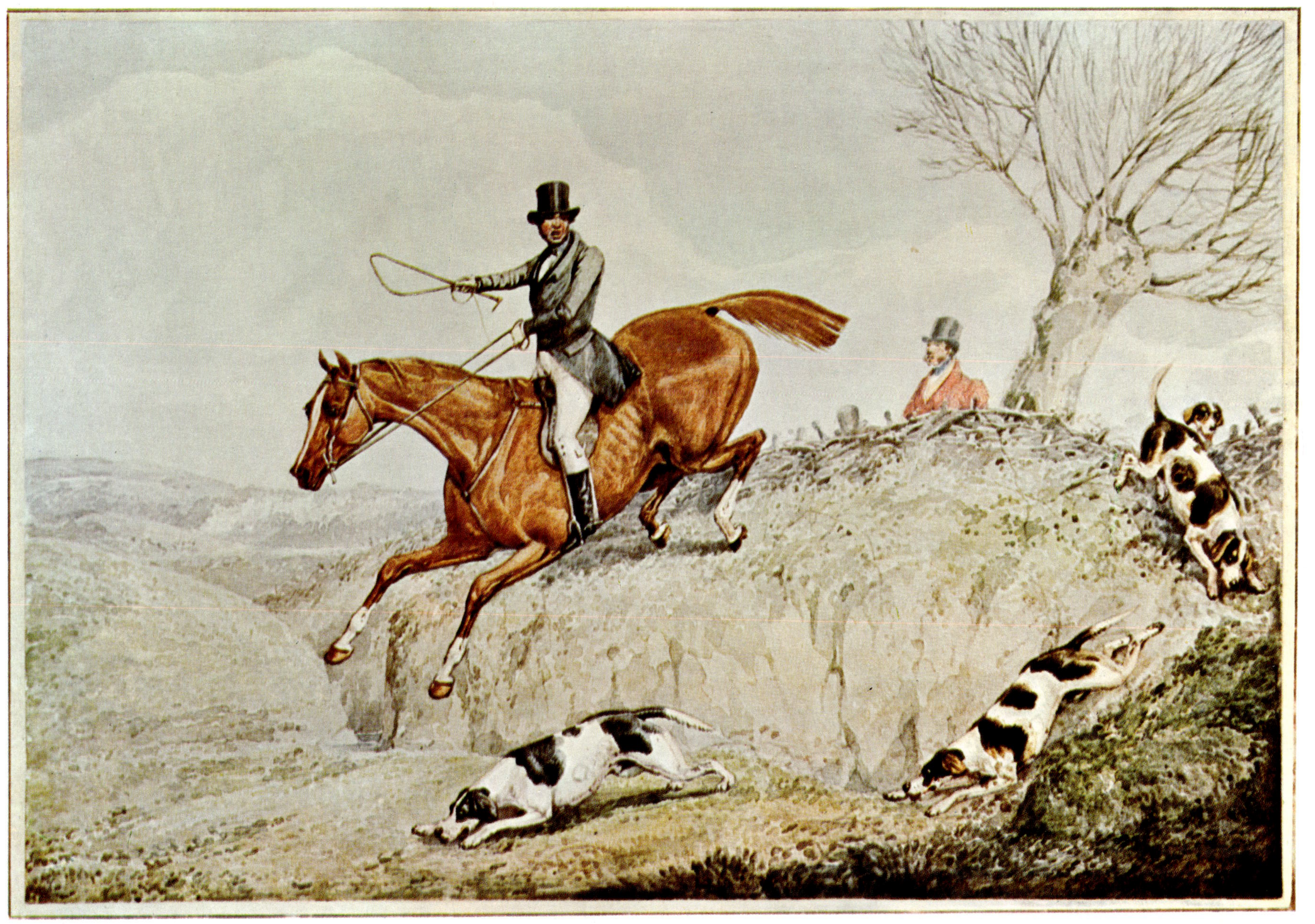

FOX HUNTING: "THE FIRST OVER"
*From an Original Drawing
By Henry Alken*

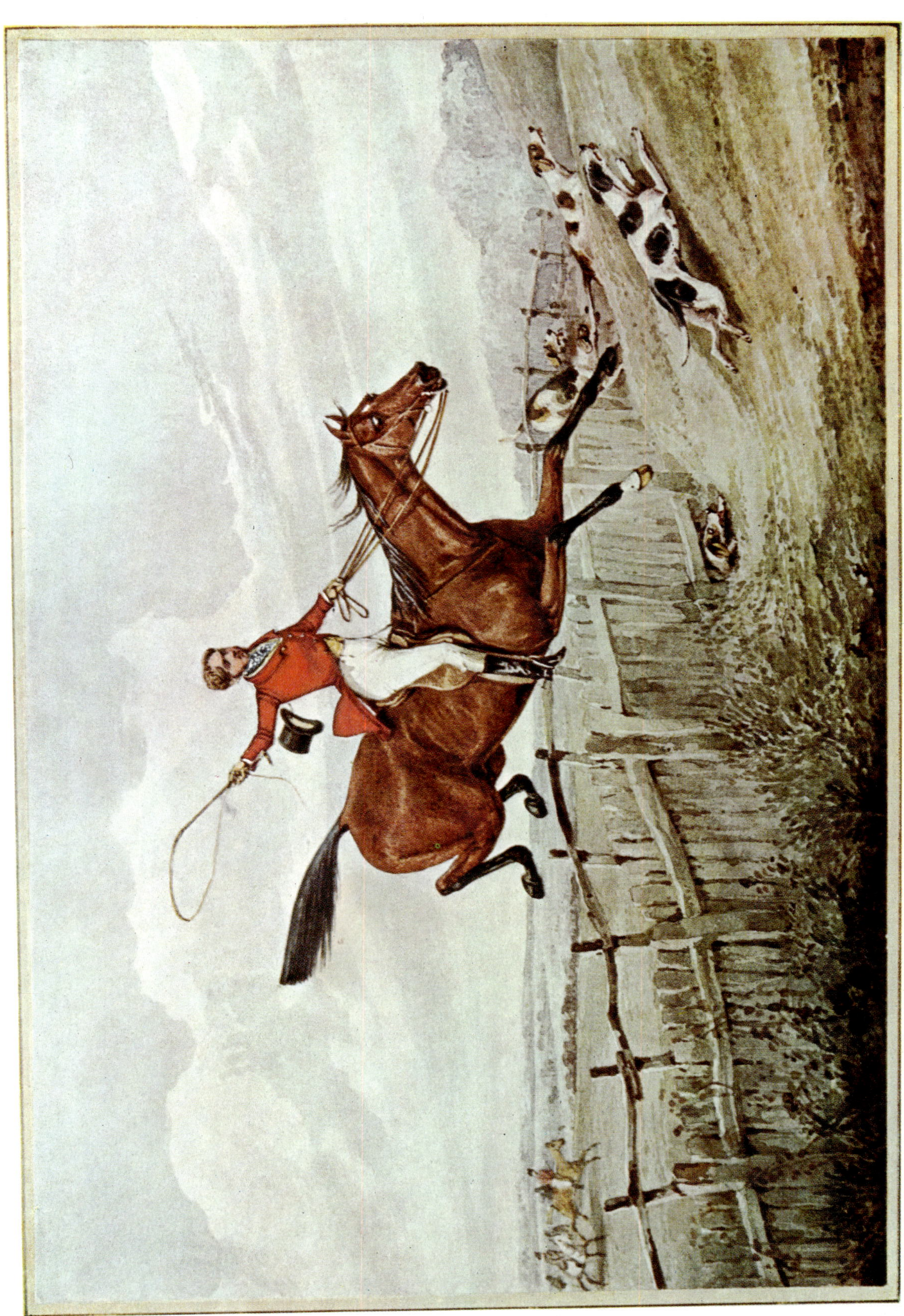

A FIRST RATE WORKMAN OF MELTON
By Henry Alken

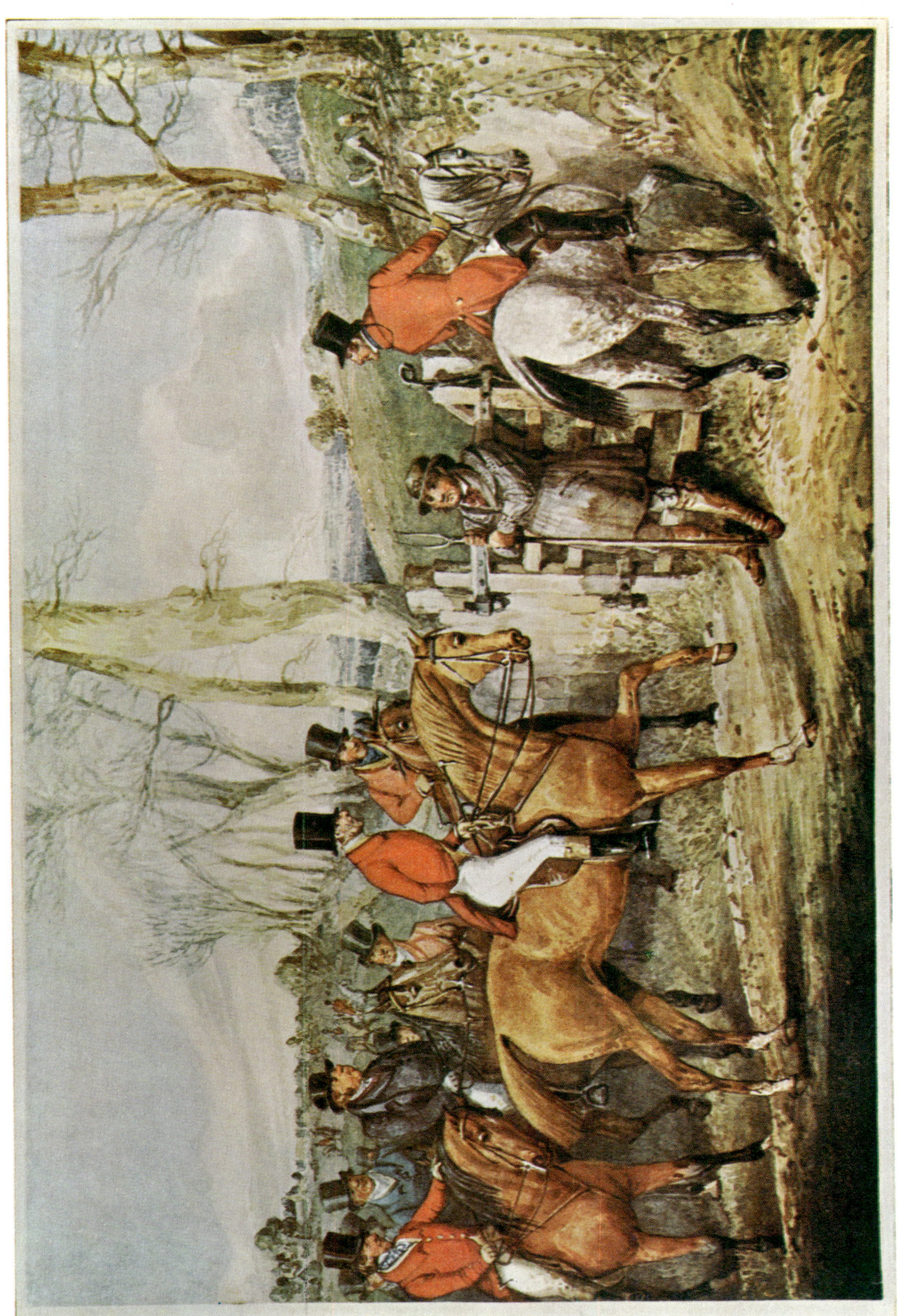

DUKE OF WELLINGTON AND HODGE
By Henry Alken

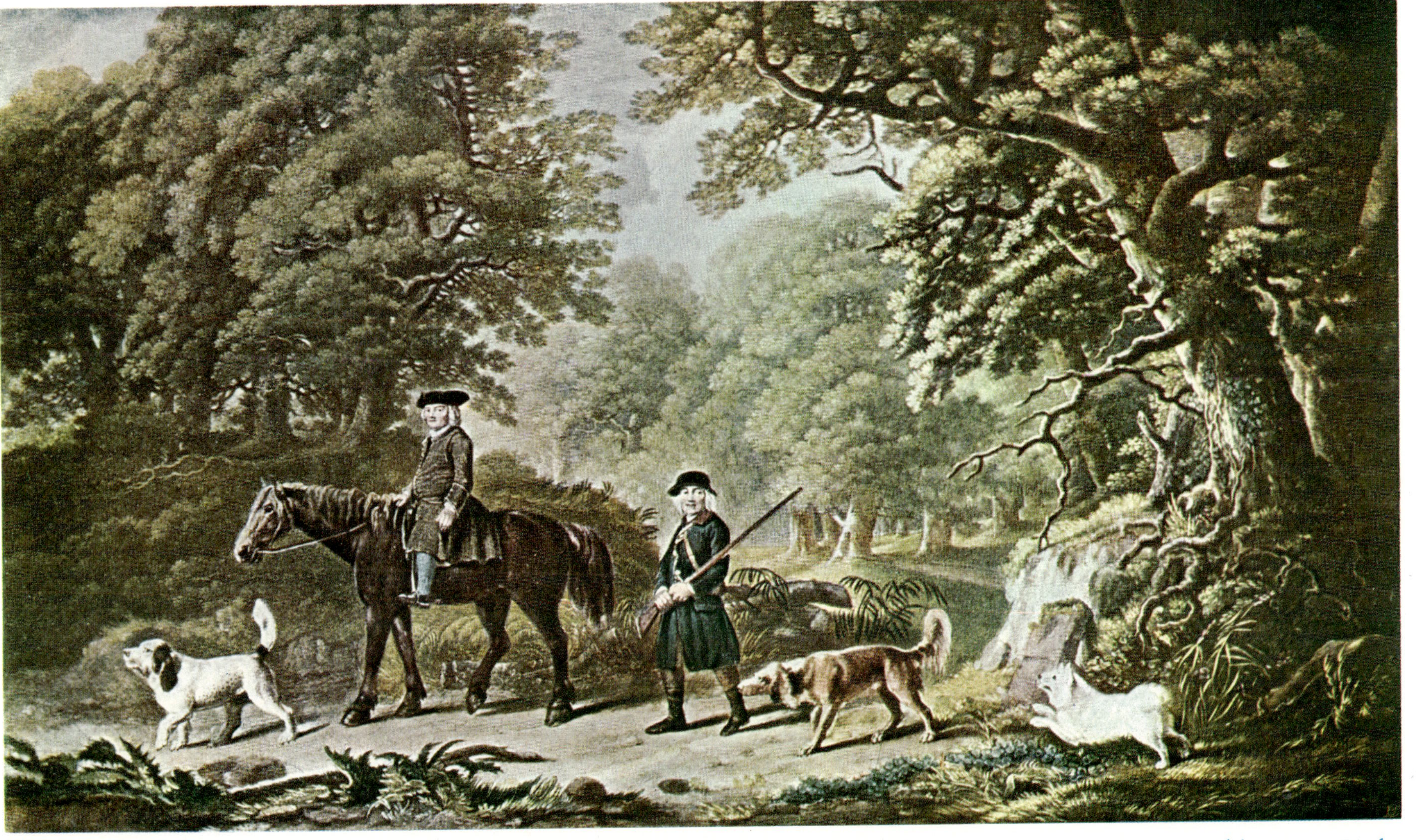

Painted by George Stubbs R A
Landfcape by Amos Greene Efq Bath

Publifhed May 25 1790 by B B Evans Poultry London

Engraved by Henry Birche

GAME KEEPERS
To the Right Honble Lord Viscount Torrington This Plate is respectfully inscribed
By his Lordship's obliged and very obedient servant
Benyn. Beale Evans

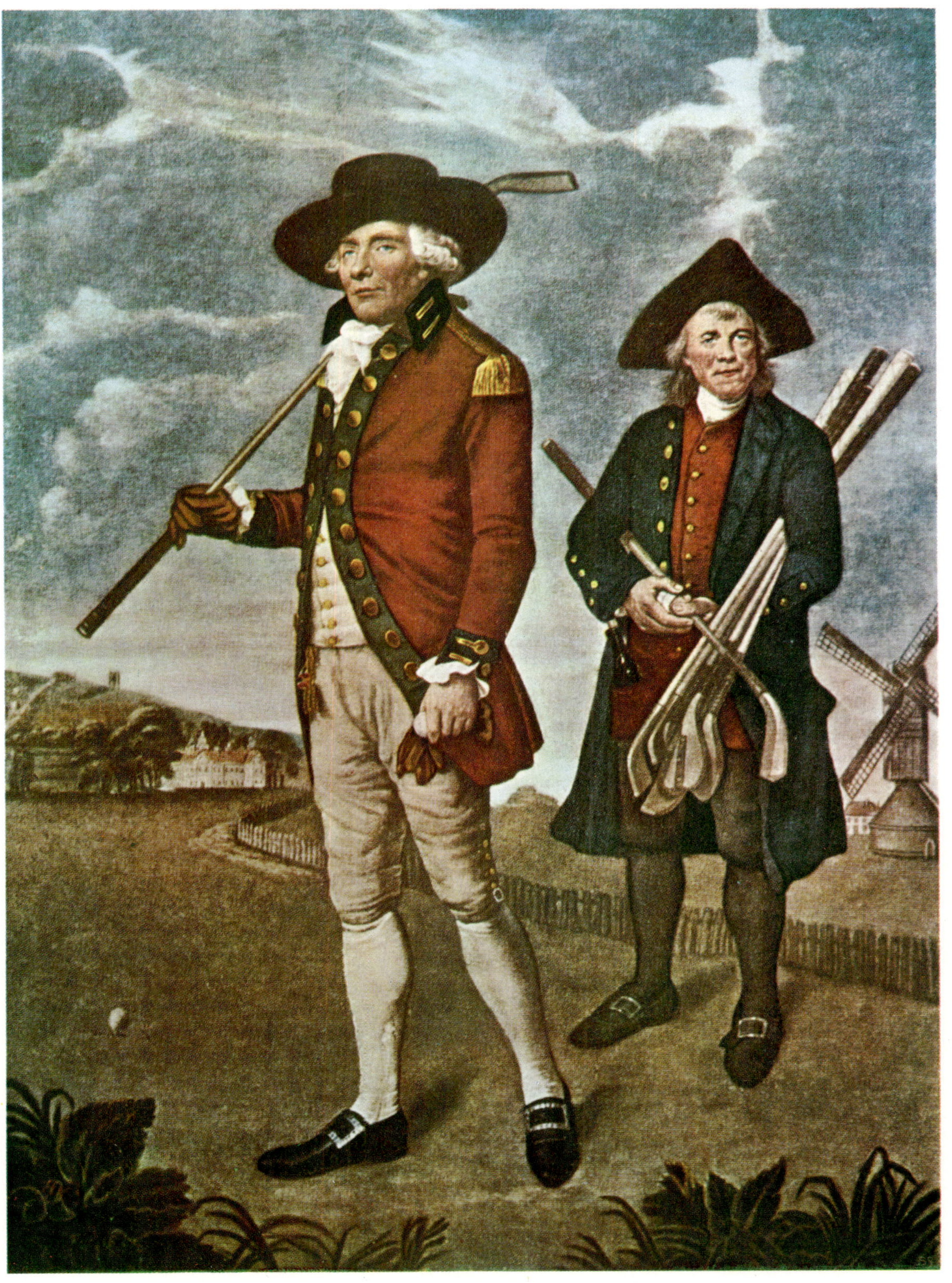

Painted by L. F. Abbott 1790   Engraved by V. Green Mezzatinto Engraver to his
Majesty & the Elector Palatine
TO THE SOCIETY OF COFFERS AT BLACKHEATH
This Plate is with just Respect Dedicated by Their most humble Servant
Lemuel Francis Abbott

List of a few Exceptionally Attractive Prints.

RACING.

Racing.—"The Walk," "Starting," "Weighing and Rubbing Down," and "The Race"	A set of four, by T. Sutherland, after H. Alken; in colours.
A Hurdle Race	Four prints, in colour, by C. Hunt, after H. Alken.
Racing Subjects	Eight plates, each about 18 inches by 12; in colours, by S. Alken. Very rare.
Life and Death of a Racehorse ...	Six plates, in aquatint, by and after Gooch.
The Aylesbury Grand Steeplechase, February, 1866...	By C. Bentley, after Alken; in colours.
Derby Stakes, 1820	After H. Alken.
Racing	By the same.
The Derby of 1820	After Alken; in colours.
Epsom Races	By Sutherland, after Alken; a pair, in colours.
The High-Mettled Racer	By Thomas Sutherland, after Alken; a series of six plates, in colours.
Race and the Road, The	Epsom 1851; a folding coloured print, by Henry Alken; opening to about 8 feet, describing scenes on the road to Epsom and the race for the Derby Stakes; published by Ackermann, n.d.
The First Steeplechase on Record...	A series of four coloured plates, by John Harris, after Henry Alken. This is also known as the Night Riders of Nacton, the jockeys being cavalry officers wearing nightgowns over their regimentals. It was published by Rudolph Ackermann.
Ascot	His Majesty's Gold Plate, after J. Pollard; in colours.
Aylesbury Grand Steeplechase ...	A set of four plates, in colours, by Harris, after Pollard.
The Derby Stakes of 1828 and 1829, and the Ascot Gold Cup, 1829 ...	After J. Pollard. A set of three, in colours.
The Derby of 1839	After Pollard; in colours.
Doncaster Races	By Harris, after Pollard; a series of four plates in colours.
The St. Leger of 1836	After Pollard, by Harris.
Epsom	After J. Pollard, by C. Hunt; a set of six, in colours.
Epsom, Goodwood, and Ascot Races	After Pollard, by Pyall; a set of three, in colours.
Epsom Grand Stand, and Goodwood Grand Stand	After Pollard, by Reeve; both in colours.
Scenes on the Road, or a Trip to Epsom and Back	By John Harris, after James Pollard; a series of four plates in colours.
Match Between Flying Dutchman and Voltigeur for £1,000	Run at York, on May 13th, 1851, by Charles Hunt, after Harry Hall; in colours.

HUNTING.

The Lucky Sportsman	A very valuable print in colours, executed by F. D. Soiron, after Morland.
Fox Hunting	Four rare coloured prints, by E. Bell, after Morland.
Going to Cover, The Chase, At Fault, The Death	By T. Burford, after J. Seymour ; in colours.
Fox Hunting	Four fine aquatints, after Rowlandson.
George III. returning from Hunting. A Royal Hunt in Windsor Park ...	By L. F. Dubourg, after Pollard ; in colours.
The Quorn Hunt...	A fine and valuable set of eight coloured plates, by Lewis, after Henry Alken.
The Meet, Breaking Cover, Full Cry, The Death	Four oblong prints, by Sutherland, after Henry Alken.
Hunting Subjects	A set of four, by J. Gleadah, after Henry Alken.
Fox Hunting	Four prints, by Harris, after Henry Alken, published by Ackermann in 1844.
Sporting Anecdotes	A series of some fourteen prints, after Alken, the best known of which is perhaps the Hunting Sweep (No. 14). This was engraved by the artist himself and published by Ackermann in 1837.
Hunting Notions...	Six coloured plates, by Henry Alken. A reprint of slight value exists.
Hunters at Grass...	By W. Ward, after B. Marshall. A fine print.
Sir M. M. Sykes' Hounds Breaking Cover	By Wolstenholme, after H. B. Chalon, the master is in the background mounted upon a white horse ; the huntsman, William Carter, being the central figure.
Leicestershire	Four fine coloured plates, representing hunting scenes, by J. Dean Paul.
Hunting Scenes	Four prints, by T. Reeve, after Wolstenholme.
Fox Hunters Meeting, Breaking Cover, Fox Chase, The Death ...	A set of four, by C. Hunt, after Pollard.
The Essex Hunt...	Four plates, by and after Dean Wolstenholme, junior, the men, horses and hounds represented being portraits.
Fox Hunting	By J. Havell, after Pollard. A set of four.
Fox Hunting	Four fine coloured prints, after Herring.
The Burial of Tom Moody. The Shade of Tom Moody	By and after Wolstenholme.

COACHING.

An Airing in Hyde Park, this shows the "Ring" in 1793	By Gaugain after Dayes. A valuable print especially in the proof state.
Hyde Park Corner	By Rosenberg after Pollard. A fine coloured print.
The General Post Office with mails departing	By Reeves after Pollard in colours. This and other views of the same building are valuable.

COACHING—continued.

North Country Mails	By Sutherland } after Pollard
West Country Mails	By Rosenberg } after Pollard
	Very fine prints.
Stage Coach Arriving, Changing Horses and Setting Off	A valuable set by Havell after Pollard.
Stage Coaches, with News of Peace and News of Reform	A very fine pair by Havell after Pollard.
Stage Coach Travelling, Opposition Coaches at Speed	After Pollard.
Mail Coach in a Flood, In a Drift of Snow, and In a Thunderstorm ...	Three good prints after Pollard, the finest of which is the first (see reproduction).
Lioness attacking the Exeter Coach...	The incident illustrated by Pollard is described in the text.
Mails changing Horses and preparing to start	A fine pair after Pollard.
Highgate Tunnel and View on the Highgate Road	By Hunt after Pollard.
The " Cambridge Telegraph " starting from Fetter Lane	By Hunt after Pollard.
West Country Mail-Coach at the Gloucestershire Coffee House, Piccadilly	By Rosenberg after Pollard.
The London Fire Engines, the noble Protectors of Life and Property ...	After Pollard.
Coaching Incidents	Three valuable prints after Cooper Henderson.
The Taglioni Coach and the Original Bath Mail	After Henderson.

The Reading Telegraph	
The Windsor Coach	
The Southampton Coach	
The Brighton Age	
The Edinburgh Express	
The Red Rover...	Fine and valuable coloured plates of coaches.
The London and Birmingham Tally-Ho	
The Paris and Dover Coach ...	
The Eagle	
The Blenheim Coach	

Royal Mail Coach	By and after Pollard. A valuable coloured print.
Two of His Majesty's State Horses	
The Earl of Chesterfield's State Carriage	By W. Ward after H. B. Chalon.

SHOOTING.

The First of September.—Morning and Evening	By William Ward after Morland. Coloured impressions are of considerable value.
Hare Shooting, Pheasant Shooting...	A pair of coloured prints by J. Ward after Morland.
Morning, Partridge Shooting, Pheasant Shooting, Snipe Shooting, Duck Shooting, Evening	Six valuable large oblong prints in aquatint by S. Alken after Morland. The majority of these were etched by Rowlandson.

79

SHOOTING—continued.

Duck Shooting, Partridge Shooting, Snipe Shooting	In colours, by Charles Catton after Morland.
The Sportsman's Return	By William Ward after Morland. A fine coloured print.
Pheasant and Woodcock Shooting ...	By Thomas Sutherland after Wolstenholme. Four plates.
Coursing Scenes	A set of four by Reeve after Wolstenholme.
Shooting, Coursing	By Robert Pollard.
Cover Shooting	A pair of coloured prints by Thomas Reeve after Wolstenholme.
The Spanish Pointer	By W. Woollett after G. Stubbs. A fine and valuable print.
Dash	A good coloured print of a Pointer in the possession of Colonel Thornton by Robert Pollard.
Setters	By R. Laurie after F. Sartorius.
Wasp, Child and Billy	Three famous Bulldogs belonging to Mr. Henry Baynton By W. Ward after H. B. Chalon.

BOXING.

The Fight between J. Broughton and G. Stevenson in 1742	By John Young, after Mortimer ; a very rare print.
The Fight between Humphreys and Daniel Mendoza	By Joseph Grozer, after S. Einsle.
The Fight between Humphreys and Daniel Mendoza	Three engravings, published by Fores, one with letter-press description underneath. This great battle took place at Odiham, on January 9, 1788.
The Fights between Mendoza and Ward ; between Randall and Martin ; and between Dutch Sam and Medley	Three prints.
The Fight between Spring and Langan	By Clements and Pitman, in colours.
The Fight between Ward and Cannon	With descriptive letterpress.
The Fives Court	After Collins.
Going to the Fight. The Return ...	Two long strips about 4 feet long by 2 inches wide. Coloured. Very rare.
The Interior of The Fives Court ...	Randall and Turner are Sparring. After Blake, by C. Turner. The first state, in colours, is the most desirable.
The Fight between Broome and Hannan	After Heath, in colours, with key.
The Fight between Crib and Molineux	After Rowlandson, coloured.
The Fight between Pearce and Gully	By Woolnoth and Lopez.
The Fight between Sayers and Heenan, 1860	In colours, after Walton, with key.

BOXING—continued.

The Fight between Sayers and Heenan	By Jem Ward, coloured.
Thomas Belcher...	The Prizefighter, after D. Guest, C. Turner.
Thomas Belcher...	By Charles Turner, after B. Marshall, mezzotint.
James Belcher	The Prizefighter of Bristol, after Allingham, by E. Clint, printed in colours.
John Broughton	A Prizefighter. Mezzotint, published by W. Richardson. A lithograph of the same, full length, after Hogarth, also exists.
Buckhorse	A Prizefighter, mezzotint.
John Gully	By Lopez.
Daniel Mendoza...	In Fighting attitude, by H. Kingsbury, after T. Robineau, very rare.
Daniel Mendoza...	A Prizefighter, by Gillray.
Dutch Sam	A Prizefighter, by and after P. Roberts, in colours.
Tom Sayers. Heenan	Both in colours.
Johnny Walker	The Prizefighter, after A. S. Henning, by G. Hunt, printed in colours.
James Ward	The Prizefighter, after Finnie, by T. Woolnoth.
Deaf Burke	After Meyer, by C. Hunt ; and Young Dutch Sam, after East ; two Portraits of Prizefighters.
Thomas Cribb	The Prizefighter, after D. Guest, by J. Young.
Molineux	A Prizefighter, by J. Young, after D. Guest.
Molineux	A Prizefighter, by Dighton.
John Gully	The Prizefighter, full length in private dress, a mezzotint.
John Gully	The Prizefighter, full length, a mezzotint.

A Record of the Principal Sporting Prints Sold by Auction, 1901—1908. By W. G. Menzies.

ANGLING.

Title.	Artist.	Engraver.	Method.	Remarks	Year of Sale.	Price. £ s. d.
Anglers' Repast and Party Angling	Morland, G.	Ward, W., and Keating	c.p.	pair	1903	215 5 0
,, ,, ,,	,,	,,	,,	,,	1903	183 15 0
,, ,, ,,	,,	,,	,,	,,	1902	173 15 0
,, ,, ,,	,,	,,	,,	,,	1901	149 0 0
,, ,, ,,	,,	,,	,,	,,	1901	126 0 0
,, ,, ,,	,,	,,	,,	,,	1906	105 0 0
,, ,, ,,	,,	,,	,,	,,	1904	99 15 0
,, ,, ,,	,,	,,	,,	,,	1907	81 18 0
,, ,, ,,	,,	,,	,,	,,	1901	63 0 0
,, ,, ,,	,,	,,	,,	,,	1903	42 0 0
Anglers, The	Westall, R.	Knight, C.	c.p.	—	1906	13 13 0
Anglers' Repast	Morland, G.	Ward, W.	c.p.	—	1905	14 14 0
,,	,,	,,	c.p.	—	1907	7 7 0
Bottom Fishing and Anglers Packing up	Pollard, J.	Hunt	c.p.	pair	1908	14 15 0
Bottom Fishing and Fly Fishing	,,	,,	c.p.	—	1908	10 10 0
Bottom Fishing; Trolling for Pike; and Anglers Packing up	Pollard, J.	Hunt	c.p.	mounted on canvas	1908	19 0 0
Fisherman's Departure and Fisherman's Return	Corbould	Ward, W.	c.p.	pair	1902	16 16 0
Humorous Fishing Scenes	—	Turner, C.	c.p.	series of four	1908	8 15 0
Party Angling	Morland, G.	Keating, G.	m.	o.l.p.	1902	55 13 0
,,	,,	,,	m.	—	1907	31 10 0
,,	,,	,,	m.	—	1906	24 13 0
,,	,,	,,	m.	—	1902	12 1 6
Trolling for Pike and Fly Fishing	Pollard J,	Hunt	c.p.	—	1908	6 6 0
Young Waltonians	Constable, J.	Lucas, D.	m.	1st state	1903	50 8 0
,,	,,	,,	m.	p.b.l.	1906	35 0 0
,,	,,	,,	m.	—	1906	2 2 0

COACHING, DRIVING, AND RIDING.

Title.	Artist.	Engraver.	Method.	Remarks	Year of Sale.	Price. £ s. d.
Airing in Hyde Park, and Promenade in St. James' Park	Dayes	Gaugain and Soiron, F. D.	c.p.	pair	1903	346 0 0
,, ,,	,,	,, ,,	,,	,,	1903	280 0 0
,, ,,	,,	,, ,,	s.	,,	1908	50 8 0
,, ,,	,,	,, ,,	s.	,,	1902	44 2 0
,, ,,	,,	,, ,,	c.p.	second in brown	1908	42 0 0
,, ,,	,,	,, ,,	s.	in bistre, pair	1905	33 5 0
Airing in Hyde Park	Dayes	Gaugain	c.p.	—	1905	131 15 0
,, ,,	,,	,,	c.p.	—	1902	92 8 0
,, ,,	,,	,,	s.	—	1906	12 10 0
,, ,,	,,	,,	s.	—	1907	3 10 0
Approach to Christmas; Mail in Deep Snow	Pollard, J.	Hunt, G.	c.p.	pair	1908	14 10 0
Arrival of the Stage Coach; Royal Mail Coach	,,	Havell, R.	c.a.	pair	1908	20 0 0
Bedford Times Mail Coach	—	Rudge, B.	—	lithograph	1908	3 0 0
Birmingham Tally-Ho Coach passing the "Crown" at Holloway	Pollard	—	c.p.	—	1904	12 12 0
Brighton Coach at the "Bull and Mouth," Regent Circus	Lambert	Hunt, G. and C.	c.p.	—	1902	17 6 6
Carlton House Gardens	Bunbury	Dickinson	s.	p.b.l.	1906	42 0 0
,, ,,	,,	,,	s.	in brown o.l.p.	1907	30 0 0
,, ,,	,,	,,	s.	in bistre p.b.l.	1904	26 5 0
,, ,,	,,	,,	s.	in brown	1903	24 0 0
,, ,,	,,	,,	s.	o.l.p.	1906	14 3 6

Title.	Artist.	Engraver.	Method.	Remarks.	Year of Sale.	£	s.	d.
Changing Horses	Henderson	Hullmandel	c.p.	—	1908	2	10	0
Coaching Scenes	Pollard, J.	—	c.a.	set of six	1908	22	1	0
Car Travelling in the South of Ireland in the year 1836 — Bianconi's Establishment	Hayes, M. A.	Harris, J.	c.p.	set of four	1908	12	0	0
Coaching Accidents	Newhouse, C. B.	—	c.p.	set of four	1908	2	15	0
Coaching Incidents	Alken, H.	—	c.p.	set of four	1904	15	15	0
Coach Horses and Chaise Horses	Garrard, G.	Young, J.	m.	pair	1907	24	0	0
Driving Tandem	Pollard, J.	—	c.p.	—	1908	9	0	0
Driving a pair	Alken, H.	—	c.p.	—	1908	5	10	0
"Eagle" — Paris and Dover Coach	Tregear, C.	Alken	c.a.	—	1906	17	0	0
Edinburgh and London Mail Coach, passing a Tollgate at night	Pollard, J.	Hunt, G.	c.p.	—	1908	5	10	0
Elephant and Castle on the Brighton Road	„	Fielding, T.	c.p.	—	1902	37	16	0
„ „ „	„	„	a.	—	1908	15	15	0
Elephant and Castle	Jones, S. E.	Hunt	c.p.	—	1902	18	18	0
Elephant and Castle with Mail Coach preparing to start	Pollard, J.	Fielding, T.	a.	—	1908	13	5	0
Excursion to Brighthelmstone, 1789	Wigstead and Rowlandson	Tinted by Alken	c.a.	eight plates	1908	9	15	0
English Travelling, or the First Stage from Dover; French Travelling, or the First Stage from Calais	Rowlandson	Jukes, F.	c.p.	pair	1908	5	10	0
Four in-hand	Pollard, J.	Gleadah	c.p.	—	1908	8	15	0
George III., His Majesty in his Chariot returning to Town from Windsor	Davis, R. B.	Turner, C.	—	—	1907	8	10	0
Hyde Park Corner	Pollard, J.	Rosenberg	c.p.	—	1908	31	10	0
London Fire Engines	„	Reeve	c.p.	—	1902	17	17	0
London Fire Engines	„	Reeves	c.p.	—	1908	5	0	0
Mail at Temple Bar	Newhouse, C. B.	Baily, J.	a.	—	1906	7	0	0
Mail Coach by Moonlight	Pollard, J.	Hunt, G.	c.a.	—	1906	17	0	0
Mail Coach-Guard dropping a bag at Post-office	—	„	c.p.	—	1908	10	10	0
Mail Coach in a Flood	Pollard, J.	Rosenberg	c.p.	—	1908	9	0	0
Mail Coach in a Storm	Morland, G.	Reynolds, S. W.	c.p.	—	1904	14	10	0
Mail Coach in a Thunderstorm on Newmarket Heath	Pollard, J.	Reeves, G.	c.p.	—	1908	6	6	0
Mail Coach with the Horses bolting from the changing place	—	—	c.p.	in the manner of J. Pollard	1908	7	0	0
Manchester Coach	Pollard, J.	—	c.a.	—	1905	7	15	0
Mail Coach—In a Flood / „ In a Thunderstorm / „ In a Drift of Snow / „ In a Snow Storm	Pollard, J.	Reeves	c.p.	set of four	1904	28	7	0
Mail Coach	„	Reeves & Rosenberg	c.a.	set of four	1907	6	15	0
Mail Coach behind Time; and Stage Waggon	Walter, H.	Pyall, H.	c.a.	pair	1907	9	10	0
Mail Coach by Moonlight; and Mail Coach in a Fog	Pollard, J.	Hunt, G.	c.a.	pair	1907	9	5	0
Mail Coach in a Flood, and Mail Coach in a Thunderstorm, on Newmarket Heath	„	Rosenberg and Reeves	c.a.	pair	1907	8	5	0
North Country Mails at the "Peacock," Islington; and "Elephant and Castle," on the Brighton Road	Pollard	Fielding, T.	c.p.	pair	1907	11	0	0
North Country Mails at the "Peacock" Islington	Pollard, J.	Sutherland, J.	c.p.	—	1907	26	5	0
„ „	„	„	a.	—	1908	16	16	0
„ „	„	„	c.p.	—	1907	4	15	0
No time to spare for Refreshment	Newhouse, C. B.	Harris, J.	c.p.	—	1907	5	10	0
Ports taken August 12th 1813 — a gentleman driving Tandem in a curious Sporting Cart	Clarke, R.	Cooke, H. R.	—	—	1908	6	5	0
Post Boys watering their Horses; and Hunters on their way to the Hunting Stables	Pollard	Pyall, H.	c.a.	pair	1907	13	5	0

Title.	Artist.	Engraver.	Method.	Remarks.	Year of Sale.	Price. £ s. d.
Promenade at Carlisle House	Smith, J. R.	Smith, J. R.	m.	—	1905	75 12 0
" "	"	"	m.	—	1903	29 8 0
Promenade at St. James's Park	Dayes, E.	Soiron, F. D.	c.p.	—	1908	198 0 0
" "	"	"	c.p.	—	1906	54 12 0
" "	"	"	s.	p.b.l.	1907	20 0 0
Quicksilver—Royal Mail	Pollard, J.	Hunt, C.	c.a.	—	1908	4 10 0
Rather Varment	Alken, H.	"	c.p.	—	1908	10 0 0
Royal Mail Coach descending a Hill	Pollard, J	Pollard, J.	c.p.	—	1908	24 0 0
Royal Mail Coach	"	Havell, R.	c.p.	—	1908	8 10 0
Rubbing down the Post Horses; and Watering the Cart Horses	Morland	Smith, J. R.	c.p.	pair	1908	36 15 0
Royal Mail starting from the General Post Office	Pollard	Reeves, R. G.	c.p.	—	1908	9 15 0
" "	"	"	c.a.	—	1907	5 5 0
" "	"	"	c.p.	—	1908	2 2 0
Royal Mails starting from the Post Office, Lombard Street	Jones, S. J. E.	Hunt, C.	c.a.	—	1907	8 0 0
Rubbing down the Post Horses	Morland.	Smith, J. R.	c.p.	—	1902	10 15 0
Specimens of Horsemanship	Pollard	Dubourg	c.p.	series of 10	1908	14 10 0
" "	"	"	"	"	1907	13 0 0
Stage Coach; London Royal Mail; and a Four in Hand	Pollard, J.	—	c.a.	—	1907	5 15 0
Sporting Anecdotes — The Blind'uns and a Bolter	Alken, H.	—	c.p.	—	1908	2 2 0
Stage Coach, A	Jones, S. J. E.	Hunt, G. E.	c.a.	—	1902	25 10 0
Stage Coach Anecdotes — Let'em go, and Take Care of Yourselves	Alken, H.	—	c.p.	—	1908	11 5 0
Stage Coach Ascending a Steep Hill	Pollard, J.	—	c.p.	—	1908	10 0 0
Stage Coach driving through Rural Scenery	Jones, S. J. E.	Hunt, C.	c.p.	—	1908	3 0 0
Stage Coach with opposition Coach in sight	Pollard, J.	Havell, R.	c.p.	—	1907	19 0 0
" "	"	"	"	—	1908	7 0 0
Stage Coach with News of Peace	"	"	c.p.	—	1907	19 10 0
" "	"	"	c.a.	—	1906	14 0 0
Turnpike Gates	Rowlandson and Dagoty	—	c.a.	set of six	1908	23 10 0
Trip to Brighton	Paul, J. Dean	—	c.a.	set of four	1908	16 16 0
Trip to Melton Mowbray	Paul, Jno Dean	—	c.p.	set of 18	1908	31 0 0
Trip to Gretna Green, pursuing Chaise meeting with an Accident	—	—	c.p.	—	1908	7 15 0
Trotting Horse	Alken, H.	—	c.p.	—	1908	6 0 0
Vauxhall	Rowlandson	Pollard, R.	a.	—	1903	27 6 0
"	"	"	c.a.	—	1906	21 0 0
"	"	"	c.a.	—	1908	9 19 6
"Very Spicy"—A gentleman driving a Trotting Horse	Alken, H.	Hunt, C.	c.p.	—	1908	13 5 0
View on the Highgate Road	Pollard, J.	"	c.a.	—	1908	19 8 6
West Country Mails at the Gloster Coffee House, Piccadilly	"	Rosenberg	c.p.	—	1908	2 18 0

COURSING.

Title.	Artist.	Engraver.	Method.	Remarks.	Year of Sale.	Price. £ s. d.
Coursing	Wolstenholme	Reeve	c.a.	set of four	1908	26 10 0
Coursing and Duck Shooting	Morland, G.	Thompson, J.	m.	—	1907	8 8 0
Going Out	Wolstenholme	Sutherland	c.p.	—	1908	3 5 0
Hounds Finding and The Chase	Alken, H.	—	c.p.	pair	1908	5 15 0
Return from Coursing, with companion	Wheatley and Hamilton	Bartolozzi and Cardon	c.p.	pair	1907	84 0 0
" "	" "	" "	"	"	1902	50 0 0
Return from Coursing	Hamilton	Cardon, A.	c.p.	—	1905	23 2 0

DOGS.

Title.	Artist.	Engraver.	Method.	Remarks.	Year of Sale.	Price. £ s. d.
Bulldogs—" Wasp," " Child," and " Billy "	Chalon, H. B. ...	Ward, W. ...	m.	—	1908	6 5 0
Famous Setter	Chalon, H. B. ...	,, ...	c.p.	—	1906	1 1 0
Fisherman's Dog ... ... Sportsman's Dog	Morland, and Northcote, J. ...	Reynolds, S. W..	c.p.	pair	1902	14 10 0
,, ...	,, ...	,, ...	m.	pair	1907	8 0 0
Fox Hounds, Stag Hounds, Harriers, and Beagles ...	Wolstenholme ...	Reeve	c.p.	set of four	1908	19 10 0
Hounds of the Berkeley Hunt	Turner, F. ...	Dunkarton, W....	m.	o.l.p.	1904	13 15 0
Kennel, The, and Bear Hunt..	Morland ...	Reynolds, S. W..	c.p.	—	1907	3 3 0
Last Litter ; and Hard Bargain	Morland ...	Ward, W. ...	m.	pair p.b.l.	1906	162 15 0
Last Litter	Morland, G. ...	,, ...	c.p.	—	1902	10 10 0
Modish—A Foxhound ; and Dash—A Pointer	Gilpin, S. ...	Pollard, R. ...	a.	pair	1907	5 0 6
Pointers and Setters	Morland ...	Ward, W. ...	m.	pair p.b.l.	1906	38 17 0
,, ,, ...	,, ...	,, ...	c.m.	pair o.l.p.	1906	31 10 0
Pointers	Sartorius					
Setters	Morland, G. ...	,, ...	m.	pair o.l.p.	1908	23 10 0
Raby Pack	Chalon, H. B. ...	,, ...	c.m.	—	1902	40 0 0
,, ...	,, ...	,, ...	m.	p.b.l.	1903	31 10 0
,, ...	,, ...	,, ...	c.	—	1903	21 0 0
Setters	Morland ...	,, ...	m.			
Setters	,, ...	Reynolds, S. W.	m.	two	1907	6 6 0
Setters ... ... Pointer Bitch	Morland ... Ward	Reynolds, S. W..	c.p.	two	1902	6 16 6
Setters	Sartorius, F. ...	Laurie, R. ...	c.p.	o.l.p.	1906	5 10 0
Setters	Turner, C. ...	Syer, R. ...	c.p.	—	1906	4 12 0
Spanish Pointer... ...	Stubbs, G. ...	Woollett, W. ...	m.	early finish proof—set of four	1902	10 10 0
Spanish Pointer...	Stubbs, G. ...	Woollett ...	m.	—	1907	5 0 0
Thunder—An old English Setter	Chalon, H. B. ...	Ward, W. ...	c.p.	—	1907	13 10 0

HUNTING.

Title.	Artist.	Engraver.	Method.	Remarks.	Year of Sale.	Price. £ s. d.
Ad Montem, The	Pollard	Pollard	c.p.	—	1902	31 0 0
,, ,, ...	,, ...	,, ...	c.p.	—	1903	21 0 0
,, ,, ...	Campion, G. B.	Hunt, C... ...	c.a.	—	1906	14 0 0
Bear Hunt, and The Kennels	Morland. ...	Reynolds, S. W.	c.p.	two	1907	3 3 0
Best Run of the Season ...	Landseer, Sir E.	Landseer, T. ...	m.	artist's proof	1907	2 2 0
,, ,, ...	,, ,, ...	,, ...	m.	,, ...	1907	1 1 0
Bilsden Coplow Day	Loraine Smith, C.	Jukes	c.a.	—	1906	28 10 0
Challenge, The	Landseer, Sir E.	Walker, H. ...	m.	1st published state ...	1906	1 1 0
Challenge, The ... ... Sanctuary, The	Landseer, Sir E.	Lewis, C. G. ... Burnet, J. ...	m.	pair, first state ...	1901	37 10 0
,, ...	,, ...	,, ...	m.	,, artist's proof ...	1903	30 0 0
,, ...	,, ,, ...	,, ...	m.	,, signed	1904	25 10 0
Chevy	Landseer, Sir E.	Landseer, T. ...	m.	artist's proof	1908	5 5 0
Death of Tom Moody... ...	Wolstenholme, D.	Wolstenholme ...	c.a.	o.l.p.	1906	8 5 0
Death of Tom Moody ... Burial of Tom Moody ...	Pollard Pollard	Duncan Rosenberg ...	c.p.	pair	1908	17 10 0
Death of Tom Moody ... Shade of Tom Moody ...	Pollard	Wolstenholme, D.	—	pair	1908	6 10 0
Deer Family	Landseer, Sir E.	Landseer, T. ...	m.	artist's proof, signed	1907	5 15 6
Deer Pass	Landseer, Sir E.	,, ...	m.	,, —	1908	14 3 6
Drawing a Cover, and Gone away	Alken, H. ...	Sutherland Landseer, T.	c.a.	pair	1907	7 5 0
Drive of Deer, and Hunters at Grass	Landseer, Sir E.	Lewis, C. G. ...		artist's proofs ...	1907	4 4 0
Drive of Deer	Landseer, Sir E.	Landseer, T. ...	m.	,, —	1901	4 4 0
,, ...	,, ,,	,, ...	m.	,, —	1906	3 13 6
Earl of Derby's Stag Hounds	Barenger ,, ...	Woodman ...	c.p.	,, —	1908	9 19 6
Easter Monday at Windsor, and Easter Monday at Epping	Pollard	Pollard	c.a.	pair (a pair uncoloured realised £3 15 0 at this sale)	1902	20 0 0
Fox Breaking Cover	Reinagle ...	Meadows & Lewis	c.p.	—	1908	5 15 0
Fox chase, Dogs having lost the right scent	Vernet, C. ...	Debucourt ...	—	pair	1907	9 0 0
Fox Chase—with verses of song underneath	Wolstenholme ...	Reeve, R. ...	c.p.	Plates one, three, and four	1908	13 15 0
Fox Hunting	Pollard	Sutherland ...	c.a.	1824, set of four, long	1902	65 0 0

Title.	Artist.	Engraver.	Method.	Remarks.	Year of Sale.	£	s.	d.
Fox Hunting	Morland, G.	Bell, E.	c.p.	set of four	1902	39	8	0
,,	,,	,,	c.p.	,,	1905	35	14	0
,,	,,	,,	c.p.	,,	1902	23	2	0
Fox Hunting	Wolstenholme,	Sutherland	c.p.	set of four	1903	37	16	0
Fox Hunting, and Hawking	Gilpin	Scott		pair	1907	9	10	0
Fox Hunting—Going Out	Morland	Bell, E.	c.p.	—	1902	19	15	0
Fox Hunting	Leech, Jno.	—	c.p.	—	1907	8	8	0
,,	Wolstenholme	Sutherland	c.p.	—	1908	5	10	0
,,	Reinagle, P.	Barney	m.	—	1907	4	0	0
,,	Smith, Loraine	—	c.p.	—	1908	3	0	0
Fox Hunting— Meeting at Cover Breaking Cover Full Cry The Death	Alken	Sutherland	c.a.	set of four	1908	56	0	0
,, ,,	,,	,,	c.a.	,,	1902	53	0	0
,, ,,	,,	,,	c.a.	,,	1903	44	0	0
,, ,,	,,	,,	c.a.	,,	1902	39	0	0
Drawing Cover Getting Away Full On The Death	Alken	Reeve	c.a.	four	1904	20	0	0
Fox Hunting	Wolstenholme	Wolstenholme	c.p.	,,	1908	2	10	0
Fox Hunters Regaling—" The Toast "	Alken, H.	Hunt, G.	c.p.	—	1908	2	2	0
Fox Hunt	Pollard	Pollard	c.p.	set of four, long	1902	38	0	0
,,	,,	Howell	c.a.	set of four	1906	33	12	0
George III., His Majesty returning from Hunting	Pollard, J.	Dubourg, M.	c.p.	—	1907	15	5	0
Going to Cover	Alken, R.	Sutherland	c.p.	—	1908	9	15	0
Going to Cover, and The Death	Alken, H.	Bentley	c.a.	pair	1907	8	0	0
Going to Cover, The Leap, Full Cry, and The Death	Alken, H.	Bentley, C.	c.p.	set of four	1908	29	0	0
,, ,,	,,	,,	,,	,,	1908	7	0	0
Going out in the Morning, The Chase, The Death of the Fox, and The Dinner	Rowlandson	—	c.a.	set of four	1908	12	1	6
Going out in the morning, The Chase, The Death of The Fox	Rowlandson	—	c.a.	three	1908	27	10	0
,, ,,	Rowlandson	Reeve, R.	c.a.	set of three	1908	16	15	0
Going Out, The Chase, Drawing Covert, and The Death	Hassell	—	c.a.	set of four	1908	4	10	0
Hare Hunting	Hodges	Reeves	c.a.	pair	1907	5	12	6
His Majesty's Harriers	Davies, R. B.	Woodman, R.	m.	o.l.p.	1904	11	0	0
,, ,,	,,	,,	m.	proof	1906	3	10	0
Hunters at Cover Side	Alken, S.	Pollard, J.	a.	—	1908	8	0	0
Hunters at Grass	Landseer, Sir E.	Lewis, C. G.	m.	artist's proof, signed by the artist	1902	127	0	0
,, ,,	,,	,,	m.	signed by the painter	1901	97	13	0
,, ,,	,,	,,	m.	artist's proof	1904	68	5	0
,, ,,	,,	,,	m.	presentation proof, signed	1905	42	0	0
,, ,,	,,	,,	m.	proof, 2nd state	1904	25	0	0
,, ,,	,,	,,	m.	signed by the painter	1901	18	18	0
Hunters on their way to the Hunting Stables and Post Boys Watering their Horses	Pollard	Pyall, H.	c.a.	pair	1907	13	5	0
Hunters at Cover side, Breaking Cover, Full Cry, and The Death	Alken, S., Sartorius, Pollard, and Gell	Pollard, J.	c.p.	set of four	1908	28	10	0
Hunted Stag and Laying down the Law	Landseer, Sir E.	Landseer, T.	m.	1st state	1907	3	3	0
Hunting Subjects	Sartorius	Peltro and Neagle	c.p.	set of four	1905	54	12	0
,, ,,	Pollard	—	c.p.	set of three & one other	1906	19	8	6
,, ,,	Seymour	Burford	—	set of four	1907	8	8	0
,, ,,	,,	,,		,,	1907	7	7	0
Hunting Subjects	Hodges, W. P.	Alken, H.	c.p.	set of eight	1905	38	17	0
,, ,,	,,	,,	c.a.	set of eight	1907	16	5	6
Hunting Scenes	Ansell	Sutherland	c.p.	set of 10	1908	2	17	6
How to Qualify for a Meltonian	Alken	Alken, H.	c.p.	set of six	1902	38	0	0
Humorous Hunting Scenes—Thrown out, Craning, Heading the Fox, and Taking the Lead	—	R. F.	c.p.	—	1908	12	10	0
Litter of Foxes	Morland & Smith C. Loraine	Grozier, J.	m.	coloured	1907	3	10	0

Title.	Artist.	Engraver.	Method.	Remarks.	Year of Sale.	£	s.	d.
Leicestershire Hunt—								
The Meet, Getting Away,								
Full Cry, and The Death ...	Alken, H.	Fielding, T.	c.p.	set of four	1908	45	3	0
,, ,,	,,	,,	c.p.	The Death, p.b.l. un-coloured	1908	14	0	0
,, ,,	,,	,,	c.p.	set of four	1908	5	5	0
Meltonians	Alken, H.	Alken, H.	c.p.	set of five (should be 6)	1902	17	0	0
Old Druid—with portraits of R. K. Sampson and John Presse ...	Henwood, T.	—	—	coloured litho.	1908	4	4	0
Otter Hunt	Landseer, Sir E.	Lewis	m.	—	1904	9	10	0
,,	,,	,,	m.	artist's proof	1906	5	5	0
Only one in at the Death, The and The Right Sort...	Alken, H.	—	c.p.	—	1908	4	0	0
Pleasures and advantages of a capital run—Young Gentlemen amusing themselves	Wolstenholme	R.F.	c.p.	—	1908	4	10	0
Quorn Hunt	Alken, H.	Lewis, F. C.	c.a.	set of eight	1907	97	0	0
,, ,,	,,	,,	c.p.	set of eight	1908	52	10	0
,, ,,	,,	,,	c.p.	set of eight	1903	27	6	0
,, ,,	,,	,,	c.p.	set of eight	1902	16	5	0
Reynard seeking Refuge in a Church and Death of Tom Moody ...	Wolstenholme	Wolstenholme	c.a.	pair	1908	8	5	0
Royal Hunt at Windsor Park and George III. returning from Hunting	Pollard, J.	Dubourg	c.p.	pair	1902	37	16	0
,, ,, ,,	,,	,,	c.p.	pair	1907	23	0	0
Royal Hunt in Windsor Park..	Pollard, J.	Dubourg, M.	c.p.	—	1907	15	5	0
Royal Hunt, The	,,	,,	c.a.	—	1906	4	5	0
Sporting Anecdotes	Alken, H.	—	c.a.	set of five	1907	9	10	0
Sportsmen Refreshing and Horse Feeder...	Morland, G.	Alken Smith, J. R.	c.p.	—	1907	5	15	6
Stag at Bay and Return of the Hunt to the Castle	Byron, H.	Rowlandson, T.	c.a.	pair	1907	4	10	0
Sanctuary, The...	Landseer, Sir E.	Burnet, J.	m.	1st state	1901	14	14	0
Sir Mark Masterman Sykes' Fox Hounds breaking Cover	Chalon, H. B.	Wolstenholme	c.p.	—	1904	39	0	0
,, ,, ,,	,,	,,	m.	o.l.p.	1905	23	0	0
Sporting Discoveries, or the Miseries of Hunting...	—	—	c.p.	—	1907	20	0	0
Stag at Bay	Landseer, Sir E.	Landseer, T.	m.	signed by the artist	1902	84	0	0
,,	,,	,,	m.	artist's proof, signed by the painter	1902	48	6	0
,,	,,	,,	m.	artist's proof	1904	44	2	0
,,	,,	,,	m.	—	1901	35	14	0
The Start, Going to Cover, Full Cry, and Hounds at Fault	—	Howitt, G.	c.p.	four	1908	13	0	0
Village Scenery—Full Cry	Wolstenholme	Wolstenholme, jr.	c.p.	—	1908	4	14	0

PORTRAITS.

Title.	Artist.	Engraver.	Method.	Remarks.	Year of Sale.	£	s.	d.
Astley, Francis Dukinfield and his Harriers ...	Marshall, B.	Woodman, R.	—	proof	1908	8	15	0
,, ,,	,,	,,	—	o.l.p.	1907	5	5	0
Blackheath Golfers	Abbott, L. F.	Green, V.	m.	—	1902	26	0	0
,, ,,	,,	,,	m.	—	1907	15	0	0
Callender, Henry, to the Society of Golfers at Blackheath ...	,,	Ward, W.	m.	proof	1907	17	17	0
Darlington, Earl of, and his Foxhounds ...	Marshall, B.	Dean, T.	c.p.	lettered proof	1908	11	0	0
Forfeit, Robert, huntsman to John Warde, Esq. ...	Biederman	Harding, E.	—	o.l.p.	1908	1	14	0
Frampton, Tregonwell, "The Father of the Turf"	Wootton	Jones, J.	m.	—	1907	6	10	0
,, ,,	,,	,,	m.	—	1907	4	15	0
Innes, William, to the Society of Golfers at Blackheath ...	Abbott, L. V.	Green, V.	m.	—	1908	28	7	0
,, ,,	,,	,,	m.	—	1905	21	0	0
,, ,,	,,	,,	m.	—	1903	15	15	0
,, ,,	,,	,,	m.	—	1908	8	15	0

Title.	Artist.	Engraver.	Method.	Remarks.	Year of Sale.	£	s.	d.
Lambton, Ralph, and his Hounds	Ward, J.	Turner, C.	m.	proof	1903	19	8	6
,, ,,	,,	,,	c.p.	—	1902	15	4	6
Ligonier, Viscount, on Horseback	Reynolds, Sir J.	Fisher, E.	m.	—	1906	2	15	0
Masson, Monsieur, "The Tennis Player"	Mortimer	Brookshaw, R.	m.	p.b.l.	1902	31	10	0
,, ,,	,,	,,	m.	p.b.l.	1908	16	0	0
,, ,,	,,	,,	m.	inscription space cut off	1907	2	12	0
Oldacre, Tom	Marshall, Ben	Ward, W.	m.	coloured	1902	50	0	0
Payne, Philip, huntsman to the Duke of Beaufort, on Horseback with Hounds	Davis, T. R.	Turner, C.	m.	—	1908	6	10	0
Tattersall, Mr.	Beach, Thomas	Jones, J.	m.	—	1908	6	15	0
Thornton, Col.	Reinagle	Mackenzie	c.p.	—	1906	4	17	6
Ward, Jno., on Blue Ruin	Barraud	Collyer	—	—	1908	7	5	0

RACEHORSES.

Title.	Artist.	Engraver.	Method.	Remarks.	Year of Sale.	£	s.	d.
Anvil	Stubbs, G.	Stubbs, G. T.	c.p.	—	1908	1	15	0
Anvil, Baronet and Dungannon	Stubbs	Stubbs, G. T.	—	o.l.p.	1908	4	0	0
Baronet	,,	,,	c.p.	—	1908	2	7	6
Dan O'Connell	—	—	—	in the manner of Herring	1908	4	15	0
Derby, Winners of—								
Caaland, 1828	After Herring J. F. and Fernley		c.a.	—	1908	6	5	0
Priam, 1830				—	—	6	15	0
Spaniel, 1831				—	—	6	15	0
Dangerous, 1833				—	—	7	0	0
Plenipotentiary, 1834				—	—	6	15	0
Dr. Syntax	Marshall, Ben	—	m.	—	1907	4	0	0
Eclipse	Stubbs, G.	Burke, Thos.	m.	—	1902	15	0	0
Eclipse	Stubbs, G. I.	Stubbs, G.	c.p.	—	1908	4	0	0
Eleanor, Penelope, Bobtail, Parasol and Metcora	Whessell, J.	Whessell	a.	—	1907	7	15	0
Grey Diomed and Escaye	Sartorius	Dodd, R.	—	o.l.p., two	1907	12	5	0
Gustavius	Pollard, J.	Pollard, J.	c.p.	—	1908	10	15	0
Hafed	Landseer, Sir E.	Cousins, S.	m.	artist's proof	1902	27	6	0
Hambletonian and Diamond	Sartorius	Whessell	c.p.	pair	1907	9	10	0
Highflyer	Gilpin	Jukes, F.	—	—	1908	1	10	0
Inkle and Jarico	Singleton, H.	Pollard, R.	c.p.	pair	1908	2	5	0
Mabrino, Pumpkin and Sharke	Stubbs	Stubbs, G. T.	—	o.l.p.	1908	4	0	0
Marske and Sweetwilliam	Stubbs, G. T.	Stubbs, G. T.	c.p.	pair	1907	5	10	0
Orville	Tomson, C.	Scott, J.	—	—	1908	3	15	0
Oscar, Lop and two others	Marshall, B.	Whessell	—	o.l.p.	1907	2	0	0
Protector, Baronet, Mambrino and another	Stubbs	Stubbs, G. T.	—	—	1907	5	0	0
Riddlesworth, winner of the Two Thousand Guineas, 1831	Herring and Ferneley	—	c.a.	—	1908	6	15	0
Selim	Chalon, H. B.	Ward, W.	m.	—	1908	9	0	0
Sir Peter Teazle	Gilpin, S.	Ward, W.	m.	—	1908	8	5	0
Slyboots	Rowlandson	Rowlandson	—	—	1908	1	10	0
Soldier	Gerrard, C.	Alken, S.	—	in brown	1908	2	10	0
St. Leger Stakes, Winners of the—from 1815-42 and 1845	Herring, J. F., and Hall, H.	Reeves, Hunt, etc.	c.p.	29	1903	69	6	0
St. Leger Stakes, Winners of the	After Herring, J. F. and Ferneley, J.		c.a.	—	1908			
Filho-da-Puta, 1815	—	—	—	—	—	3	15	0
The Duchess, 1816	—	—	—	—	—	4	12	0
St. Patrick, 1820	—	—	—	—	—	4	13	0
Jack Spigot, 1821	—	—	—	—	—	4	4	0
Barefoot, 1823	—	—	—	—	—	4	12	0
Jerry, 1824	—	—	—	—	—	4	12	0
Memnon, 1825	—	—	—	—	—	4	13	0
Tarrare, 1826	—	—	—	—	—	4	16	0
Matilda, 1827	—	—	—	—	—	5	5	0
The Colonel, 1828	—	—	—	—	—	4	10	0
Rowton, 1829	—	—	—	—	—	4	18	0
Birmingham, 1830	—	—	—	—	—	6	0	0
Chorister, 1831	—	—	—	—	—	5	10	0
Margrave, 1832	—	—	—	—	—	4	10	0
Touchstone, 1833	—	—	—	—	—	4	12	0

Title.	Artist.	Engraver.	Method.	Remarks.	Year of Sale.	Price. £ s. d.
St. Leger Stakes, Winners of the, at Doncaster from the year 1815 to the year 1824 inclusive	Herring	Sutherland	c.a.	Set of 10	—	56 0 0
Sweetbriar, Sweetwilliam and Volunteer	Stubbs	Stubbs, G. T.	—	o.l.p.	1908	3 18 0
Tiresias	Pollard, J.	Pollard, J.	c.p.	—	1908	10 5 0
Velociped, winner of the St. Leger at the York Spring Meeting, 1828	Herring and Ferneley	—	c.a.	—	1908	6 0 0
Violante, Trumpeter and Dick Andrews, from the Set.—Portraits of celebrated Running Horses	Whessell, J.	Whessell	a.	—	1907	18 10 0
Wellesley Arabian, The	—	—	m.	p.b.l.	1907	13 0 0

RACING AND STEEPLECHASING.

Title.	Artist.	Engraver.	Method.	Remarks.	Year of Sale.	Price. £ s. d.
Adventures of Knutsford Race-course	Hazlehurst, E.	Reeve, R.	a.	—	1908	16 0 0
Aylesbury Grand Steeplechase	Pollard, J.	Harris, J.	c.a.	set of four	1906	36 0 0
,, ,,	,,	,,	c.a.	,,	1905	22 0 0
,, ,,	,,	,,	a.	,,	1907	18 18 0
Brighton Hurdle Race, 1833	Earp, E.	Hunt, C.	c.a.	pair	1906	6 5 0
Chances of the Steeplechases	Pollard, J.	Various		set of eight	1908	16 10 0
Country Race Course	Mason, W.	Jenkins, I.	—	pair	1907	12 10 0
Derby Stakes at Epsom, 1828	Pollard, J.	Reeves, R. G.	c.p.	—	1901	10 0 0
,, ,,	,,	,,	c.a.	—	1907	6 15 0
Derby Day ; and The Railway	Frith	—	a.	proofs, pair	1907	7 17 6
Derby Stakes at Epsom ; and Gold Cup at Ascot, 1829	Pollard	Gleadah, J. Edge, J.	c.a.	pair	1907	12 15 0
Doncaster Races—The Horses Starting ; and the Horses passing the Judge's Stand (Great St. Leger Stakes)	Pollard, J.	Smart and Hunt.	c.p.	pair	1908	30 10 0
Doncaster Races	,,	Harris, J.	c.p.	set of four	1902	26 15 0
,, ,,	,,	,,	c.p.	,,	1907	20 1 6
,, ,,	,,	,,	c.p.	,,	1905	12 1 6
Doncaster and Epsom Races	,,	Smart, J. & Hunt	c.p.	,,	1903	42 0 0
,, ,,	,,	,, ,,	c.p.	,,	1905	39 18 0
,, ,,	,,	,, ,,	c.p.	,,	1902	31 10 0
Epsom Races	Pollard, J.	Hunt, C.	c.p.	set of six	1908	42 0 0
Epsom	,,	,,	c.p.	,,	1905	38 17 0
Epsom Races	,,	,,	c.p.	,,	1902	37 0 0
Epsom Races, with Horses preparing to Start ; and The Race for the Derby, 1818	Alken, H.	Sutherland T.	c.p.	pair	1907	24 0 0
Epsom Races	Pollard, J.	Hunt, C.	c.p.	—	1907	13 10 0
Epsom Races	Alken	Sutherland, T.	c.p.	proof	1902	11 0 6
Epsom — Settling Day at Tattersall's	Pollard, J.	Hunt, C.	c.p.	—	1908	10 10 0
Epsom—Saddling in the Warren	,,	,,	,,	—	1908	7 10 0
,, Preparing to Start	,,	,,	,,	—	1908	6 5 0
,, The Grand Stand	,,	,,	,,	—	1908	6 0 0
,, The Race	,,	,,	,,	—	1908	6 0 0
Epsom Race Course, with Mr. Thornhill's "Sam" winning the Derby Stakes, 1818	Alken, H.	Sutherland, T.	c.p.	—	1908	17 10 0
Epsom Race Course, with the Horses preparing to start for the Two Mile Heat	,,	,,	,,	—	1908	15 10 0
Extraordinary Steeplechase	Alken	Alken and Duncan	c.a.	—	1902	25 0 0
Fairlop Fair	Pollard	Dubourg	p.c.	—	1907	14 0 0
First Steeplechase on Record	Alken	Harris, J.	c.p.	set of four	1902	20 5 0
,, ,,	,,	,,	c.a.	,,	1907	8 8 0
Grand Leicestershire Steeple-chase	Alken, H.	Bentley	c.a.	set of eight	1908	56 14 0
,, ,,	Alken	Alken, H.	c.p.	series of eight plates	1902	49 0 0
Grand Stand, Doncaster	Pollard, J.	Ryall, J.	c.p.	—	1908	5 17 6
High Mettled Racer	Alken, H.	T. Sutherland	c.a.	set of six	1907	53 0 0
High Mettled Racer	Rowlandson, T.	—	c.p.	set of four	1907	5 15 6

Title.	Artist.	Engraver.	Method.	Remarks.	Year of Sale.	Price. £ s. d.
Horse Racing Subjects	Alken	Sutherland, T.	c.p.	set of four	1903	48 6 0
Hurdle Race, A	,,	Hunt, C.	c.p.	,,	1902	48 0 0
High Mettled Racer	Rowlandson	—	c.a.	—	1908	3 3 0
Leicestershire	Paul, J. D.	Paul, J. D.	c.p.	,,	1902	30 0 0
Life of a Racehorse	Ansell	Jukes	a.	,,	1908	3 5 0
Liverpool Grand National Steeplechase, 1853.	Laporte, G. H.	Reeve, R. G. and A. W.	c.p.	,,	1908	13 10 0
Life of a Race-horse—TheFoal; Breaking-in; and the Death Leap, The, The Sporting Sweep, etc.	Alken, H.	—	c.p.	three	1908	9 0 0
	Alken, H.	—	—	—	1907	7 15 0
Match between Hambletonian and Diamond...	Sartorius	Whessell	c.p.	proofs, pair	1906	22 1 0
,, ,, ,,	,,	,,	a.	pair	1907	5 5 0
Newmarket, Ascot, Epsom, and Ipswich	Alken	Sutherland	c.p.	set of four	1903	32 11 0
Newmarket, Racing at	,,	,,	c.p.	,,	1907	7 10 0
Northampton Grand National Steeplechase, 1840— The Start, The Brook, The Fence, and Coming In	Hunt, C.	Hunt, C.	p.c.	set of four—long	1908	27 0 0
Newmarket Races	Alken, H.	Alken	c.a.	pair	1906	14 15 0
Newton Races, 1831	Towne, C.	Hunt, C.	c.a.	—	1902	59 0 0
,,	,,	,,	c.a.	—	1904	21 10 0
(Fylde beating Halston and Recovery)	,,	,,	c.p.	—	1908	39 0 0
Newtown Races	Towne, C.	Hunt	c.a.	full margin	1904	22 0 0
Newmarket Racecourse	Alken	Alken, H.	c.a.	—	1902	18 10 0
Newmarket Races	Pollard, J.	Pollard, J.	c.p.	—	1902	10 0 0
Noblemen's and Gentlemen's Trains of Running Horses taking their exercise up the Warren Hill, Newmarket	—	—	c.p.	with letterpress key	1908	36 0 0
,, ,,	—	—	c.p.	uncoloured, without the key	1908	20 0 0
Preparing to Start, Doncaster Race Course	Walker, G.	Havell, H.	c.p.	—	1908	2 10 0
Qualified Horses aud Unqualified Riders	Alken, H.	—	c.p.	—	1907	13 0 0
Racing	Alken	Sutherland, T.	c.a.	set of four	1902	70 0 c
Racing Subjects	Alken, H.	Sutherland	c.p.	,,	1908	29 8 0
Race Horses Exercising, Preparing to Start, The Race, and after the Race	—	—	c.p.	,,	1908	20 0 0
Rubbing Down the Racehorse	Vernet, C.	Debucourt	—	p.b.l.	1908	20 0 0
,, ,,	,,	,,	c.p.	—	1908	20 0 0
Steeplechase, A...	Alken, H.	Bentley, C.	c.a.	series of three	1907	11 0 0
,,	,,	,,	,,	,,	1907	7 5 0
Steeplechase, A	Alken	Alken, H.	c.p.	set of six	1902	23 10 0
,,	Alken, H.	Bentley	c.a.	,,	1906	19 0 0
St. Albans "Tally Ho" Stakes 1834	Pollard, J.	Hunt, G. and C.	p.c.	pair	1908	14 15 0
St. Albans Steeplechase, 1832	Pollard, J.	Reeves and Hunt	c.p.	plate II.	1906	3 5 6
Sir Joshua beating Filho-da-Puta at Newmarket, April 15, 1816	Pollard, J.	Havell, R.	c.p.	—	1907	18 0 0
Starting and Training	Pollard, J.	Hunt, C.	c.p.	—	1908	6 0 0
Subscription Rooms at Newmarket...	—	Pollard, R.	c.p.	—	1908	13 0 0
Tradesmen's Plate, Chester, 1839	Turner, F. C.	Harris, J.	—	—	1908	8 10 0
Training at Newmarket	Alken, H.	Sutherland	c.p.	—	1907	9 0 0
Trip to Epsom and back	Pollard, J.	Harris	c.a.	set of four	1906	55 0 0
Warren Hill, Newmarket, with Portrait of the Prince of Wales	Burney	Collyer	—	—	1908	7 5 0
Welter Stakes, June 16th, 1801	Chalon, H. B.	Turner, C.	c.p.	—	1908	43 10 0
,, ,,	,,	,,	m.	—	1905	21 0 0
Welter Stakes, Bibury Club, 1801	,,	,,	—	—	1904	12 1 0
Wolverhampton Stakes	Turner, F. C.	Turner, G. A.	c.p.	—	1908	5 15 0

SHOOTING.

Title.	Artist.	Engraver.	Method.	Remarks.	Year of Sale.	£	s.	d.
Amorous Sportsman	Wheatley, F. ...	Hodges	c.p.	—	1903	29	0	0
Benevolent Sportsman, and Sportsman's Return... ...	Morland... ...	Ward, W. ...	c.p.	pair	1907	29	8	0
Duck Shooting, Pheasant Shooting, Snipe Shooting, and Partridge Shooting	Morland, G. ...	Alken, S. ...	c.a.	four	1907	37	6	0
Duck. Hare, Woodcock and Snipe Shooting	,,	Simpson, & Calton	—	in bistre, four ...	1907	18	7	6
Duck Shooting	Morland... ...	Simpson... ...	s.	Plates I. and II. ...	1907	11	0	0
Duck Shooting and Coursing	Morland, G. ...	Thompson ...	—	—	1907	8	8	0
Duck Shooting	,, ...	Simpson	c.p.	—	1908	11	15	0
,, ,, ...	Alken, H. ...	—	c.p.	—	1908	6	10	0
Evening, or the Sportsman's Return	Morland, G. ...	Grozer, J. ...	c.p.	—	1907	12	1	6
,, ,, ...	,, ...	,, ...	m.	—	1907	10	10	0
First of September	Sadler, Dendy ...	Lowenstein ...	—	early artist's proof ...	1907	6	6	0
First of September—Morning, and Evening ...	Morland... ...	Ward, W. ...	m.	o.l.p. pair	1906	113	8	0
,, ,, ...	,, ...	,,	c.p.	pair	1906	52	10	0
,, ,, ...	,, ...	,,	m.	,, ...	1907	36	15	0
,, ,, ...	,, ...	,,	c.p.	,, ...	1903	22	1	0
,, ,, ...	,, ...	,,	c.p.	,, ...	1902	17	5	0
,, ,, ...	,, ...	,,	m.	,, ...	1903	15	0	0
,, ,, ...	,, ...	,,	c.p.	,, ...	1907	6	6	0
Fowler, The	Graham, P. ...	—	m.	artist's proof	1906	5	15	6
Gamekeepers	Stubbs	Birch, H. ...	m.	—	1906	2	10	0
Gamekeepers, and Labourers...	Stubbs	Birch, H. ...	m.	pair o.l.p.	1903	37	16	0
,, ,, ...	,, ...	,,	m.	,, ,, ...	1905	26	5	0
Gamekeepers' Midday Meal, and Return from the Shoot...	Alken, H. ...	Sutherland, T. ...	p.c.	pair	1907	4	10	0
Going to the Moors, and going to Cover	Henderson, C. C.	Harris, J. ...	c.a.	,, ...	1907	5	5	0
Grouse, Wild Duck, Pheasant and Partridge Shooting ...	Alken	Hunt, G. ...	a.	set of four	1902	23	10	0
Grouse Shooters in The Forest of Bowland, (Mr. Ashton and Mr. Haste)	Northcote, J. ...	Dawe, G. ...	—	o.l.p.	1908	12	15	0
,, ,, ...	,, ...	,, ...	c.p.	—	1908	6	15	0
,, ,, ...	,, ...	,, ...	m.	proof in colours ...	1907	6	10	0
Hare Shooting, and Woodcock and Pheasant Shooting ...	Morland, G. ...	Simpson, T. ...	s.	pair	1907	10	0	0
Leicestershire Covers	Alken	Sutherland, T. ...	c.a.	set of four	1902	26	0	0
Moor Shooting	Reinagle, P. ...	Lewis & Nichols	—	—	1908	3	15	0
Morning, or the Benevolent Sportsman	Morland... ...	Grozer, J. ...	c.p.	—	1907	37	16	6
Morning, or the Benevolent Sportsman, and Evening, or the Sportsman's Return ...	Morland... ...	Grozer, J. ...	c.p.	pair o.l.p.	1902	112	15	0
Morning, or the Benevolent Sportsman, and Evening, or the Sportsman's Return ...	,, ...	,,	m.	pair framed	1907	86	0	0
Morning, or the Benevolent Sportsman, and Evening, or the Sportsman's Return ...	,, ...	,,	c.p.	pair	1906	18	18	0
Newcastle, Duke of, Return from Shooting ...	Wheatley, F. ...	Bartolozzi	c.p.	—	1907	44	2	0
,, ,, ...	,, ...	,, ...	c.p.	—	1904	26	5	0
,, ,, ...	,, ...	,, ...	c.p.	—	1902	17	17	0
,, ,, ...	,, ...	,, ...	c.p.	—	1904	16	16	0
Newcastle, Duke of, Return from Shooting, (and Companion after Hamilton)	Wheatley ...	Bartolozzi	c.p.	pair	1907	84	0	0
,, ,, ...	,, ...	,, ...	c.p.	,, ...	1902	50	0	0
,, ,, ...	,, ...	,, ...	c.p.	,, ...	1905	39	5	0
Partridge Shooting	Alken, H. ...	Hunt, G. ...	c.p.	—	1908	1	1	0
Pheasant shooting, and Woodcock shooting	Ibbotsen, J. ...	Dodd, R. ...	c.a.	,, ...	1907	6	15	0
Pheasant shooting, and Partridge shooting	Alken, H. ...	—	c.p.	,, ...	1908	6	5	0
Pigeon Shooting	Alken	Alken, H. ...	c.a.	1828, with key plate	1902	18	0	0
Poachers...	Turner, J. L. ...	Turner, C. ...	a.	set of eight	1904	30	0	0
Random Shot	Landseer, Sir E.	Lewis, C. G. ...	m.	artist's proof	1907	3	13	6
Retriever and Woodcock, and Spaniel and Pheasant ...	,, ...	Landseer, T. ...	m.	pair—artist's proofs...	1904	19	19	0

Title.	Artist.	Engraver.	Method.	Remarks.	Year of Sale.	£	s.	d.
Shooting Pieces...	Alken	Alken, S.	c.a.	set of four	1908	31	10	0
Shooting Subjects	,,	Catton	c.p.	set of four	1906	3	5	0
,, ,,	,,	,,	—	set of four proofs	1907	9	9	0
Shooting Pieces	Stubbs, G.	Woollett, W.	m.	set of four, early finished proofs	1902	40	0	0
,, ,,	,,	,,	m.	set of four	1907	39	0	0
Shooting ...	,,	,,	m.	,,	1903	37	16	0
,,	,,	,,	m.	,,	1907	18	7	6
,,	,,	,,	m.	,,	1908	5	10	0
Shooting—Illustrations to a Song ...	Wolstenholme	—	c.p.	,,	1908	11	0	0
Snipe Shooting, and Partridge Shooting ...	Morland, G.	Catton, C. Junr.	s.	colour print—pair	1907	81	0	0
Snipe Shooting, and Partridge Shooting ...	,,	,, ,,	c.p.	pair	1908	20	0	0
,, ,,	,,	,,	m.	,,	1907	7	7	0
Snipe Shooting, and a Pigeon Shooting Match ...	Alken, H.	—	c.p.	,,	1908	4	10	0
Sportsmen Refreshing, and The Rabbit Warren ...	Morland, G.	Alken, S.	—	pair o.l.p.	1907	5	15	6
Sportsman's Return ...	Morland	Ward, W.	m.	p.b.l.	1906	46	4	0
,,	,,	,,	m.	p.b.l.	1902	44	2	0
,,	,,	,,	c.p.	—	1907	37	16	0
,,	,,	,,	c.p.	—	1902	33	12	0
,,	,,	,,	m.	p.b.l.	1904	24	0	0
,,	,,	,,	c.p.	—	1905	15	15	0
,,	,,	,,	—	—	1907	11	11	0
,,	,,	,,	—	—	1908	5	15	0
,,	,,	,,	c.p.	—	1906	4	14	0
Weary Sportsman ...	Morland	Bond, W.	c.p.	—	1907	16	10	0
,,	,,	,,	c.p.	—	1906	6	16	6
,,	,,	,,	c.p.	—	1906	1	1	0
Wild Fowl Shooting from a Punt ...	—	—	c.p.	—	1908	3	18	0

MISCELLANEOUS.

Title.	Artist.	Engraver.	Method.	Remarks.	Year of Sale.	£	s.	d.
Archery ...	Rowlandson	—	—	drawn and etched in colours—pair	1908	3	10	0
Boxing—The Great Contest between "Spring" and "Langan" upon Worcester Racecourse, January 7, 1824	Clement	Gleadah, J.	c.a.	—	1908	7	0	0
Boxing Match between Richard Humphrey and Daniel Mendoza, at Odiham ...	Einsle, S.	Grozer, J.	—	—	1907	2	0	0
Cock Fighting—Col. Mordaunt's Cock Match...	Zoffany	Earlom, R.	m.	with the key	1901	23	2	0
,, ,,	,,	,,	m.	o.l.p.	1907	5	15	0
Falconer, The ...	Northcote, J.	Reynolds, S. W.	m.	p.b.l.	1908	26	0	0
,,	,,	,,	m.	p.b.l.	1902	9	5	0
Fores Sporting Scraps...	Henderson, C. C.	Harris, J.	c.a.	pair	1907	3	0	0
Game Larder ...	Snyders	Earlom	m.	p.b.l.	1906	1	10	0
Game Market ...	,,	,,	m.	p.b.l.	1906	2	10	0
Interior of the Fives Courts, with "Randall" and Turner Sparring ...	Blake, T.	Turner, C.	c.a.	—	1908	10	15	0
Sporting Table, wherein all the Laws touching Game are shown at one view, a printed broadside with engraved border of Hunting Incidents, etc. ...	—	Paton, F.	—	—	1908	3	0	0
Wrestling ...	Alken, H.	—	c.p.	—	1908	4	4	0
Wrestling — A Match at a Country Fair ...	—	Turner, C.	c.p.	—	1908	2	6	0

ABBREVIATIONS.

c.p.—colourprint. s.—stipple. a.—aquatint. c.a.—coloured aquatint. m.—mezzotint. p.b.l.—proof before letters. e.l.p.—etched letter poof. p.b.t.—proof before the title. o.l.p.—open letter proof.